Expedition Escape from the Classroom

CONFIGURATIONS: CRITICAL STUDIES OF WORLD POLITICS

Patrick Thaddeus Jackson, series editor

Recent Titles:

Expedition Escape from the Classroom: Political Outings on the Campus and the Anxiety of Teaching IR
Oded Löwenheim

Chasing Greatness: On Russia's Discursive Interaction with the West Over the Past Millennium
Anatoly Reshetnikov

Decisiveness and Fear of Disorder: Political Decision-Making in Times of Crisis
Julius Maximilian Rogenhofer

The Politics of Military Force: Antimilitarism, Ideational Change, and Post-Cold War German Security Discourse
Frank A. Stengel

Interspecies Politics: Nature, Borders, States
Rafi Youatt

Decency and Difference: Humanity and the Global Challenge of Identity Politics
Steven C. Roach

State of Translation: Turkey in Interlingual Relations
Einar Wigen

The Politics of Intimacy: Rethinking the End-of-Life Controversy
Anna Durnová

Angry Public Rhetorics: Global Relations and Emotion in the Wake of 9/11
Celeste Michelle Condit

The Distinction of Peace: A Social Analysis of Peacebuilding
Catherine Goetze

For a complete list of titles, please see www.press.umich.edu

Expedition Escape from the Classroom

POLITICAL OUTINGS ON THE
CAMPUS AND THE ANXIETY
OF TEACHING IR

Oded Löwenheim

University of Michigan Press
Ann Arbor

Copyright © 2024 by Oded Löwenheim
Some rights reserved

This work is licensed under a Creative Commons Attribution-NonCommercial 4.0 International License. *Note to users:* A Creative Commons license is only valid when it is applied by the person or entity that holds rights to the licensed work. Works may contain components (e.g., photographs, illustrations, or quotations) to which the rightsholder in the work cannot apply the license. It is ultimately your responsibility to independently evaluate the copyright status of any work or component part of a work you use, in light of your intended use. To view a copy of this license, visit http://creativecommons.org/licenses/by-nc/4.0/

For questions or permissions, please contact um.press.perms@umich.edu

Published in the United States of America by the
University of Michigan Press
Manufactured in the United States of America
Printed on acid-free paper
First published November 2024

A CIP catalog record for this book is available from the British Library.

Library of Congress Cataloging-in-Publication Data

Names: Lowenheim, Oded, 1970– author. | Michigan Publishing (University of Michigan), publisher.
Title: Expedition escape from the classroom : political outings on the campus and the anxiety of teaching IR / Oded Löwenheim.
Other titles: Expedition escape from the classroom : political outings on the campus and the anxiety of teaching international relations | Configurations (Ann Arbor, Mich.)
Description: Ann Arbor [Michigan] : University of Michigan Press, 2024. | Series: Configurations : critical studies of world politics | Includes bibliographical references (pages 229–246) and index.
Identifiers: LCCN 2024030245 (print) | LCCN 2024030246 (ebook) | ISBN 9780472077113 (hardcover) | ISBN 9780472057115 (paperback) | ISBN 9780472904723 (ebook other)
Subjects: LCSH: International relations—Study and teaching. | International relations—Philosophy. | Lowenheim, Oded, 1970– —Political and social views.
Classification: LCC JZ1237 .L68   2024 (print) | LCC JZ1237 (ebook) | DDC 327.071—dc23/eng/20240813
LC record available at https://lccn.loc.gov/2024030245
LC ebook record available at https://lccn.loc.gov/2024030246

DOI: https://doi.org/10.3998/mpub.12876215

The University of Michigan Press's open access publishing program is made possible thanks to additional funding from the University of Michigan Office of the Provost and the generous support of contributing libraries.

Cover photo: The main inner path within the Hebrew University's Mt. Scopus campus, Jerusalem. In the foreground, a display from the well-known photograph "Albert Einstein Riding a Bicycle" [1933, Leo Baeck Institute]. This path serves the author and his students in many of their campus expeditions. Photograph courtesy Oshri Löwenheim.

Contents

FOREWORD   vii

ACKNOWLEDGMENTS   xi

LIST OF ILLUSTRATIONS   xiii

Introduction: My Teaching Anxiety and Its Sources   1

ONE   Out of the Classroom: A Conceptual and Pedagogical
         Rationale for This Book   27

TWO   To the British Jerusalem War Cemetery:
         Heterotopia and Associative Encounters with the
         (Foreign, Imperial) War Dead   57

THREE   Looking for Roots in the Mt. Scopus Botanical Garden:
         Ideological Flora, Buffer Zones, and Seeing/Ignoring   98

FOUR   The Enigma of Portrait Busts: Exploring Power, Art,
         and History in Honorific Sculpting on Campus and Beyond   138

FIVE   Layers of Memory and Identity: Exploring the Spaces
         and Stories of the Harry S. Truman Research Institute
         for the Advancement of Peace   172

         Conclusions: Analytical Axes, Writing Drawbacks, and the
         Author-Book Separation   204

EPILOGUE   223

BIBLIOGRAPHY   229

INDEX   247

Digital materials related to this title can be found on
the Fulcrum platform via the following citable URL:
https://doi.org/10.3998/mpub.12876215

Foreword

So much of what we scholars write and publish in international studies operates with a *detached* perspective and tone: we scholars stand *here*, making sense and producing explanations of some phenomena over *there*. Whether we do this as an analytical pose or out of a genuine commitment to the mind-independent externality of the objects we study, the rhetorical stance is similar, and it interpellates the reader as a fellow-observer along with the author. We come to texts constructed in this standard way expecting to learn something about the object, something portable and definite that we can take with us—and that we can place into our individual reliquaries to add to the stock of things that we know.

Other modes of writing don't do this. It's hard to say what we learn from reading a novel, and even if we treat a narrative depiction as a metaphor, it's often impossible to say just what it is a metaphor *for*. (As Ursula Le Guin once commented that, if a writer could simply say what something was a metaphor for, they should just have said so instead of writing the novel in the first place.) At the same time, it is undeniable that we *do* learn things from narrative accounts, even if precision about what we have learned remains elusive.

Oded Löwenheim has not written a novel, but he has written a brilliant piece of autoethnography that works by taking the reader into the narrative as two intertwined dilemmas are explored. First, the location of Löwenheim's professional life—the Mt. Scopus campus of the Hebrew University—is simultaneously an academic enclave and a highly political site, implicated in even while holding itself apart from the wider Israeli-Palestinian conflict. Second, Löwenheim experienced a crisis in his teaching and writing (so, in both parts of the "scholar-teacher ideal") and went actively searching for a way to confront his often paralyzing anxiety. The blunt *honesty* of his disclosure of those dilemmas was in fact the first thing that attracted me to this manuscript; how many of us suffer from similar anxieties, and how many of our institutions are far from the pristine ideals they purport to be and which we often emotionally need them to be? In this way, the highly personal and local elements of Löwenheim's account speak to broader experiences more widely shared, and his unsentimental discussion provides points of connection for a circle much wider than himself and his university.

viii   Foreword

Löwenheim's account is simultaneously a marvelous illustration of the power of autoethnography as a methodological approach, a trenchant criticism of the organization and practices of the contemporary research university, and a compelling case for conceptualizing International Relations not as politics and economics "out there," but as part and parcel of our everyday lives not just as citizens and workers and consumers, but as students and teachers. I am particularly pleased by the book's focus on pedagogy as a site for the production of thinking subjects, and by Löwenheim's courage in moving pedagogy beyond the classroom environment in order to expand its range and depth. Here we have a configurational account of what might be the aspect of international affairs that is closest to us as academics: our teaching, and the kind of critical awareness it can produce in our students.

What we find here is nothing less than a critical reimagining of the very purpose of "teaching IR." We are well past the transmission model of education, in which a body of more or less certain knowledge has to be imparted to the students. And we are not operating in the realm of professional socialization, as we would perhaps be with graduate students; the goal of teaching here is not to form our students into junior colleagues. Instead, the goal is to equip the students with tools and strategies that they can use to, in Löwenheim's words, "IR-ize" their own experiences—that is, to connect them to a broader global context involving borders and border-crossings of myriad varieties. His proposal for doing this involves promoting reflection and reflexivity on the part of his students by taking them on "tours" around campus, encouraging them to draw connections between the campus and the international environment. The resulting reinvigorated teaching and learning—Löwenheim is unflinchingly honest about his struggles and disillusionment with the traditional classroom environment—reveals the campus, and the kind of knowledge it produces, as concretely situated in a social and political context that needs to be taken into account.

Löwenheim's account also resists the temptation of easy answers. Aspects of the Mt. Scopus campus are not reductively explained by pointing to aspects of Israel's politics or the Israeli-Palestinian conflict; instead, those important factors are shown to be elements in the complex configurations that produce botanical gardens and bomb shelters. Theory is wielded judiciously as a way to pry apart these configurations analytically, letting us—and the students involved in the classes Löwenheim taught—appreciate the complexity that underpins seemingly simple and seamless spaces. And while there is no claim here that general lessons can be drawn from the author's experiences, there are certainly ample parallels and what Wittgenstein might call "family resemblances" between his experiences and ours. This is of course precisely what a good configurational account delivers: a set of analytical elements that recur in diverse combinations. Teachers and students of IR thus have here a rich resource on which to draw in rethinking their own pedagogy.

At the end of the day, complicating the simple stories of nationalist righteousness and scientific knowledge production by refracting such stories through the prism of individual experience may not seem like a major contribution. It may not even seem like "IR." But that, I think, is ultimately because we have a far too restrictive sense of what *counts* as international studies scholarship, and a far too heroic expectation of what our scholarly writing can accomplish. Critical reflexivity in our teaching and in our writing probably won't save us, but it might make us (and our readers and our students) less susceptible to the siren songs and hollow idols offered as a quick and easy alternative to dwelling in the pain and ambiguity. Honesty is, after all, the first necessary step on the road to any sort of improvement.

Patrick Thaddeus Jackson
Series Editor, Configurations

Acknowledgments

First and foremost, my deepest gratitude goes to Patrick Thaddeus Jackson, the editor of the "Configurations" series. Without his unwavering support and encouragement, this book would have remained a mere thought. Thank you, PTJ.

I am indebted to all the students I've had the privilege to teach over the years in the course "The Mt. Scopus Enclave: Hebrew University's Campus as a Security-Political-Academic Space." Your enthusiasm and dedication transformed this course into the pages of this book.

To Dr. Daphna Sharef-Davidovich, my partner in both life and ideas, thank you for being a constant sounding board during this project. Your innovative solutions often guided me through my writer's block.

Within the International Relations department at the Hebrew University, I extend my appreciation to Dr. Orit Gazit. Her broad theoretical and conceptual perspectives have been invaluable in shaping and refining the narrative of this book. Heartfelt thanks to Prof. Gadi Heimann and Prof. Dan Miodownik as well for their positive feedback and genuine interest in this work. While I could enumerate also those who offered less favorable views, I choose to focus on the positive (;

Lastly, to Dror Löwenheim and Oshri Löwenheim, the radiant lights of my life, my enduring source of joy—as always, this book is for you.

Oded Löwenheim
Jerusalem, October 30, 2023

Illustrations

1 *The Siege and Destruction of Jerusalem by the Romans under the Command of Titus, A.D. 70*, painted by David Roberts   36

2 The Mount Scopus enclave, as represented on Google Maps (November 2023)   39

3 "An eternal memento from unified Jerusalem, 1967": the Scopus open theater   42

4 Laying of the cornerstones for the Hebrew University on Mt. Scopus (July 24, 1918)   53

5 Hebrew University, looking West along Olivet Road (1933)   58

6 A view of the cemetery from the direction of the guardhouse   60

7 The main gate to the cemetery   73

8 The Stone of Remembrance and the Memorial Chapel   74

9 Inscriptions in Arabic on the outer wall of the cemetery   83

10 The Cross of Sacrifice   84

11 "A Soldier of the Great War"   88

12 Fasces on an Italian soldier's headstone   91

13 The botanical garden in low resolution   104

14 In the oak grove, within the garden   110

15 Black smoke from burning waste in Issawiya   111

16 Issawiya, from within the botanical garden   113

17 The roots tunnel   115

18 The Nicanor burial cave plot   122

19 Eig's phytosociological map of Palestine   128

20 Relocation of a cedar from Eig's cedar grove in 1993   136

21 The raven perching on the bust of Pallas Athena   141

xiv   Illustrations

22 Author Sholem Asch, by Sir Jacob Epstein, in the foyer of the Senate Hall, Hebrew University of Jerusalem — 143

23 US Senator Edward Kennedy presenting a bust of his late brother John F. Kennedy to Prime Minister Yitzhak Shamir (December 1986) — 145

24 The head sculpture of Professor Norman Bentwich, at the Faculty of Law — 146

25 Prime Minister Ehud Olmert with the Bonds delegation at the Knesset, Jerusalem, May 5, 2008 — 147

26 Rembrandt, *Aristotle Contemplating a Bust of Homer* (1653) — 148

27 Bernini's bust of Louis XIV — 152

28 Elisabeth, Queen of the Belgians, appreciates her portrait bust (Giv'at Ram Campus, 1958) — 156

29 The bust of Moshe Dayan, and Maurice B. Hexter, its sculptor (April 1976) — 157

30 The busts of Tagore, Weizmann, and Herzl turned into "strange attractors" — 159

31 A close up of "Tagore" by Ramkinkar Baij — 170

32 In the foyer of the Truman Research Institute for the Advancement of Peace at the Hebrew University — 179

33 Four marble busts in the bomb shelter of the Truman Institute — 182

34 Close-ups of the Truman Institute busts — 186

35 Eliyahu Elath with his bust, sculpted by Maurice B. Hexter — 193

36 "A Bust of an Oriental Jew," by Maurice B. Hexter, in the storage room — 194

37 Dedication ceremony with Maurice Hexter and Eliyahu Elath (March 1968) — 195

Introduction

MY TEACHING ANXIETY AND ITS SOURCES

At the age of 45, sometime during the fall semester of 2015, I experienced a serious episode of teaching anxiety that eventually evolved to include writer's block. This book is an autoethnographic account of how I found and developed innovative pedagogical and conceptual-theoretical methods to cope with this anxiety—and thereby also return to writing.

The book has three goals. The first is to explore the issue of the teaching anxiety university professors can experience—a relatively understudied topic compared to the learning anxieties of students. I describe the underlying causes of my anxiety, how it manifested in my teaching, and how I eventually managed to transform it into a valuable resource for revitalizing my pursuits in both teaching *and* research. Writing from the perspective of an Israeli International Relations (IR) professor at the Hebrew University of Jerusalem, I place my teaching anxiety in the context of an ever-radicalizing society entrenched in protracted conflicts. And given that IR is a social science among the other social sciences, I believe that the ideas and lessons contained here will speak to scholars from related fields as well.

The second goal arises from and continues the first: I seek to create the possibility for a meaningful connection with the reader by sharing an honest and personal account of vulnerability and doubt, closure, and healing. I want to foster empathy and solidarity within IR—a field that is not traditionally associated with creating spaces for vulnerability and healing.[1] By bringing these issues to the fore, I try not simply to create solidarity and empathy per se but also help others who experience crises of teaching or research in the neoliberal university to use their period of difficulty as a resource for professional and personal progress. I also want my narrative to serve as a source of strength and resilience for academics who struggle under the heavy weight of

---

1. I thank the anonymous "Reviewer B" for phrasing this idea for me.

2   EXPEDITION ESCAPE FROM THE CLASSROOM

managerial pressures to constantly "excel."[2] There are times, as my account shows, when one cannot excel. It is precisely during such times that one can engage in the original purpose of the university—"to inculcate the exercise of critical judgement" (Readings, referring to Fichte 1996, 6).

The third goal of the book is to further advance the notion of cultivating critical judgment. I want to demonstrate how an academic can transition from a state of striving for "excellence" to consciously rejecting "excellence" as the fundamental principle for teaching and research while still maintaining a high standard of scholarly work. I achieve this by showcasing how, alongside my students, I engaged in a mode of thinking that encompassed the "IR-zation" of different locations and objects on our campus of Mt. Scopus. We continually asked, "Does this seemingly irrelevant place or object have relevance to IR?"

As I explain in this introduction, to help cope with my teaching anxiety I developed a university course—entitled "The Mt. Scopus Enclave: Hebrew University's Campus as a Security-Political-Academic Space"—that involves physical, intellectual, and emotional investigations of the boundaries of IR as both a real-world phenomenon and a scholarly discipline. I performed these investigations using interdisciplinary knowledge (including from IR, political geography, history, literature, art, architecture, botany, and archaeology) while "escaping," along with my students, from the regimented environment of the classroom to various spaces on the university's Mt. Scopus campus. Mt. Scopus is, effectively, an Israeli enclave within mainly Palestinian neighborhoods in northeastern Jerusalem, providing many opportunities to observe various current and historical manifestations of international politics in and around the campus. I was surprised that only a few students and faculty members perceive this space in such a way. In fact, most campus dwellers on Mt. Scopus see the campus as a place to spend as little time and to know as little about as possible. In contrast, during my campus outings, I seek to show the students how to uncover various manifestations of the international sphere in our everyday environment. By identifying how the state and politics are constructed in these university spaces, I critique how power operates through diverse institutions and is embodied in everyday locations.

This process of "IR-zing" the campus was an extensive and time-consuming

---

2. One of the first and best analyses of the appearance of the concept of academic excellence as the main mission of the university since the 1980s is that by Bill Readings (1996). Readings sees the postmodern university mainly as a corporation for degree dispensing and the concept of "excellence" as an empty category.

journey, fraught with various inconsistencies and methodological and episte-mological challenges. I had to gather and become familiar with a substantial body of interdisciplinary knowledge, whose parts did not always align seam-lessly. This process goes against the prevailing "prime directive" of academic excellence, which prioritizes specialization within a well-defined subfield of knowledge and the rapid publication of polished, defensible, and stream-lined articles in leading "Q1 journals."[3] It also emphasizes transmitting this knowledge to students in the most organized and comprehensible way to meet our university's underlying expectations to ensure high student "reac-tion yield"—a term (from chemistry, no less! in Hebrew: ניצולת) referring to the highest possible number of students successfully completing the course within the allocated time frame.

Against these trends, the campus escapades seek to develop and maintain skills such as the capacity for critical observation of physical and ideational landscapes and to support curiosity, "idleness," and imagination in an aca-demic setting that stresses utilitarian and strategic performance (Hansen and Triantafillou 2022). The "Mt. Scopus Enclave" course resists what I con-sider to be external political pressures and internal organizational incentives to avoid investing the time people need to look critically at their physical *and* mental and emotional environments and to reflect on what they see there. The course also encourages intellectual openness by emphasizing reading and learning about topics and issues outside the cage of one's "proper" discipline and expertise. By narrating the stories of these campus outings, this book advocates this approach to both teaching and research.

Finding, exposing, and sometimes even playfully inventing the inter-national in our immediate campus environment is also a way to "trick" (or "make do" / "rip off" in Michel de Certeau's terms—see the next chapter) the "proper" of IR. The outings have a strong element of an active, even adven-turous, shared learning experience, which is usually absent from the con-ventional four-walled classroom. This active experience helps me to contest students' established notions of "important" or "proper" subjects for an IR university course and, consequently, allows me to overcome a major source of my teaching anxiety: that is, student misunderstanding, alienation, sus-picion, and even mockery of my conception of the "I" in "IR" (Löwenheim 2010). I believe that the "international," the "everyday/ordinary," and "per-

---

3. On "fortress writing," see Ravecca and Dauphinee (2018). Projects that did not materialize or fail also can teach us a great deal. See, in this regard, Scott (2018).

4   EXPEDITION ESCAPE FROM THE CLASSROOM

sonal experience" are not mutually exclusive categories. And this, in turn, has a direct, reinvigorating impact on my research.

Thus, overall, the narratives in this book describe a mid-career professor's search for meaning and belonging in the academic profession in what was once considered "the last German university in the world" (Mosse 2000, 197) and is now just another neoliberal institution for higher education and the 'production and transmission of knowledge.' By sharing stories of interaction and encounter with the university campus and the students, the book explores aspects of how a person can come to feel at home on campus and in academia despite the increasing obstacles to attaining such a feeling (Korica 2022). Finally, these narratives are also self-reflective, inquiring how—during and after a personal/professional crisis—I was able to regain the desire and confidence to teach and, consequently, return to writing and to research.

The Rise of My Teaching Anxiety

In the fall of 2015, when I started to experience physical symptoms of anxiety before and during classes, I was not in any position of vulnerability or risk at my university.[4] These feelings started five years *after* I received tenure in the Department of International Relations at the Hebrew University of Jerusalem and, perhaps ironically, during my service as chair of my department (2014–17).[5] And yet, I started experiencing physical symptoms of anxiety before and during classes. I taught only small classes then—advanced seminars and workshops—and although I was very busy with the administration of the department (we had around 700 students in the three different degree programs and more than 30 senior and adjunct academic staff), I did have "time to class" (Jackson 2020)—that is, to properly plan the classes and make myself available for the students.

---

4. Stress and anxiety at work are not only related to personal attributes and factors, but also influenced by systemic factors. In the university, such systemic factors can include the "balance of power" between students/"clients" and professors, the question of tenured versus nontenured employment, the degree and quality of the management's backing of professors' academic freedom, political pressures from political parties and figures, and student (usually, right-wing) groups. See Loveday (2018).

5. In this sense, my case is somewhat opposite to Brent J. Steele's, who writes, "But I now know that one of the benefits of tenure in higher education is not what it necessarily does for a research program, but rather, how it liberates instructors in the classroom. I felt *free* to engage my students, or perhaps, much freer than I had been before" (Steele 2020, 284).

Nonetheless, and despite being otherwise a physically healthy person, I began to experience, before and during classes, phenomena such as increased heart rate, fast breathing, dryness of the mouth, sweating, and hot flashes. I also developed an emotional and psychological aversion to teaching IR. I suffered before each class, sometimes even canceling sessions. I was afraid I would not have enough to say during the lesson, or the opposite—that I would have too much to say, in terms of both the number of subjects and stories I would cover and the degree of disclosure and elaboration. More seriously, I increasingly felt misunderstood by the students and estranged from them. I sensed that many of them were angry with me or were mocking me because of what and how I taught them. For *what* I teach is intricately connected to *how* I teach. I'll return to this point soon.

My reading on IR pedagogy revealed much more discussion about student learning challenges and anxiety than about professors' apprehensions and fears of teaching. Despite this, I believe I am probably not the only professor who has experienced teaching anxiety (Sterling-Folker 2020; Park Kang 2022), and I think that exploring this anxiety and my consequent dealing with it could convey something significant about our academic discipline and international politics in the real world too. For the anxiety emanated from political and theoretical sources.

I didn't always have teaching anxiety. In fact, from the time I was hired as an assistant professor at the Hebrew University in 2003, I was almost always excited before entering a classroom. One year into the tenure track, I was given the "double prize" of teaching "Introduction to IR" at the undergraduate level *and* "Qualitative Research Methods" at the graduate level. I not only felt excited to teach but also sensed (as a new and young professor often feels) a special responsibility, pride, and belonging in the discipline for being given these "core" modules. Both were very large and demanding courses and sapped a great deal of mental energy. But I was not afraid to enter the lecture hall. I had confidence in my teaching abilities, and I felt I was in "command" of the taught material. In fact, I enjoyed the performance. I had a very defined script for each class, approaching it like a presenter or an actor in a play. The specter of exams and other assignments greatly influenced the orientation of discussions in class. Because of the subject matter as well as my naive perception then of IR as a positivist science, these classes had a constant atmosphere of "seriousness" and "importance."

But after finishing my "tour" in these large survey courses in 2009, and especially after the death of my father following a long and painful illness in that year, my research interest shifted toward personal narrative, autoethnography, and experimental writing (Löwenheim 2010). My father's death and my sudden state of orphanhood made me realize several important things: he had lived and died within a political and societal structure of violence (aka, "Israel in the Middle East"), and even though I am "in" IR (writing in English about the "Great Powers," for example in Löwenheim 2007), I, too, am embedded within the same political-cultural structure. In other words, I realized how the trauma and pain he suffered because of living in Israel contributed to his illness, and how turning away my gaze to IR might not protect me from similar consequences. I also understood that I have questions for him about my identity that I will now never receive the answers to, and that this uprootedness will haunt me for the rest of my life. Finally, it became clear to me that I cannot remain professionally oblivious to such matters.

Consequently, I started to teach mostly small classes that explored what I have since deemed the hollowness, absurdity, and arbitrariness of conflict and violence, especially in the context of the Israeli-Palestinian conflict. By this, I do not mean to belittle the pain and suffering of people and societies in conflict—on the contrary. I also do not try to claim that groups and states, and individuals within them, are not guided by just, real, and grave considerations and interests that lead them to employ violence. By "hollowness, absurdity, and arbitrariness of conflict and violence," I refer to how these practices, behaviors, and structures *take a life of their own and create and dominate the purpose, identity, and ontological security of people who live in societies that are embroiled in protracted conflicts*. In other words, I talk about the automatization of violent conflict, not least by the many practices that we adopt to ignore violence around us and disregard how violence eventually constitutes our subjectivities. I try to show how violence and conflict drain us of reflexivity and empathy, and I seek to expose how they sweep away the human spirit.

I strive to reveal the naturalization mechanisms that construct violent conflict as a taken-for-granted fact. By this, I don't necessarily refer to IR Realist perceptions about the endurance of violence in international politics (whether due to classical realist factors such as human nature's proclivity to violence[6] or neorealism's focus on structure, anarchy, and the constant pursuit of security). Instead, I talk with the students about that baffling (but perhaps not so unique) Israeli mode of thinking and being in the world that on the one hand refuses to acknowledge the multiple manifestations and per-

---

6. But see Ferguson (2018).

vasiveness of the violence we exert in our existence here, and on the other hand valorizes life in violent conflict as a destiny that cannot be overwritten and should not be questioned.

Of course, mine are not the only classes where the students encounter such ideas and notions. In many other courses in the IR department, they learn concepts and topics such as the way violence constitutes the ontological security of people within protracted conflicts (Mitzen 2006); how collective memory is selective and hostile to counternarratives (Barak 2007); the resilience of unintended consequences and the high potential for miscalculations in the use of force; and the political psychology of biases, blind spots, and routines in intergroup conflicts.

However, in my courses, I don't use supposedly scientific, theoretical, objective, or detached terms or deal mainly with "case studies" from other places in the world or outside it (for that, I also teach a seminar called "Science Fiction and [International] Politics," where it is easier to talk about such realities in the "universe" of *Star Trek*). Instead, I usually focus on the emotional costs of violence and protracted conflict in everyday life, mainly in Israel and Palestine. More specifically, using autoethnography and personal narrative as my main teaching methods, I share with the students how I experience the culture of conflict and violence in our country and ask them to reflect on how they are, as much as I am, products and carriers of this culture, and sufferers of it.[7] While some students find this approach interesting and even stimulating, many others, sometimes most of the group, resist it.

Student Resistance to Autoethnography and Critical Personal Narratives

Autoethnography involves a reflexive discussion of the self as part of a particular culture and employs an evocative personal narrative. It talks about the author's doubts, pains, vulnerabilities, and regrets. These are not observable or tangible things that can be measured and quantified or reproduced in an experiment, or enumerated in the data section of an article. Autoethnography is subjective, complex, and inconsistent by definition and requires students to look critically into their hearts and open up to others' stories and

---

7. "Carriers" in the sense of bearing it as well as conveying it to others; "sufferers" as victims but also as tolerators.

emotional worlds. It invites honesty and sincerity on topics that otherwise remain unspoken (A. Beattie 2019), but it also provokes, at least in some people, strong objections. Beyond the fact that many, if not most, of the topics and theories in the IR syllabus, not just mine, are perceived by many students in our department as biased toward political liberalism and the Left (Gross and Fosse 2012), my use of autoethnography sometimes becomes the last straw. Students (but also many of my colleagues) often complain and dismiss this research and teaching as not being scientific or academic. They are not comfortable hearing my personal stories and are reluctant to share their own. Why is this so?

Many possible reasons exist for this resistance to autoethnography. The claim about the method's inherent lack of objectivity is probably the most prominent. But I think that there is a more fundamental cause. After all, many other theories, methods, and debates in IR are imbued with subjectivity and hidden or implied ideological assumptions and worldviews (Gilpin 1996). I believe that a significant motivation to resist autoethnography is that it and related forms of personal narrative focus on regular, seemingly "unimportant" people's stories and accounts (Hülsse 2010; Khosravi 2010; Enloe 2014). Even though they are increasingly practiced by scholars in IR (for example, Dauphinee 2013; Bleiker 2019; Sucharov 2021; Inayatullah 2022; Park-Kang 2022), autoethnography, memoir, and personal narrative are rarely seen in the discipline's mainstream. Such narratives vary from the conventional IR storyline, which tends to focus on observable and recurring big patterns (think "hegemonic rivalries"), main actors/agents, pivotal events, and influential practices and institutions. In contrast, autoethnography and personal narratives evocatively show how history or politics is experienced and felt by the author's soul and body. As a result, they are perceived, perhaps also unconsciously, as not only criticizing the so-called important elements of the international political order for their impact on individual men and women (Sylvester 2013), but also questioning the ontological preeminence of what is conventionally considered from the outset as "important."

Autoethnographic texts argue that micro-level knowledge is legitimate, even desired and required in IR. I should note in this context that this focus on the micro is not unique to autoethnography. Recent years have seen a turn in IR toward the study of the everyday: objects, places, and practices such as "pissing on the [figurines of British oppressors from the] past" in Scottish pubs (Saunders and Crilley 2019), the private home in international politics (Shim 2016; Berger Ziauddin 2017), the colors of military uniforms (Guillaume et al. 2016), and passports and airports (Salter 2007), among many other examples. Yet, in such works, the author's voice usually takes the standard omniscient and remote/objective form that characterizes "conventional" academic writing (namely, explaining what *other* people do and think). And even though the emphasis is on some micro or "small" phenomenon, artifact, space, or practice, the aim is often to shed light on the bigger structures and actors of the international system *through* these examples. In autoethnography, on the other hand, the author's voice is almost always subjective and personal by definition, and the purpose is not necessarily to learn something about the bigger structures and actors as such.[8] Often, the aim is to put the individual human being at the center and see how each personal experience is unique and worthy of knowing, even if it is formed within larger social and political systems and structures and even if it shares similarities with or parallels the personal experiences of others. Isaiah Berlin's interpretation of Tolstoy's understanding of history is instructive here:

> History, as it is normally written, usually represents "political"–public-events, as the most important, while spiritual–inner-events are largely forgotten; yet *prima facie* it is they—the inner events—that are the most real, the most immediate experience of human beings; they, and only they, are what life, in the last analysis, is made of; hence, the routine political historians are talking shallow nonsense. (Berlin 2013:17)

With its focus on the micro/everyday *and* the inner world of the particular narrator, and with its attention to "unheroic" and inconsistent elements of the political as experienced by individuals, autoethnography turns upside down the very concept and understanding of "importance" in social and political life and analysis. And studying about important mainstream phenomena and people—perhaps also aspiring to become such a person or to be hired by important institutions of the state—is commonly among the most desired goals of the students I teach. Perhaps this is why the personal accounts of vulnerability, doubt, regret, contradiction, failure, and irony that I share with them in class make many of them fidgety, alienated, and sometimes even angry. This is not what they expected to hear when they enrolled in the IR department.

---

8. Except for "analytic autoethnography," which is "committed to developing theoretical understandings of broader social phenomena." See Anderson (2006).

On the Conditioning of "Importance"

Over my twenty years of teaching IR as a faculty member at the Hebrew University, I have come to realize that a strong motive for many students to study IR is their need to belong to something bigger—to feel they rub shoulders with political power. There are, of course, the more obvious and professed reasons to enroll in our department: an interest in current world affairs, a hope to get a steady job in a governmental bureaucracy such as the foreign ministry or the security services of the state, or even a desire to develop a career in politics, civil society, or international organizations. But I also think that they also seek to study IR because of the feelings of self-esteem, pride, meaning, and connection the discipline can generate.[9] The "stuff" that makes up much of the IR curriculum—great historical figures, epic stories of strategic struggles, the pursuit of systemic understandings of international politics (Grand Theory)—often excites and inspires people. IR's key actors, its "heroes" (Campbell 2008), seem to be elements of a bigger world drama. These include actors such as the state as an institution, specific states (Great Powers, for instance), famous historical state leaders, state organs (ministries, militaries, treasuries), or even challengers of the state or entire states system (think, transnational terrorists, pirates—Thomson 1996) and competitors of the state (multinational corporations).

This drama imparts some of its importance to those who study its mechanisms, dynamics, and components. The learner acquires knowledge, judgement, and expertise, often accompanied by a sense of intimacy with (the holders and institutions of) power and the undercurrents that shape international politics. Even if power-holders or officials are revealed in this drama

---

9. I did an intensive search for academic literature on the determinants of student choice to enroll in IR programs but found none. This gap seems to reveal that we in the discipline don't bother to consider why students come to learn from us. It validates my sense that the subject matter of the discipline is so obviously important in the eyes of its researchers and teachers that they don't concern themselves with student motivation to study this field. Even an author such as Aaron Ettinger, who specializes in pedagogy in IR, does not ask what initially drives students to enroll. What he does note is that "the classroom is on the front line in the battle for resources. Student recruitment and retention are essential to the economic viability of academic departments including political science and international relations. Turning students off the subject matter through an unreflexive pedagogy, boring classes, or mediocre lecturers has real economic implications for the future. Without students prepared to part with tuition dollars, or governments prepared to unlock activity-based funding, no department can thrive, even with a roster of productive researchers" (Ettinger 2020, 351).

as weaker or more shortsighted than initially imagined or are shown to err in wielding power, students still feel a proximity to power and a familiarity with how it works. They may even think they know better what to do in certain situations and how to avoid repeating past mistakes (Molloy 2020). Alternatively, such analytical knowledge can enable the learner-knower to normalize terrible realities of conflict and violence by subjecting them to rational and removed analytical frameworks and concepts.[10] Students learn to detect and supposedly understand recurring patterns that perhaps cannot be changed or abolished ("hegemonic cycles") but at least can be given a name and conceptualized.[11]

Moreover, I think that students choose to enroll in our department—over "regular," domestic political science—because of the allure of the larger and greater world the program conveys. Domestic politics is perhaps seen as corrupt, boring, self-evident, and increasingly, at least in Israel, hopelessly deadlocked in eternal struggles between Left and Right, liberals/seculars and conservatives/religious, and, more specifically, the Netanyahu and the anti-Netanyahu factions. Enrollment in the department of political science has fallen considerably in the last decade compared to the IR department[12] (we have been two separate departments since the early 1970s due to some historical faculty strife). Unlike the perceived murky and shallow waters of domestic politics, IR contains the promise of the global, the faraway, and the unknown. The demand for our program rises yearly, and the department chair must argue annually with the university's administration to close admission because of limited teaching resources. Yet almost every year, enrollment continues even after admissions officially close, and we get not a few additional students due to "computer problems."

Against this background, my courses do not offer the allure of the inter-

---

10. In this regard, see Carol Cohn's (1987) description of her immersion in the security experts' discourse.

11. On the opposite process of giving up control by un-naming, read the very short story by Ursula K. Le Guin, "She Unnames Them," *The New Yorker*, January 21, 1985. In this story, "Eve," who is never identified as such in the story because she has rejected her name, removes the names that "Adam" gave to the animals and thus releases them from human domination.

12. In the 2019–20 academic year, for example, we had a total of 599 undergraduate students, and in 2020–21 (the first year of COVID), the number rose to 638. The Department of Political Science had a total of 361 and 425 undergraduate students in those years, respectively. Source: Department of International Relations, Self-Evaluation Report as part of the Council for Higher Education External Review Process, September 2022.

12   EXPEDITION ESCAPE FROM THE CLASSROOM

national or its mystique of power. Instead of talking about IR—the academic discipline and international politics itself—in the self-empowering and self-congratulating manner sketched above,[13] I introduce and highlight locality, specificity, confusion, contradictions, inconsistencies, and a fractured narrative. I share stories with the class about, for example, my father's post-trauma after the 1973 Yom Kippur War and what it was like it to grow up in the 1970s in such a home. I tell them about my own post-traumatic experiences as a result of my military service in Hebron in the West Bank in the early 1990s and about the suicide of my cousin during his military service in 2003 (Löwenheim 2015). I share with them the process I went through during my exposure of—and exposure to—the Palestinian disaster, the Nakba, in 1948 as I rode my mountain bicycle along the frontier of Jerusalem (Löwenheim 2014). Yes, I embed the stories within larger historical and political backgrounds and contexts. I also show movies and documentaries that deal with related themes. The resistance I feel from my students is not, I believe, due to their perceiving me as self-absorbed or a navel gazer, as autoethnographers are often accused by their critics. At least, such criticisms do not appear in my teaching surveys. I think, though, that what bothers many students is my sharing of personal pain.

For university professors, there is always tension between building rapport with students and keeping a professional distance from them. We are not allowed to become friends with our students; but most of us don't want to be overtly removed or distanced from them either. It's a delicate balance—especially as I get older and the age gap between me and the students widens[14]—to establish close enough but not too close relations with them. I think students are also occupied with the proper relationship they should have with their professors. Most of my students call me "Oded," not "Dr. Löwenheim"—a typical Israeli practice. But within these limits of accepted amicable student-professor relations, most students also feel that my job is not to tell them too much about myself.

Because of the proportional sizes of the various degree programs in the

---

13. This studying of IR because it is "important" is reminiscent of the process of mutual empowerment among sovereign states in the early-modern period, as described by Spruyt (1996).

14. While one might assume that the professor-student tension around maintaining appropriate boundaries would ease as the age gap widens, I have found that this gap actually contributes to an increasing sense of tension in the classroom. As a man in my fifties, I am often seen as a tiresome "boomer" by my students.

department, I teach mainly undergraduates. These students usually want a professor to be a mentor and facilitator. From many conversations I have had with students during class or office hours and throughout my years as department chair, I believe they mainly want professors to facilitate clear and orderly structure for the various classes. They want predictability around final exams and practical knowledge and learning opportunities—for example, on how to prepare a presentation or a policy paper or how to arrange meetings or lectures with practitioners. These practitioners could include state officials, spokespersons, social and political entrepreneurs, representatives of international organizations, or other "important" or "key" professionals in the field of international politics and public diplomacy. They also want the professor to mentor and tutor them by showing active and continuous interest in their personal academic advancement.

It is not that they have no interest in basic conceptual and theoretical research in IR. But it seems that "Introduction to IR" and a few similar extensive introductory courses suffice for most of them. In addition, as young people, they tend to seek more reassuring or "positive" knowledge than what I provide them with. It's challenging for them to witness the bodily and environmental scars of violence (in Brent J. Steele's terms [2013]) because of the accountability they demand: who let this horrible violence erupt and why? Similarly, emotional scars place a burden of accountability on those who hear about them, especially if they're from the speaker's ingroup (Kurowska 2020). Of course, I don't demand the students to be accountable for the pain I share with them, but I do place a part of that obligation on the state.

The problem I encounter is that in Israel, which is a state that is in a continuing acute struggle for survival, the education system and then the military instill in young people a strong identification with the state. As the IR literature on emotions tells us, people are rooted in the state's emotional structure—thus, the emotions of many of my students are constructed and conditioned by the emotional structures of the Israeli state. The great majority of them deeply identify with the state. Every year, for example, students miss classes to participate in activities of state-sponsored/supported organizations such as "Stand with Us—Supporting Israel and Fighting Antisemitism" and "Taglit—Birthright Israel." Some miss because of reserve service in the Israel Defense Forces (IDF), which is a legal obligation for many former mandatory conscripts. Never in my career have I encountered any student who asked permission to miss a class because of an activity of "Breaking the Silence" or other anti-occupation organizations. The narrative of the state is

14 EXPEDITION ESCAPE FROM THE CLASSROOM

coherent, omniscient, and smooth, with no real bumps or pitfalls and little space for doubts or regrets.

As young people conditioned by the state, many of my students are upset to hear about the violence of the state and the outcomes of this violence, both in general terms (e.g., Walter Benjamin's or Carl Schmitt's concepts of state violence: that while political order is supposed to address the problem of violence, violence is ineliminable from the political domain) and in the more specific terms of the Israeli-Palestinian conflict. Some of them enacted violence in the name of the State of Israel during their mandatory military service and are reluctant to acknowledge that, talking instead about the legitimate employment of *defensive* force. "Violence" has a common connotation of unruly, even criminal, offensive use of force. Yet what is "legitimate" and "defensive" almost always depends on one's (ideological and political) standpoint or social position and role. By definition, the wielding of physical force *violates* the integrity of the other's body or property or disrupts someone's freedoms. (As the Dire Straits lyrics go, "You could even catch a bullet from the peace-keeping force.") Others suffered themselves (or their dear ones suffered) from Palestinian violence. But they are hesitant to see themselves as victims also of the broader conflict rather than only of specific circumstances within it or of the nefarious and supposedly independent actions of the other side. I will sometimes posit, or even hint, that the conflict is not just a historical, religious, or territorial struggle between two opposing ethnic and national groups but that it has, during the years, transformed Israel almost completely into a complex political structure of domination over the Palestinians—within Israel "proper" (the 1949 borders of the Green Line) and the Occupied Territories (after 1967). This polity not only inflicts pain on the oppressed and conquered native Palestinian Arabs but also is saturated with the pain of occupation and domination from within. But when I suggest these things, the discussion almost always reverts to the question of the validity of the ("so-called") Palestinians' claim of nativity or to the blame game: who refused to this or that peace or partition plan, and who started the current "round" of violence. On other occasions, many of the students deny that there is even such a reality as the "occupation."

I don't mean to portray my students as heartless, unkind, or unsophisticated people. On the contrary, most are pleasant, positive, enthusiastic, and smart young individuals. But within their learning objectives and expectations, within their political upbringing, within what they identify as the "material" that an IR university course should contain; within the format of a university class or seminar ("where is the presentation here?", "what part of this will be in the exam?"); within their emotional conditioning by the State of Israel; and within their image of IR as a phenomenon in the world, my sharing of personal rupture and pain is not deemed by many of them as useful knowledge. And it comes with what they perceive as an onus of accountability.

The Difficulty of Listening to "Chaotic Narratives"

Arthur W. Frank (2013) distinguishes between "restitution" narratives and "chaos" narratives in the context of sharing stories of bodily illness. Restitution narratives contain a future and are infused with optimism. Chaos narratives are the opposite of this: they are incoherent, describing vulnerability and rupture caused by illness. They convey the inevitability of illness, pain, suffering, and even death. These narratives arouse anxiety. Unlike restitution narratives, which are easy to listen to, chaos narratives are not appealing to the listener, and people tend to avoid them. This denies storytellers the opportunity to tell their stories and achieve a sense of meaning. It also denies the recognition of the storyteller's suffering (Vroman, Warner, and Chamberlain 2009).

I think that many of my students perceive my stories as "chaotic" and politically "biased" narratives. Yes, my stories and narratives are political and subjective, and they are not optimistic or "positive." I do not follow the advice of the historian from the preface of the novel *Penguin Island*, by Anatole France, who recommends the novel's prospective author to

> lose no opportunity for exalting the virtues on which society is based—attachment to wealth, pious sentiments, and especially resignation on the part of the poor, which latter is the very foundation of order. Proclaim, sir, that the origins of property—nobility and police—are treated in your history with all the respect which these institutions deserve. Make it known that you admit the supernatural when it presents itself. On these conditions, you will succeed in good society. (France 1948, vii)

Instead, I try to adhere to Max Weber's notion that the role of the professor is to present uncomfortable facts to the students (Weber 1958)—namely, that the structures of domination and the culture of violence extensively permeate the Israeli condition and cannot be compartmentalized spatially, temporally, and even psychologically, as the state would like. My talking about my personal chaos narratives of trauma and post-trauma in the classroom, and the students' resisting this as "political" or "biased," precisely attests to this effort to restrain pain and trauma to the "right place and time" and its failure.

Naeem Inayatullah writes, "Teaching is impossible. Learning is unlikely. Encounter is the remainder. You already know this, as do I" (2022, 1). He sees learning as a painful process of deep and internal change: "It ruptures the self, alienates us from our families and communities, and threatens the national identity. Often, it's simply not worth the risk" (2022, 3–4). Moreover, he sees learning as "a kind of social death that produces loss, grief, and mourning. Hence the impossibility of teaching. Students lie. Students lie when they provide the appearance of wanting to learn. No one is ready (until suddenly, unexpectedly, unintentionally, and miraculously they are) to risk social death, loss, grief, and mourning. Hence the impossibility of teaching." (Inayatullah 2020, 21). Inayatullah openly and intentionally adopts a polemic style. I am not as determined as he is about these issues, and I am definitely not trying to be polemical in the classroom. But I think he underlines an important truth. Meaningful learning indeed involves profound personal changes. In the political realm, "what they/we most do *not* want to learn is that it might be impossible to be good in a world structured by tragedy. None of us wants to apprehend our constitutive role in the very problems we are trying to solve" (2020, 25).

Thus, when I talk with students about my pain and doubts and share with them my misgivings and ruptured narratives of the self, although they are sometimes empathetic and attuned to what I say, they also seem to assume two things. The first is that I expect them to engage in a similar reflexive process, which might be emotionally costly and difficult, as Inayatullah rightly notes. The second is that I put some of the onus for these experiences and feelings on them, as they are part of the social-political structure that produces these experiences. As I said earlier, most of my students are recently discharged soldiers from the IDF, the very organ of the state that features in many of my stories of post-trauma. Service in the IDF instills a reported sense of self-maturation among many of the ex-soldier students (male and female), but I feel that it mainly hardens their hearts to "weakness." Many students retain military body postures when they present their seminar papers to the class, for example, or still use military jargon or diction, even though they are often in their mid-twenties, several years after their discharge. The age gap between us thus grows and widens every year.

This background in the classroom was thus a major source of my teaching anxiety. I increasingly felt like a foreigner among my students. I felt the tension and sometimes their hostility or ridicule. This was rarely overt or aggressive, and some students did open up to my stories and narratives and wrote excellent personal narratives of their own. For example, one student wrote about her childhood aversion to the Arabic language due to her parents' origin from Iraq and her consequent wish to stress her unquestionable Israeliness and how she recently came to terms with her family's Iraqi-Arabic legacy and identity. Another student wrote about how he left religion and became secular following his experiences as a youth during the 2005 Israeli unilateral disengagement from Gaza. Despite these moments, however, I lacked a sense of joint purpose and common ground with many, perhaps most, students. I mainly felt *loneliness* while standing before my students, and to this feeling was added a growing sense of unworthiness as a teacher—I felt I scarcely had an impact on them.

Professional Impasse

On top of the tension and even occasional friction in my relations with the students, another source of my teaching anxiety was related both to my commitment to autoethnographic writing and to the pressures from the management of our neoliberal factory of knowledge to produce and publish more and more research. Much of this can be illustrated through an email exchange I had in 2019 with the rector of the Hebrew University, Prof. Barak Medina, following his announcement that department chairs are asked to publish quarterly lists of the new publications of their faculty members. In response, I sent him an email to express my offense at his posting and to explain the reasons for this offense.

I began by pointing out that "I'm one of those faculty members who has not published in several years" and went on to explain the autoethnographic approach I took in my second published book, in 2014, as well as an article I published in 2015—my only two publications since tenure. The 2014 book describes a daily mountain-bike trip/commute I took from my home in Mevaseret Zion to our campus of Mt. Scopus and the experience

18 EXPEDITION ESCAPE FROM THE CLASSROOM

of being exposed to the landscape of the Israeli-Palestinian conflict along the bike trail:

> In fact, it is a book about a daily transition through a space of violence and pain. . . . With this story, I hoped to crack, if only slightly, the ideological-cultural structure known as our "conflict." I wanted that, through my story, people who read the book will think about their experience and see how they are, at the same time, a product of this culture and its replicators, and perhaps thus acquire a more active and agentive role. The book was, in effect, a call for conversation and humanization of our "situation," and thus I hoped that I might contribute my share, however small, to the facilitation of a human ground towards finding some way out of the terrible complexity of our conflict.

I explained in the email that the book, while a personal narrative, had an academic conceptual-theoretical framework (qualifying the epistemological and political importance of sharing personal experiences) and presentation (including references, presentation of arguments and counterarguments, and reliance on primary sources, first-hand observations, and semi-structured interviews). Despite this, it was "not necessarily received in the way I had hoped for in the IR community. In fact, it was pretty much ignored." I also described the article I published in 2015 ("the most important text I have written in my life") about my military service and the suicide of my cousin Eran during his military service, which also received little critical attention in the IR field. I then described the negative effects of this "relative disregard for these two texts" on me and on my self-confidence as a writer.

> In terms of the systemic incentives of the university, I had to conclude that if I wanted to win back professional respect and honors (e.g., citations and promotion), I must return to mainstream writing. But I felt that if I was to stay true to myself, I had to keep writing like that. Let me emphasize that, in my opinion, and in the eyes of many other researchers from around the world, narrative and autoethnographic writing in IR and the social sciences generally is a legitimate academic pursuit. My [bicycle] book came out with the University of Michigan Press, a respected publisher in IR. . . . But unlike mainstream writing, personal narrative involves, I believe, more complex internal deliberations and longer processes of thought and internal discussion with the self, and with others as well.

In my email to Prof. Medina, I went beyond my personal response to his requirements and addressed problems I saw with the worldwide "neoliberal processes of quantification and commercialization of knowledge" of universities, where

we have to "produce" as much as we can, and the meaning of the things we write is sometimes lost. I feel like we are sawing off the branch we are sitting on—producing a steady stream of articles that often replicate themselves in different titles while also chasing grants just to get more grants and hire research assistants who are usually not needed.

I pointed out my love for the Hebrew University, reflected through my service to it as chair of the department for over three years and my upcoming role as acting head of the Harry S. Truman Research Institute for the Advancement of Peace. I had agreed to this role out of a belief that the university was a "safe space, where my voice—and the voice of others—can be heard, and where I can devote the time—as much time as I need—to thinking about the next book or article":

For our words to have meaning, for them to have wisdom and genuine content, I think that sometimes one needs time to think and process personal experiences and crises. I believe that in one way or another, the same applies to experimental science researchers. . . . I believe that if you as the academic director of the institution seek to increase the number and quality of publications, you should also consider the time dimension and become more familiar with the personal stories of faculty members. To provide the staff with this all-too-essential security and confidence, which ultimately binds us to the institution and to our profession. We must ask ourselves what the purpose of all these publications is. For people to write articles and books that have a purpose and meaning that may benefit the world, I do not think you should shame them—even if unconsciously or unintentionally—by publishing lists as you suggested in your letter.

In response to my email, Prof. Medina thanked me for sharing my personal experiences. He noted that he would do his best to read the article on my military service in the Hebron fort and to read my (2014) book. He said that the suggested quarterly list was not intended to shame anyone but to positively publicize the faculty's work. He did not deem the harm or dam-

20   EXPEDITION ESCAPE FROM THE CLASSROOM

age caused to those not included as high. Within the "rules of the academic game," he added, we cannot abandon any external judgment and review, and as proof of that, he mentioned that I chose to publish my work in English and not Hebrew. His email to the faculty indicated, he said, our duty as faculty members to try to contribute to science and that he's searching for "soft" ways to encourage the faculty to do this. I replied by thanking him for his thoughtful response and stated that, while I did not see eye-to-eye with him on many of the points he raised, in order not to burden him any further I would leave things as they are. I thanked him for reading my words carefully and seriously.

Soon after this, the Department of International Relations, like many other academic units, posted an ongoing list of faculty publications on its website, from which I was absent, of course. We were also asked to open individual faculty ORCID and CRIS accounts to facilitate greater international visibility and to simplify the tracking/surveillance of faculty's publications for the Council for Higher Education's funding formula. Consequently, the vice dean for research (a new appointment in our faculty of social sciences) announced in June 2022:

> Every year, a sum of one billion NIS is distributed in the publication component [of the Council for Higher Education's budget], an amount divided according to the relative number of publications in each and every field (plus a bonus, as mentioned, for the first places). Last year our faculty's share of the pie was 3.7%. This year, thanks to you, the university will receive 4.7% of the budget pie (an increase of 10.5 million NIS compared to last year).

During the decade of the 2010s, I had looked at such developments a bit dismissively. I saw the intensification of these trends of fetishizing journal lists, CVs,[15] impact factors, h-factors, i-factors, budget formulas, and pursuit of research grants as things that did not concern me. I thought I was protected by tenure. And indeed, I am still protected by tenure—even though I have not published since 2015, they cannot fire me. But I saw colleagues hired much later than I was promoted swiftly, as they were quick to internalize these newly stepped-up norms and rules of the profession, while my heart kept sinking, along with the 2014 book and 2015 article, into the pond of oblivion.

---

15. See this interesting piece on the changing academic CV: Hamann and Kaltenbrunner (2022).

Introduction **21**

In classes, when I presented my "mountain-biking book," students were at first intrigued or amused—after all, the subject is unusual in IR. But when they realized it was another "personal story"—and in fact a "leftist" and so-called "anti-Zionist" one—many became indifferent or sometimes even openly opposed it. Indeed, others were more interested and open-minded, but no MA or PhD student wanted to write an autoethnography (or even an autoethnographic chapter in their thesis) under my supervision—I think they sensed that this might lead them to an academic impasse or that the risk was too high. All this increased my intellectual loneliness in the department along with an intensification of teaching anxiety and writer's block. And then, in early 2018, after nineteen years of marriage, I went through a painful divorce and the breaking up of my family. This, combined with my teaching anxiety and my declining self-image as an author and researcher, resulted in crushing depression, and I could not see myself publishing again. I was ashamed and humiliated.

But in the spring semester of 2018, I started to teach the "Mt. Scopus Enclave" course, and something in it brought back the desire to write again. It was not a quick or easy process, and each chapter of this book took a great deal of time and emotional energy to write. But I did write this book.

The Plan of the Book

Following this introductory chapter, chapter 1 of this book, "**Out of the Classroom: A Conceptual and Pedagogical Rationale for This Book**," lays out a rationale for the practice of "escaping from the classroom." I recount how I initially started taking sporadic excursions from the classroom to cope with my teaching anxiety. Outside the classroom, in the open spaces of the campus, I noticed a significant reduction (but not disappearance) in tension between me and the students, as well as a considerable decline in the physical symptoms of my anxiety. I also noticed that the students showed a heightened capacity for empathetic listening. Stepping away from the classroom environment provided a dynamic and refreshing learning experience. As simple as this might sound, the change in surroundings—accompanied by fresh air, sunlight, and the absence of confining walls—created a more relaxed atmosphere. Students no longer felt compelled to summarize every word I said,[16] which brought them a sense of some liberation from traditional teach-

---

16. As many students use laptops during classes instead of paper notebooks, being

22   EXPEDITION ESCAPE FROM THE CLASSROOM

ing norms and academic hierarchy. Additionally, the outdoor setting fostered social interaction and strengthened connections among students. Chance encounters with various people and unexpected surprises during our outings added an element of adventure, enhancing the "we-feeling" of the group.

As time went on, these spontaneous excursions transformed into planned tours with specific themes. This prompted me to delve deeper into researching the history and current politics of the places we went and to uncover the IR-ish dimensions in them. The result was scattered notes that gradually evolved into more coherent chapters and eventually a book manuscript that also contemplated the meaning of the tours themselves. Writing these lessons, based on outing notes, complemented the tour narratives. The book, like the outings, is a means for students to witness first-hand how learning can be a collaborative effort between themselves and the professor. It also provides a deeper understanding of the inherent tension and occasional friction that exist between teacher and students. The chapters freeze moments and tours in time, serving as a baseline for each cohort of the course to compare past and present outings and see how the same place can inspire different interpretations on each visit or generate meanings similar to those depicted in the book. (I ask them to read the chapters *after* the tours, along with other relevant bibliographical materials. The take-home exam at the end of the course combines questions on the reading materials with questions about what happened during that specific group's outings.)

The outings also create a strong emotional connection to the campus as a site of revelation and exploration and thus enhance the sense of joint purpose between me and the class. They foster a sense of belonging and ownership by deciphering the hidden meanings and realities the campus holds. Simultaneously, the tours cultivate critical distance and estrangement by unveiling the control, power, and sometimes violence embedded within the familiar and mundane. By seeing these phenomena first-hand *together*, we can engage in more empathetic and meaningful conversations, even if we don't necessarily agree on the interpretation. (But we usually agree that it is better to spend the ninety minutes enjoying the sunlight and open green spaces of the botanical garden than sitting within the gray-walled classroom.)

The IR-ization dimension of the tours seeks to sustain our sense of wonderment and interest—even hope, joy, respect, and sometimes awe—

---

in the open spaces of the campus limited their ability to use the computers (no electric sockets, no stable platform to put it on) and decreased the level of digital distraction.

regarding the act of learning about the political realm in the institution of the university. These facets led to a more positive and enriching encounter with my students. And if the encounter with students is one of the main avenues for a professor to have a real impact in the world—certainly more influential than the "impact factor" of one's articles[17]—then a more meaningful encounter with the students is something worth exploring.

After this conceptual chapter come the excursion chapters themselves. Chapter 2, **"To the British Jerusalem War Cemetery: Heterotopia and Associative Encounters with the (Foreign, Imperial) War Dead,"** deals with the first field trip in the "Mt. Scopus Enclave" course. The cemetery, established in 1927, is the resting place for over 2,500 soldiers, predominantly from Britain, Australia, and New Zealand, who met their fate during the British conquest of Palestine in WWI. Surprisingly, despite its prominent location near campus, it remains largely unnoticed by most students. When I guide them through the cemetery, it serves as a backdrop to discuss international landmarks often overlooked in daily life. We speculate on its relative obscurity and consider the unsettling aura cemeteries often emanate.

This visit grants me an avenue to delve into Foucauldian concepts of heterotopy. I challenge the students with questions designed to blur temporal and spatial distinctions: Are we in Jerusalem or the English countryside? Are we in the post–World War I era or the 2020s? Such inquiries stir deeper reflections on war's aftermath, where lines distinguishing enemies often become porous. The presence of enemy and imperial soldiers buried side by side in the same cemetery accentuates this ambiguity. I emphasize to students the profound impact these fallen soldiers, particularly the imperial ones, have on our current Israeli identity. Their sacrifices laid the groundwork for what we recognize today, including institutions like the Hebrew University. The tour thus aims to reshape perceptions, erasing clear demarcations between "us" (Israelis) and "them" (British or others), and between familiar locales like Jerusalem and distant ones like England.

This British cemetery, though managed by the Commonwealth War Graves Commission, stands as a testament to the duality of state borders: evident in its existence, yet blurring as we recognize its integral role in our shared history. Most students might not feel compelled to return, but my annual visits with new students, and my solitary reflections in between, constantly remind

---

17. "Teaching is a more influential and political site of scholarly action than commonly acknowledged" (Hagmann and Biersteker 2014, 310).

24   EXPEDITION ESCAPE FROM THE CLASSROOM

me of the thin and permeable boundaries that separate the familiar from the foreign. Therefore, my personal connection to the cemetery conditions the way I present it to the students during the class visit to this place, and the description of these dimensions aligns with the three goals of this book: to discuss how my teaching anxiety plays out during these tours in the cemetery (goal 1), to present an evocative and lively narrative of the place we visit and try to engage the reader's capacity for empathy (goal 2), and to problematize IR as an elusive political practice that can be found or ignored in everyday places (goal 3).

Chapter 3, "**Looking for Roots in the Mt. Scopus Botanical Garden: Ideological Flora, Buffer Zones, and Seeing/Ignoring**," takes us to the largest open space on campus. This garden, planted in the 1930s, is a site where I discuss with the group the relations between science and settler colonialism, between plants and ideology, and how the garden serves today as a "buffer zone" between the campus and the adjacent Palestinian neighborhood, Issawiya. The chapter was written about a class I taught in 2020, during the virtual-teaching period of the COVID-19 pandemic, and it describes how I toured the garden by myself prior to the class, planning what (and what not) to say, and how to present the place to the students on Zoom. Hence, the chapter reflects on the translation of the spatial environment of the garden to the medium of Zoom and the opportunities that arise with distance learning. In addition, the garden, as opposed to the British cemetery, is less political/IR a place at first sight. It is a botanical garden, after all. But, after more closely examining it, I IR-ize the garden by showing the students its relations with the space around it—the university campus, on the one side, and the Palestinian neighborhood, on the other side. Also, while preparing for the tour, I reflect on the possibility of creating an understanding and a sense of community with my students, in light of the feeling of common purpose that the founders of the garden in the 1930s shared with *their* students. Can IR as a field of teaching and research resemble the clearer shared purpose that characterized the establishment of the botanical garden in the 1930s? These aspects of the chapter align with the first and second goals of the book—to engage the reasons of my teaching anxiety and to present an evocative narrative about it.

Chapter 4, "**The Enigma of Portrait Busts: Exploring Power, Art, and History in Honorific Sculpting on Campus and Beyond**," describes a process I went through over several years of developing an interest in portrait bust sculptures. Scattered throughout the campus corridors and halls of the

Hebrew University, portrait busts attracted my attention while I wandered in these spaces before classes to ease my tension before teaching. I describe what these artifacts came to symbolize for me and how I see manifestations of political power and authority in them. Within this chapter, after offering a "theory of busts," I elaborate on my experiences with a sculpture of Rabindranath Tagore: specifically, when I took my "Science Fiction and Politics" students to observe it after we studied Arthur C. Clarke's novel *Childhood's End* as a eulogy to British colonialism in India. Tagore seems sad and pensive in this portrait, and I took the class to see the bust as a representation of a person who was at least partially defeated by colonialism. I narrate a fleeting moment of connection that I shared with an East Jerusalem Palestinian student from the group as we stood there, in the courtyard of the humanities, where the bust of Tagore is placed.

This chapter IR-izes the portrait busts and tries to show the students how to "make do" with what we find on campus to infer interesting insights about political and historical issues and phenomena through the stories of the persons sculpted and the art of sculpted portraiture itself. Perhaps more than previous chapters, this one "questions the boundaries of the profession and what is considered worthy/unworthy within its framework; its conservatism in the face of random or fleeting opportunity."[18] Moreover, the "pilgrimage" to Tagore's bust after discussing *Childhood's End* utilizes the presence of the sculpture on our campus (it was donated by the Indian Ministry of Culture in 2012) to contemplate whether and how we can consider colonialism and post-colonialism in our Scopus campus, given its complex spatial-political positionality. Accordingly, this chapter focuses mainly on the third goal of the book, IR-ization and problematization of the everyday.

Chapter 5, "**Layers of Memory and Identity: Exploring the Spaces and Stories of the Harry S. Truman Research Institute for the Advancement of Peace**," narrates my excursion with the students to the Truman Institute in our university. I tell about how the students reacted to the naming of the peace institute after President Truman, who authorized the bombing of Japan with nuclear weapons. We also view four portrait busts of important Zionist leaders. These busts were "exiled" to the bomb shelter of the institute by a once-powerful university official who disliked what they represented politically and historically. But the real person I focus on during this chapter is the sculptor who created these pieces of marble, and, through his story, I

---

18. Quoting my friend and colleague in my department, Dr. Orit Gazit.

26   EXPEDITION ESCAPE FROM THE CLASSROOM

ask the students to think with me about fact and fiction in history and the role of historical coincidence. I also narrate a crucial experience I had on the roof of the Truman building, which led me to stay in Israel instead of immigrating to Canada and, consequently, hastened my divorce.

This chapter also shows how I try to delve into the mind of another person—the sculptor of these busts in the bomb shelter—as I remove the dust from the gray marble busts and offer to look at them in a different or new light. I seek to uncover my deep emotional connection to the Hebrew University through tracking the story of the sculptor and his work, and I reflect on how the possibility of immigration to Canada informed my pursuit of historical and conceptual knowledge in this case and how the search for academic knowledge stems from deep feelings and emotional commitments. Accordingly, this chapter mainly pursues the second and third goals of the book—to present an evocative autoethnography that seeks to give meaning to the pursuit of knowledge in academia and to show how personal life in this profession intertwines with the university campus as a site that becomes intimately connected to one's subjectivity; and to show how the spaces and artifacts of the campus carry IR meanings.

The concluding chapter summarizes the four outings along the lines of three conceptual axes: space and history-politics-security; space and profession; and space and mind–knowledge production. I also interpret the lessons from these outings in relation to IR and to several issues around the conflict in Israel/Palestine that the chapters did not mention. I then consider the process of writing this book and the issue of writer's block in academia and in IR. Finally, I ponder how to avoid the experience of grief and paralysis should this book, too, fall into the pond of professional oblivion. I believe this is relevant not only to me, but to all writers in academia.

CHAPTER 1

Out of the Classroom

A CONCEPTUAL AND PEDAGOGICAL
RATIONALE FOR THIS BOOK

In the introduction to this book, I mentioned that leaving the classroom with my students to go on short walks and tours around the campus and to conduct classes in the university's open spaces helped ameliorate the teaching anxiety I had developed since the mid-2010s. The reasons for this anxiety related to my political interaction with the students and my use of autoethnography during classes, as well as to pressures from my university's management to intensify faculty publications numbers and ratings: "to excel." In this chapter, I delve into the conceptual and political meanings of the practice of leaving the classroom, and also discuss how effective it was as a pedagogical tool in reducing my stress and helping me return to writing.

Leaving the Classroom, Easing the Tension

Initially, the excursions from the classroom were sporadic and spontaneous, depending mainly on my degree of anxiety on a given day. Yet increasingly, whenever the weather permitted or when the students themselves started to request it, we went out to the lawns, gardens, and shaded spaces of the campus to sit there and conduct the classes. I immediately noticed that the students and I were much less tense outside of the classroom. A retired colleague in the department once told me that he is not in this profession to be loved or admired—instead, he saw his job to be to tell students the truth, as he perceived it (relatedly, see Steele 2010). I concur, but I don't think love, admiration, or even truth-telling is the sole issue here. Teaching anxiety, with its bodily signs, and writer's block, with its emotional pain, taught me that beyond the ideas I communicate as a professor, equally vital is the manner in which this communication occurs and the lasting impact that the process imparts upon both students and myself. Hence, when leaving the classroom, the movement of our bodies, the fresh air, and the sunshine—or perhaps simply the absence of walls around us—somehow greatly increased the students' capacity for empathic listening (Zembylas 2012). I often impart "troubled knowledge" (Jansen 2009, 49–50) to the students, which includes discomforting stories, ideas, and concepts about various sides of our divided community. This knowledge, which stirs negative or defensive responses because it challenges existing emotional and ideological attachments, became easier to teach outside the classroom.

Why is that? First, I think that being outside frees us from the regimented thinking or practices induced by the classroom's dull and depressing design and architecture (gray/white walls, rectangular spaces, neon/white LED lights, rows of desks and plastic seats, whiteboards, and a door painted in "coagulated blood-Bordeaux"). Going outdoors not only adds some color and liveliness to our learning process (Perks, Orr, and Al-Omari 2016) but also loosens the implicit Weberian assumption—which still exists even as the university adopts new teaching methods and technologies—that the students must remain silent and passively absorb information while *seated* in front of a lecturer ("In the lecture-room we stand opposite our audience, *and it has to remain silent*" [Weber 1958, 124, italics added].)[1] Outside the classroom, hierarchy is blurred, though not abolished, of course (Bowdridge and Blenkinsop 2011). For example, as we walk the campus paths, sit under a tree or around the frog pool, gather around artifacts, or stand at a lookout point, students don't have to keep summarizing everything I say. This in itself is often experienced by students as emancipation from "preaching" and, therefore, is welcomed by them. I, too, am less defensive and stressed outside the classroom. Walking to or from our destination on the campus also provides a short time-out or delay, allowing us to gather our thoughts or regulate emotions. The absence of plastic seats and rows of desks reduces the sense of the fixed roles in the classroom and creates a calmer atmosphere. The resentment and fatigue that builds up in a body when it is rigidly seated in the classroom dissipate when sitting in the shade of trees in the botanical garden or when walking to some destination on the campus.

These observations about fostering a different mindset by getting out of

---

1. Sometimes, though, I think that the students themselves have a dualistic approach regarding "docility": they resist it emotionally but, at the same time, often expect—even yearn for—this passive absorption, as it still seems to many as the most efficient way to maximize their grades.

the classroom correspond to Stephen Kaplan's (1995) highly cited "attention restoration theory" (ART), which suggests that natural environments provide a respite from the mental fatigue and stress caused by the demands of modern life. Furthermore, in their book *The Experience of Nature*, Rachel and Stephen Kaplan explore the concept of "soft fascination," which refers to the gentle and effortless attention elicited by natural environments. They suggest that incorporating elements of soft fascination into educational settings, such as views of nature or natural materials, can enhance students' well-being, creativity, and cognitive functioning (Kaplan and Kaplan 1989).

The open spaces of the campus are perhaps not the pristine or open wilderness environments that may come to mind when thinking about "nature," but the Kaplans' notion of nature is very broad, and it includes almost any open, outdoor space. Even when we go to the bomb shelter of the Harry S. Truman Research Institute for the Advancement of Peace, a claustrophobic and fortified place no doubt, I take the students through the botanical garden, and this fosters a mindset of an "expedition" nonetheless. Indeed, I feel students are more at ease saying what they want when we're out of the classroom. There is less formality, too: students, for example, can eat a sandwich or drink a cup of coffee during the tour without feeling guilty for violating the university's regulations. (The university can feel like an "empire of signs" [Barthes 1982]: "do not eat in the classroom," "no use of cellphones in the classroom," "no smoking," "keep quiet," "emergency exit.") And while distractions exist outside the lecture hall, I find these generally better than distractions inside the classroom (e.g., Facebook, Twitter, TikTok, YouTube), which are often tactics of student resistance against boredom or perceived political imposition.

Moreover, some of the outdoor "distractions" allow the students to get to know each other better. They find themselves more at liberty to talk with one another, on the walk to our destination, for example, or to talk with students they haven't spoken with before. In the classroom, students tend to sit in relatively fixed seats, which spatially restricts their social interaction (Sa'di-Ibraheem 2021). During the walks or tours, we sometimes also encounter "surprises." This opens our minds to unexpected questions and adds a sense of variety, spontaneity, and "adventure" to our act of leaving the classroom.[2]

---

2. On the place of adventure in education, see the *Journal of Adventure Education and Outdoor Learning* at: https://www.tandfonline.com/journals/raol20. See also Simmel (1971). Simmel considers adventures as distinct experiences that break from the routine and mundane; they are episodes that punctuate the ordinary flow of life. This

EXPEDITION ESCAPE FROM THE CLASSROOM

The fact that we walk as a *group* and that other people on campus curiously watch us (and may think about us, "Who are they?," "Where are they going?," "What are they talking about?") builds a sense of partnership or cohesion among us, which brings us closer and raises the chances of empathic learning. Leaving the classroom together and meeting *out-group* people around the campus also puts into play some elements of the minimal-group paradigm in social identity theory, whereby even arbitrary or random assignment into groups tends to make people favor their in-group members (Mercer 1995). Thus, for example, sometimes we encounter a colleague of mine from the International Relations Department or from some other unit along our path. We stop, and a brief conversation ensues with the person, who often says they should also take their students on a campus tour. Again, this momentarily fosters a sense of closeness between the students and myself, as they suddenly perceive themselves as "my" students in the presence of that colleague (unless that person also teaches some of them, which brings interesting "loyalty" conflicts into the situation). On other occasions, when students encounter friends from different courses, those friends often end up accompanying us as "guests" on the campus tour, which further enhances the positive and enjoyable nature of the "expedition."

Building the Course Book

Gradually, though, the outings from the classroom became more recurring and planned over the years, and from "regular" classes simply conducted in the open air they turned into designated tours and "expeditions." Instead of just teaching something *in* the botanical garden, I began teaching *about* the garden itself. Simultaneously, I conducted research on the history of the garden, delving into the university's archive and the garden's library, among other sources. I also explored the broader concept of botanical gardens to gain a comprehensive understanding. As a result, I began taking detailed notes and making observations both before and after the tours with the students. These notes served not only as references for future classes but also began to form the foundation for the individual chapters of this book. The process of discovery during the tours, coupled with subsequent research, instilled a

---

breaking away from normality provides a fresh perspective and can create meaningful memory that lasts. I am thankful to Orit Gazit for this reference.

Out of the Classroom   **31**

genuine sense of curiosity within me. Furthermore, the students were happy to hear about my findings during our subsequent outings. It became evident some of them possessed an authentic interest in the campus stories, and occasionally current *and* former students accompanied me to explore the campus outside of class hours.[3]

Consequently, I introduced new outings that expanded beyond the initial scope. These included visits to various locations such as the British Jerusalem World War I cemetery near the campus, or the inner courtyard of the humanities building to admire a portrait bust sculpture of the Bengali poet Rabindranath Tagore. Tagore was not only a renowned poet but also a great educator and founder of Visva-Bharati University in West Bengal, where classes are predominantly conducted in the open air (Kumar 2015). Additionally, I organized a tour to explore the bomb shelter beneath the Harry S. Truman Research Institute. (Yes, such a place exists on our campus—a peace institute named after the US president who made the decision to drop the atomic bombs on Japan, with an underground bomb shelter located directly beneath the peace institute.[4])

Then, I tried to develop a theoretical logic to justify these ventures to the students and establish a conceptual meaning for the outings. After several years of wandering in and around the campus with my students (with some conceptual bases), and after I formally started teaching a specific course based on these journeys, "The Mt. Scopus Enclave," the notes turned into more coherent chapters. After finishing writing the stories of these outings, I understood that beyond my wish to capture something of those fleeting experiences and to draw interesting insights (and, no less importantly, anecdotes and vignettes!) from them, the chapters also contained the things I could not say during the tours with the students and the things I did not understand or could not articulate then.

Writing these lessons from the lessons complemented the narratives of the tours, but they were more than just post-factum or supplemental material. The four full tour narratives in this book, in addition to the specific topic or theme of each chapter, employ autoethnographic and associative-

---

3. I need not expand on the significance of former students—who have no vested interest in grades—joining us for such explorations.

4. I was surprised to learn that the philosopher Elizabeth Anscombe was the single person who openly objected the awarding of an honorary degree to Truman in Oxford in 1956. She considered the atomic bombings as mass murder. "Choosing to kill the innocent as a means to your ends is always murder" (see Anscombe 1958).

narrative writing to explore the recursive process of searching for and exposing the international/political in a daily environment (the campus) as well as the impact of finding the political and being exposed to it in this manner (Guillaume and Huysmans 2018). The process of exposing/exposure continues through my communicating it to the students and interacting with them about it. Narrating these processes and interactions, reflecting on them, and publishing them in a book that I can then assign as part of the reading material for the course, will, in its turn, further develop these interactions (with the campus environment and the students) and allow me to share and develop some of the thoughts and questions I could not initially raise with previous students. The printed word has a different status and effect in this context.

Moreover, perhaps the stories of the tours, which students in my course will hopefully read, will let them see through a "live action" narrative how learning can be a joint endeavor of the students and the professor. They may also help them to understand more deeply the innate tension, and sometimes friction, between teacher and students from the perspective of the teacher. The chapters freeze some moments and tours in time and thus testify to what took place during certain outings. But they can also be a baseline for comparing past and present tours. And perhaps other readers of this book will find similar issues and processes in their own experience as students or teachers of the political, across topics and time, and thus be able to think about their stories of exposing/exposure through mine. They can consider how similar or different they are, what they see that I missed or ignored, and how they tackle such issues at a certain point in time or during longer processes. In other words, this book is informed by writing the teaching of the political and how teaching writes back.

Touring the Campus to Engage and Connect

Also, this is a living account of gaining self-knowledge through exploring a daily environment. Journeying the campus is done to open the various senses—of the students, of myself, and of the readers—to diverse political spaces, practices, and artifacts that are not usually perceived as such (i.e., as international, political) or that seem so banal they typically leave no impression. My impetus in the tours is to seek the hidden or unnoticed power relations embedded in such instances and situations, in this way highlighting the abundance of international and political manifestations on the campus (Guillaume and Huysmans 2018).

Uncovering and seeing with our own eyes political power in action or its mark on the places we frequent daily is more emotionally intense than merely reading about it or discussing it in the classroom. I've learned that students become more engaged when they experience these things in a sensory or bodily way. Many of them remember what we saw and talk about it even several years later. I often receive emails from alumni describing how they came back to visit the campus and went to the places I took them on the tours. One former student wrote to me from Poznań, Poland, in November 2021, about a tour he took of a British war cemetery that closely resembled "our" own in Mt. Scopus, which reminded him of our course. This seeking for engagement is related to my worry that what we do in academic fields that are mostly theoretical or abstract, such as IR, is quickly forgotten by the students after the final exam. If education is still one of the top goals of the university, then we should seek new ways to help students retain the knowledge we impart to them. I want my students to remember more of what I taught them and how I taught them.[5]

In this vein, I realized that the sense of physical discovery of the political in unexpected places or objects on the campus (or sometimes even imagining such discoveries) allows students to connect more strongly to the campus as the site where these revelations and events took place. It creates a feeling of belonging and situatedness, even ownership, through knowing or deciphering the unnoticed or hidden meanings and realities this place holds or the legends we create about it.[6] This stronger connection increases the potential for mutual understanding between them and myself, because they can clearly sense that I belong on this campus, that I am part of it. Enhancing the students' connection and fostering a sense of belonging to the campus and the university also holds political significance. In a country like Israel, where academia faces ongoing government restrictions, and freedom of thought and research are increasingly jeopardized, solidarity among students and profes-

---

5. Compared to "regular" lecture courses, in which students are often more passive, courses that engage the students in actively "doing" something on their own tend to be more remembered by university graduates. See Edward C. Page (2015, 349), and also Phillips and Jones (2018). On experiential learning in IR and political science, see Brock and Cameron (1999); Bennion (2015); Bradberry and De Maio (2019); Baer and Nichols Haddad (2023).

6. Pahre and Steele (2015) report a similar effect when traveling with political science students in US national parks as part of a module on environmental politics.

34   EXPEDITION ESCAPE FROM THE CLASSROOM

sors—in this case, through a shared, meaningful experience in the campus—becomes crucial to safeguarding the university from such assaults. The course is thus also a place-making project. Michel de Certeau writes, "There is no place that is not haunted by many different spirits hidden there in silence, spirits one can 'invoke' or not. Haunted places are the only ones people can live in—and this inverts the schema of the *Panopticon*" (1984, 107–8).

At the same time, the tours help to foster a sense of critical distancing, sometimes estrangement. They do this precisely through the process of discovering those ghosts and understanding that the familiar or taken-for-granted is no longer so and that what was perceived before as mundane, innocent, and banal contains elements of control, power, and sometimes violence, hardship, or injustice. Thus, as opposed to the closed classroom discussions—in which I talk, for example, about the emotional pain of riding a mountain bike through a landscape of conflict and violence—the students' experience of seeing, through their own eyes, similar things during campus outings or from certain lookouts in Mt. Scopus is often much more instructive. We don't necessarily have to agree about the meaning or interpretation of what we see. Yet, seeing some place or reality *together* can at least open more empathic conversations.

The act of journeying is transitory by definition, but it nonetheless opens the possibility of affecting something more permanent in a person's soul. Thus, unlike Claude Levi-Strauss's opening sentence in his *Tristes Tropiques*, I admit from the beginning: I *do not* hate traveling and explorers![7]

Mt. Scopus: AD 70, 1918, 1925

The Mt. Scopus campus of the Hebrew University of Jerusalem is one of the institution's four campuses. It is the largest in acreage and in number of students, and it houses the humanities, social sciences, business, law, education, and social work faculties and schools, as well as the university's central administration offices (e.g., the offices of the president, rector, human resources, and finance). It is the oldest campus of the university, established in 1918 by the Zionist Organization (and officially dedicated in 1925).

The campus is located in northeastern Jerusalem on the watershed of the

---

7. "I hate travelling and explorers. Yet here I am proposing to tell the story of my expeditions" (Lévi-Strauss 1973, 17).

Judean Mountains, and Scopus's eastern slopes fall sharply into the Judean Desert toward the Dead Sea. Mt. Scopus is part of the ridge of the Mount of Olives, a crest on which, according to the Roman-Jewish historian Flavius Josephus, the Roman Tenth Legion, commanded by Titus, camped before it broke into Jerusalem and destroyed the city and the Jewish Temple. Scopus was chosen as a site for establishing the Hebrew University in the late 1910s partially because of that history. The university was conceived as a secular temple, a shrine of science and scholarship that watches over the Temple Mount and thus symbolizes the modern rebirth of Jewish and Hebrew spirituality.

A large lithograph of *The Siege and Destruction of Jerusalem by the Romans under the Command of Titus, A.D. 70*, originally painted by David Roberts probably in 1848, hangs in the meeting room for the management of the Hebrew University today (see fig. 1).[8] This is a very impressive example of orientalist painting, and, if the room's doors are open and no one's there, I will sometimes take my students to see it. Of course, we can view the painting through the computer on the projection screen in the classroom assigned to the course (there is such a designated classroom—the university's course system cannot handle/tolerate a course without a specific classroom). Still, I feel the students are much more moved by the large and detailed lithograph, which has more "aura" than the projection. In addition, the "trespassing" into the meeting room involves a small act of subversion without open resistance: we only enter if the door is open and no one's there. The students are excited, as they feel they have entered a forbidden or "classified" place (again, the desire to rub shoulders with power), and I am happy if some of them suddenly recall my critical discussion from the first or second class about the notion of "importance." The lithograph shows Jerusalem (as Roberts imagined it) starting to go up in flames, refugees fleeing it, captives being taken, and the Romans readying themselves to storm it and break into its inner walls. I ask the students to appreciate the painting for a while. Then, if no one's around to scold us for trespassing, we sit around the table (there are about twenty seats, the typical number of participants in the tour) and try to guess why this specific painting is hung here. Although I could seek the answer through the university's curator of art, I prefer to keep the ambiguity to allow the students to advance even wild speculations while we're in the room.

I have heard two recurring speculations from students over the years

---

8. The original painting was lost many years ago.

Fig. 1. *The Siege and Destruction of Jerusalem by the Romans under the Command of Titus, A.D. 70*, painted by David Roberts. (Courtesy of Wikimedia Commons.)

regarding the decision. One is that it serves as a reminder of Flavius Josephus's account of the destruction the Jews experienced due to internal divisions and fanaticism during the Jewish Revolt of AD 67–73. In this context, the painting could be seen as a warning against the potential consequences of the disappearance of moderation and rational thinking from the public sphere in Israel and a reminder that the university must retain its mission of nurturing rational thinking. Other students interpret the painting as a representation of how the university's management perceives the institution—an ivory tower under siege and about to be invaded by enemy forces. However, I suggest to the students that there is another interpretation to consider. The painting may be hanging here as a reminder of the historical fact that the Tenth Legion camped on Mt. Scopus before launching the destructive assault on the city. The hill on which the Romans mass in the right foreground of the painting corresponds to the supposed location of Scopus in this imagined scene. It was from this very spot that the Romans initiated the destruction of Jerusalem in AD 70. In our present era, the Hebrew University stands atop this hill, symbolizing a reborn sanctuary of knowledge and learning.

These various interpretations highlight the multifaceted nature of the painting's symbolism, inviting contemplation and discussion about the historical and ideological underpinnings of the university, its location, and its mission. I present to the group the allegory of Mt. Scopus as seen through the eyes of the university's founders, likening it to a new temple. Thus, I read to them the words of Itamar Ben-Avi, who was known as the "first native Hebrew-speaking child" in modern-day Palestine. He was the son of Eliezer Ben-Yehuda, a significant figure in the revival of the Hebrew language. Itamar, the chief editor of *Doar HaYom* Hebrew daily, wrote the following on April 1, 1925, the day the Hebrew University was dedicated officially:

> In those days, perhaps, the boat of the Hebrews will sail to the waters of Italy in its renewed greatness, and a delegation from the boat will descend upon the wonderful capital which was erected on the ruins of ancient Rome, to tell the king and governor: not with swords or machine guns, not with gas or airplanes the People of Israel [Am Yisrael] reconquered their land. Only through their vigor and belief, only with their spirit and moral, and therefore Mount Scopus was chosen to symbolize the People's third revival. Titus destroyed the Ancient Temple, [Lord] Balfour erects the New Temple. [Balfour, the former British Foreign Secretary who granted the "Balfour Declaration" in 1917, was the keynote speaker in the university's opening ceremony.] (Quoted in Paz 1997, 292)

These words on reconquering through spiritual and moral forces connect us to the first trip we have in the course: to the British Jerusalem War Cemetery, the burial ground of thousands of imperial soldiers killed in the battles with the Ottomans in the region of Jerusalem in 1917–18. Conquests of lands are made by such sacrifices, I remind the class in the management's meeting room, and with airplanes and machine guns, not by spiritual and moral power alone. From here, the conversation sometimes trails off in various directions—to romantic and orientalist depictions of the "Holy Land" in the nineteenth century, or to World War I, the 1948 War, the 1967 War, and the ongoing occupation of the Palestinians and of East Jerusalem. Questions about whom Jerusalem belongs to, who belongs in it, and what the lessons of history are, if any, all arise from trespassing into the management's meeting room and the appreciation of Roberts' painting there.

We then go to the viewing balcony of the Maiersdorf Faculty Club to watch the Old City of Jerusalem from a vantage point similar to that in Roberts's painting. An explanatory plaque at the viewing balcony pinpoints various sites and buildings along the city's skyline. I leave the students there to

38   EXPEDITION ESCAPE FROM THE CLASSROOM

view Jerusalem and to think about the theme of conquest by airplanes and machine guns versus spiritual and moral powers, and to compare the real view in front of them with the imaginative landscape of Roberts's painting.

Enclave Years and Return from Exile

The Mt. Scopus campus sits beyond the Green Line, the 1949 armistice line between Israel and the Kingdom of Jordan, but most of the campus is not within the occupied West Bank/Palestinian Jerusalem: following the 1948 War until after the 1967 Six-Day War, it was an Israeli enclave within the Jordanian-controlled West Bank (see fig. 2). During that period, academic activity ceased on the Mt. Scopus campus, which was effectively under Jordanian siege. The campus was guarded by Israeli soldiers (dressed as policemen) who were rotated biweekly in an armored convoy.[9] The books in the libraries of the campus were evacuated in the returning convoys, and the laboratories and classrooms slid into dereliction and became military positions. (Israel did not abide by the armistice agreement's ban on keeping military personnel and heavy military equipment on the mountain, but it did this covertly. The Jordanians' conduct was similar.) In the meantime, a new campus was built in Giv'at Ram, in central West Jerusalem near the Knesset (parliament) and the government precinct. This was closer to the eye of Prime Minister David Ben-Gurion, who thought that government's financial support of the exiled university also meant that he could decide the boundaries of its autonomy (Cohen and Sapir 2016).

After the 1967 Six-Day War and the Israeli occupation of East Jerusalem, Mt. Scopus ceased to be a besieged military enclave and was reconnected to the Jewish parts of the city (West Jerusalem). Immediately after the war, a "return" fervor started among many of the university's professors. A few weeks after the war's conclusion, the 1967 honorary doctorate awards ceremony took place on the mountain. Yitzhak Rabin, then lieutenant general

---

9. One of the two roads ascending to Mt. Scopus from West Jerusalem is named Mt. Scopus Convoy Street, to commemorate the April 13, 1948, convoy that transported medical and academic staff to the Hadassah Hospital and to the Hebrew University. Seventy-eight men and women of the convoy were killed in an ambush by Palestinian forces in the Sheikh Jarrah neighborhood below Scopus. Ever since then, and even after the 1948 War, the biweekly convoy's journey to the mountain was always made in the shadow of the April 1948 massacre.

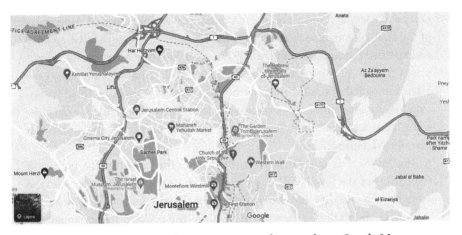

Fig. 2. The Mount Scopus enclave, as represented currently on Google Maps. There is no boundary on the ground, but the map shows Google's [and the rest of the world's] rejection of the Israeli "reunification of Jerusalem"—the dotted line is the "Green Line." (Courtesy of Google Maps.)

and chief of the general staff of the IDF, received an honorary doctorate from the university and was the keynote speaker during that event. "The question could be asked," said Rabin in his speech, "why did the university decide to grant an honorary doctorate of philosophy particularly to a soldier, as a token of appreciation for his actions in war? What do military men have to do with the world of academia, which signifies the life of culture? What do those who deal in violence by their profession have in common with values of the spirit?"[10]

I play this speech for the students when we visit the university's open theater (sometimes I bring a portable speaker, and other times we reenact the ceremony with one of the students reading the speech aloud), where the institution was dedicated in 1925 and where Rabin spoke these words in 1967. Every time I hear them, I think about Itamar Ben-Avi's assertion about the reconquest of the land through moral and spiritual powers. Most of the students don't initially ponder Rabin's tough and frank question. (Later in his speech, Rabin does answer why he, as a "violent" soldier, received this hon-

---

10. To listen to the speech, see "Chief of Staff Yitzhak Rabin's Speech at the Ceremony of Receiving an Honorary Degree—IDF Archives and the Defense System" [in Hebrew], YouTube, https://www.youtube.com/watch?v=8cwqk2y4A0k (the portion quoted begins at 57:00).

40   EXPEDITION ESCAPE FROM THE CLASSROOM

orary PhD. He also speaks about the moral power and spiritual superiority of the IDF soldiers who fought in the Six-Day War as strengths that enabled and justified the conquests of the IDF.) Instead, my students typically are surprised that there is such a thing as an honorary doctorate.[11] But when I call attention to Rabin's point that IDF officers "deal in *violence* by their profession," many students do not receive the idea easily. They cannot relate the term "violence" to the practice of the IDF, which most of them conceive as literally a defensive force.

The Mt. Scopus open theater is also where, the day after the ending of the battles of the Six-Day War (June 11, 1967), the Israeli paratroopers who occupied the Old City and other parts of East Jerusalem convened to commemorate their fallen comrades. These were the soldiers Rabin would talk about some two weeks later in the same place. One paratrooper, Meir Ariel, performed a song he wrote, "Jerusalem of Iron." The song takes the melody of the "unofficial" national Israeli anthem, "Jerusalem of Gold," which is full of nationalistic kitsch and pathos, and replaces the words with descriptions of what it really meant, in human lives, to "liberate" Jerusalem. I have never cried when hearing "Jerusalem of Gold." Still, I almost always shed tears when listening to "Jerusalem of Iron":

> The shelled battalion pushed forward
> covered in blood and smoke
> and one mother after another came amidst
> the crowd of the bereaved
> Biting its lips, and not without drudgery, the battalion continued fighting
> until finally, the flag was hoisted over the [Rockefeller] Museum . . .
> The regiments of the king [Hussein] were scattered, sniper—his turret fell
>   silent.

In 1967, the song was not perceived as a protest song but as the lamentation of a soldier who saw his comrades—and enemies—dying and injured in battle (Sharon 2016). But when I play it in the open theater today, to my students, most of them interpret it as a protest song that derides the semi-sacred "Jerusalem of Gold" theme. The song stirs uneasiness for many of them. Ariel sings about "red dawn," "Jerusalem of lead," and "expanding [Jerusalem's]

---

11. A graduate student once asked me, entirely seriously, whether the recipient of an honorary doctorate has to find a supervisor and submit a research proposal.

borders" and implies that the cost of human lives was not entirely worth the outcome.[12] The supposed "unity" of Jerusalem is almost a taboo in current Israeli politics. To question the perceived teleological course of history, that Jerusalem had to be "united" in 1967, verges on blasphemy. But listening to Ariel's voice singing his "Jerusalem of Iron" here, as well as Rabin's own voice uttering his question about violence and the honorary degree he received for wielding it (in the exact place he delivered his Mt. Scopus speech), invests their words with an undeniable dimension of authenticity. This prompts the students to reflect deeply on the questions arising from both texts—the speech and the song.

Thus, while venturing to the outdoor spaces of the campus does not annul the element of inconvenience or tension in the discussions, it induces some degree of open-mindedness and stimulates curiosity that reduces, for me at least, the perceived level of strain and resentment in the situation. It does this to the extent that I sometimes feel comfortable enough to send the students a personal photo through the course's Moodle site of my father and his girlfriend in the Mt. Scopus open theater after the war (see fig. 3).

The photo of the young couple (Dina is not my mother) was taken at the place where the speech and the song were performed not long before, with the crowd in the background looking with fascination toward the Judean Desert from within the theater's arch. This image, accompanied by the solemn words Dina wrote on the back of the photograph, helps to show the postwar excitement and euphoria that Rabin talks about later in his speech, the same euphoria that Ariel bemoaned just one day after the war. But, I tell my students that the image of the two young students also sharpens the precarity of victory: six years after this image was taken, the Yom Kippur War erupted as a result of Egypt's and Syria's desire to turn over the humiliating outcomes of 1967 and the Israeli government's dismissal of their determination and, at least Egypt's, willingness to conclude a negotiated settlement before that.

---

12. A documentary of "Meir Ariel's election campaign" captures a conversation between Ariel and an IDF major whose soldiers are about to hear Ariel in a live performance at their base in 1987. "But [what about] love of the country, love for the People of Israel?" the major asks. Ariel retorts, "What is love of the country? Give me an example." "'Jerusalem of Gold," says the major. "*You know I sang a song against 'Jerusalem of Gold,'* but I will not sing it here [italics added]," comments Ariel, as the major continues to leaf through Ariel's booklet of songs to see which of them is "beneficial" so that he can approve it to be performed in front of the soldiers. See *The "Election Campaign Journey" of Meir Ariel*, film, dir. Edo Sella, 1989, available at https://www.youtube.com/watch?v=yFXUEoXCkT8&ab_channel=LiorSiman-Tov (from 20:37).

Fig. 3. "An eternal memento from unified Jerusalem, 1967." My father, Avigdor, and his girlfriend, Dina, in the Scopus open theater, after the war. (Courtesy of the Löwenheim family album.)

In 1973, my father was among the few survivors of the IDF's Jerusalemite Brigade in the Suez Canal. He returned from that war with memories that haunted him for the rest of his life and perhaps affected his death in 2009 from Parkinson's disease. Again, something in the reality and authenticity of us being in the theater helps my words sink into my students' minds without raising too much emotional objection—or sometimes any resistance at all—and the visual power of the photo of the ordinary couple can become a part of the students' memory of this place and of the broader history of the period.

In any event, several years passed between the honorary doctorate ceremony of 1967 and the opening of the new campus in Mt. Scopus in 1981. Yet only the "human faculties" (humanities, social sciences, education, social work, law) of the university "returned" from their "exile" in Giv'at Ram to the mountain. The natural and mathematical sciences remained in Giv'at Ram, to the envy of many Scopus campus-dwellers today, who, I know, yearn to relocate to the garden campus in central Jerusalem.[13]

---

13. On the planning and design of the Giv'at Ram campus, see Dolev (2006).

Out of the Classroom   **43**

Bolting of the Campus to Jerusalem

For there is something stressful and eerie about the current Mt. Scopus campus. To begin with, the arrangement of the campus is strange and confusing. Within an area of about 700 dunams (173 acres), there are actually two campuses: the original one—several scattered buildings built mainly in the 1930s and '40s and designed in orientalist and modernist styles (Dolev 2016)—and the new campus, which "swallowed" the older one. The swallowing effect is felt viscerally by anyone who arrives at the university. They enter through a long concrete bus tunnel (now transformed into a light-rail tunnel). Coming up the escalator, they are led into a megastructure (Levin 2011) that sprawls in endless concrete corridors, with lecture halls arranged and numbered in a system that can cause innocent students and even veteran faculty members to lose their way and become marooned on campus for days (Dai, n.d.). Faculty offices are organized in strange hexagonal "honeycombs," and the megastructure features castle-like elements such as narrow windows that resemble firing loopholes and inclined outer walls that evoke images of medieval glacises.

The fortified megastructure towers over Jerusalem. It is highly visible, especially from East Jerusalem: The Old City and the Palestinian neighborhoods of A-Tur, Wadi el-Joz, and Sheikh Jarrah on one side; Issawiya, A-Zeim, and Abu Dis on the other side. But a great part of the campus is built in a way that directs inward the gaze of those inside it—inner courtyards and enclosed lawns, an indoor central forum connecting the humanities and the social sciences faculties, and windowless main corridors that prevent one from seeing what lies outside. Expansive underground parking compounds, a long bus tunnel, and large bomb shelters are at the foundation of the megastructure. The campus's largest open space is the botanical garden, from which one can observe the nearby Palestinian neighborhood Issawiya, the separation wall, and Shuafat Refugee Camp. But the garden lies outside the megastructure, a "remainder" from the original campus of the 1930s, and students and faculty hardly know it even exists.[14]

---

14. Selzer and Paz (2009) distinguish between two concepts: "relicts" (Mish'ar in Hebrew משאר) and "remainders." "Relicts" refers to remnants or leftovers from the past that can be found in the landscape but currently serve no practical purpose. They serve as evidence of the place's history and its cultural development, carrying a sense of preservation value. In contrast, "remainders" are artifacts or structures that have been brought back into use after a prolonged period of nonuse. For instance, certain

44   EXPEDITION ESCAPE FROM THE CLASSROOM

The castle-like features and planning of the campus are said to be an architectural statement that affirms the campus shall never be disconnected from Jerusalem again (Dolev 2017). In this vein, the Israeli neighborhoods that were built on the area that was occupied in 1967, between Mt. Scopus and pre-1967 Israeli Jerusalem (i.e., French Hill, Giv'at HaMivtar, Ramot Eshkol, and Ma'alot Dafna) are called the "latch" or "bolt" neighborhoods, as they were designed to "lock" Mt. Scopus to Israeli Jerusalem. When I first learned about this bolting concept, I thought it was strange to "bolt" a mountain and a campus on top of it to a city. Locking the campus, in a way, is a continuation of the siege and enclave ethos, but in reverse. Perhaps not surprisingly, I consequently developed an interest in the engineering field of moving entire buildings and structures (Curtis 1979; Paravalos 2006), as well as the fantastic genre of traveling countries and planets (e.g., the flying island of Laputa from Swift's *Gulliver's Travels*, the sailing Iberian Peninsula from Saramago's *The Stone Raft*, and *The Wandering Earth* by Liu). A university campus is a place that should not be bolted so tightly to any city. It can be connected, related, or linked, but "bolted/latched" is too strong a metaphor. There is something too decisive and rigid, too irreversible, and even forceful, in bolting. True, bolts can be pulled open, but if you close them too hard and leave them permanently locked, they often get stuck (and rusty). The cover of Diana Dolev's (2016) book on the planning and building of the early, historic campus of the Hebrew University depicts a very large plaster cast model of the pre-1948 Scopus campus being wheeled to the Levant Fair in Tel Aviv in 1936. Our current campus is too large to be transported to Tel Aviv this way. I tell the students that one of the purposes of the campus tours is to loosen this bolt a bit, to experience some freedom of movement and thought.

Places We Can't Tour

Whether the university campus is bolted to Jerusalem or not, freedom of movement is quite restricted in the environs of Mt. Scopus, because it is

---

original buildings of the Hebrew University, which were abandoned during a specific period, underwent renovation after 1967 and were reintegrated into the revitalized university campus. These buildings are now functional again, although not necessarily serving their original purpose: for example, the chemistry building, which currently houses the Institute of Contemporary Jewry. Selzer and Paz also classify the botanical garden as a "remainder" in this context.

Out of the Classroom **45**

edged on its other sides by potentially hostile Palestinian neighborhoods and areas that we cannot visit during the course because of university security regulations. Thus, for example, we cannot take the short walk to the compound of Augusta Victoria, which is just a few hundred meters south of the campus. After the 1898 visit of the German kaiser Wilhelm II to Ottoman Palestine, imperial Germany constructed this complex: a church and a hostel for German pilgrims and a center for the German Protestant community of Palestine. Following the British occupation in 1917–18, the place served for several years as the headquarters of the British forces, and then it was the official residence of the High Commissioner of the Palestine Mandate until 1927. Between 1948 and 1967, it was used as a military hospital by the Arab [Jordanian] Legion. Today, it is the second-largest Palestinian hospital in East Jerusalem. Recently, in July 2022, US president Joe Biden visited the hospital as part of his visit to Israel. Still, his visit was defined as "private," without Israeli escort, thus only half-acknowledging Palestinian authority (but not the "Authority") in that place.

I visited Augusta Victoria several times, alone or with friends and family, but, like President Biden, not in any "official" capacity related to my work at the university. The place is fascinating architecturally and historically, but the several times I went there, I always felt danger. No one showed any hostile intentions toward my companions or me; in fact, everyone I spoke to was pleasant and happy to share their knowledge and stories of the place. I did not hide my Israeli identity, even though I could have passed as a European. But being "outnumbered" by Palestinians there made me realize how they might feel in reverse situations, which are much more common in Jerusalem in general, and on Mt. Scopus campus, specifically (Kerzhner, Kaplan, and Silverman 2018). It was an instructive, somewhat humbling experience. University regulations prohibit visitations to such places without an armed security escort, which would be unthinkable in the context of a course tour like mine, and would surely garner trouble instead of "security."

Similarly, we cannot visit the Issawiya neighborhood, located just a few dozen meters from the perimeter security fence of the Mt. Scopus campus, below Martin Buber Street. Every morning, at dawn, the security department of the university patrols this road with dogs specially trained to detect explosives. In August 2002, a bomb thrown over the security fence of the campus was smuggled into the Frank Sinatra Center's cafeteria in a backpack by a Palestinian terrorist and exploded there, killing nine students and university employees and injuring dozens of others. While the plotters were not

48   EXPEDITION ESCAPE FROM THE CLASSROOM

from Issawiya but from the "Silwan Cell"—another Palestinian neighborhood in East Jerusalem—campus security was increased, and police blocked off Haruba ("carob" in Arabic) Street,[15] a road to Issawiya off the roundabout at the main entrance of the campus, with large concrete cubes.[16] Despite recurrent requests and applications from the residents of Issawiya, the road remains blocked. Residents believe that the street was blocked at the request, or at least the implicit approval, of university management. From what I know, this is not true. However, the roadblock notably reduces the traffic congestion at the busy roundabout at Avigdor HaMeiri Square, near the main entry gate of the campus; that might explain the university's lack of protest at this measure. (This slowdown of traffic also benefits a large IDF medical base on Buber Street.)

In 2016 and 2019, activists from Issawiya came to the campus and spoke, in Hebrew, with hundreds of students and faculty about the problems of the neighborhood. These include sewage spillovers from the campus to the neighborhood, the blocking of Haruba Street, police harassment of the neighborhood, and the lack of construction permits and plans in the zone. They pointed out that the only available area that could be used for new construction was being developed into a "national park" (the Mt. Scopus Slopes National Park). Following these meetings, I went on a few "police watch" activities in Issawiya (accompanied by residents) and was alarmed by the terrible condition of the infrastructure in the neighborhood. I witnessed and was disturbed by how the police routinely harassed the residents (even when "moderated" by the presence of the Israeli police watch group that followed them). But I also

---

15. There is no street sign in the actual place. I know the name of this road only from Google Maps. The street leads to a sacred carob tree in Issawiya (see Morin 2019).

16. Since 2002, the Hebrew University has implemented various security measures to enhance campus safety. These include the use of bomb-sniffing dogs, the installation of metal detectors at entry gates, electronic sensors on fences, a stricter policy of searching and examining backpacks upon entry, and the requirement for individuals to present a student or employee card when entering. According to Shmulik Dahan, the former head of the security division (which has been upgraded from a department in recent years), the annual budget allocated to the university's security division amounts to "tens of millions" of New Israeli Shekels. This represents approximately 50 percent of the combined total security budgets of the other six research universities in Israel. These details were mentioned in the minutes of the Knesset Committee for the Public's Inquiries, during a meeting focused on the security and inspection apparatus of the Hebrew University's Mt. Scopus campus on December 2, 2014, https://oknesset.org/meetings/5/6/560376.html. For an ethnographic analysis of the culture of everyday security in Israel, see Ochs (2011).

saw the marks of fire that had consumed trees in the botanical garden after Molotov cocktails were thrown into it from Issawiya, and I watched in fear and anger when students and professors were locked inside the campus for several hours after dozens of youths from the neighborhood clashed with the police at the gate of the university.[17]

So, we're supposedly guarded within the bolted campus, but the situation around us is volatile and we can watch over it only from inside the gates and fences. But in recent years, an increasing number of Palestinian students from East Jerusalem (Issawiya included) have enrolled in the Hebrew University and the university acknowledged the Al-Tawjeehi, the Palestinian General Secondary Education Certificate Examination.[18] Hundreds of East Jerusalem Palestinian youths now study on the campus, some in my department (7.82 percent of the total number of undergraduate students [47 of 601] in the International Relations Department during academic year 2021–22). This means that the next time I take my class to tour the fences of the campus (from within) and watch over Issawiya or Augusta Victoria, the chances are higher that I will have students from these areas in the group. This will surely add new information, viewpoints, and narratives to what I tell the class (Mantz 2019; Zidani 2021; Sondarjee and Andrews 2023).

Explaining the Rationale of the Outings and the Course

The "Mt. Scopus Enclave" course is part of the second- and third-year undergraduate elective courses of a three-year BA program offered by the Department of International Relations. Touring the campus is not typical of an IR course. Yet, if IR is "anything that crosses state borders and is political" (as my PhD supervisor, Professor Benny Miller, told me more than twenty years

---

17. See Nir Hasson, "Palestinians and Police Clashed at the Entrance to the Hebrew University," *Haaretz*, May 9, 2021, https://www.haaretz.co.il/news/law/1.9788337 [in Hebrew].

18. As part of the Hebrew University's economic "recovery plan" (actually, a bailout by the government), the institution committed to increasing the share of "Arab" (not "Palestinian"—thus, not recognizing this national identity) students to 18 percent in the BA and 12 percent in the MA, as well as to increase the number of Jewish Haredi ultraorthodox students to 1,000 (the total university student body is 24,000). This appears under the clause "The Institution's Enlistment to the Advancement of National Goals." See "A Plan Was Devised to Help the Hebrew University Recover," [Israel] Council for Higher Education, February 28, 2018 [in Hebrew], available at https://che.org.il

48   EXPEDITION ESCAPE FROM THE CLASSROOM

ago), then the university, as an institution and as a physical campus, is an international entity worthy of our attention. To begin with, so much of what the faculty members of the Hebrew University do is primed toward the international: we publish chiefly in English in international outlets (publications in Hebrew count little toward promotions in most fields), we participate in international conferences, and we host and keep in touch with colleagues from overseas. Most of our promotion procedures also require a considerable degree of input from foreign scholars (even though some boycott Israeli universities and academics openly or in subtler ways).

Much academic work is done from home or other places, not necessarily on campus. But teaching mainly happens on campus, at least when no global pandemic sends us to the virtual world. Teaching brings the international to the course through the topics in the syllabus (and also explicitly through the course itself: so many items on the IR syllabus include the term "international" in their title). Exchange students also sometimes take a prep year in Hebrew and then enroll in our program. While teaching is done predominantly in Hebrew in the IR Department at the BA and MA levels, the PhD program is English, even if all the students are Israeli Hebrew speakers. If the "international" or the "global" is sometimes an abstract or elusive realm and concept (Walker 2002; Salter 2007),[19] then the very act of studying them on the campus reifies and validates such notions and embodies the international on the campus. In other words, the campus is a site on which we actually perform the international. This raises the question of whether the specific features and stories of the campus as a unique place matter in this regard: is performing the international done differently on various campuses because of something endemic to each campus per se? I think that, while perhaps not necessarily or in every case, the uniqueness of each campus *can* make a difference in this respect if we examine it more deeply and actively *engage* with the campus.

Thus, for example, on many North American, Australian, and New Zealand campuses, it is customary to acknowledge the traditional land rights of Indigenous people on whose territories the campuses are located (Ambo and Rocha Beardall 2023). Such territorial rights acknowledgements can be seen

---

19. Xavier Guillaume aptly writes, "The international still tends to be thought and presented as a decontextualized, homogenous and universal historical 'reality' in contemporary international studies from which International Relations scholars are shopping for events and facts supporting or 'falsifying' their theories." "Historicizing the International," *E-International Relations*, June 8, 2013, https://www.e-ir.info/2013/06/08/historicizing-the-international/

as relevant to the discipline of IR, given the growing recognition that certain internal dynamics play a crucial role in shaping international relations or stem from IR influences, such as the historical context and ongoing processes of settler colonialism. Likewise, in the context of Israel, analyzing the dynamics between Palestinian nationalism and Zionism and the Israeli state can be seen as a part of IR, despite being focused on internal dynamics within national borders. This perspective recognizes that domestic factors can have a profound impact on international relations, and vice versa. The campus is a site where we see the dynamics of this conflict play out. As I discussed previously, the campus overlooks the Palestinian parts of Jerusalem and some of the Israeli settlements in the West Bank (including Ma'ale Adumim, one of the largest settlements), and its presence affects daily life in the nearby Palestinian neighborhoods. Students from East Jerusalem enroll in the university. And the Israeli-Palestinian conflict often "spills" onto the campus in myriad ways or stops at its gates and fences (the latter being themselves a symbol of this conflict). Moreover, the campus offers many opportunities to physically explore key moments in the history of the conflict (think, the Six-Day War and Rabin's speech at the open theater of Scopus). Thus, studying and teaching about the campus can open our minds to questions of positionality and historicity, and, as in my case, become an inspiration or source for the knowledge we "export" from here to the international sphere. (On such a way of utilizing one's own experiences as sources for research, see Riemer 1977; see also Brannick and Coghlan 2007.)

But beyond being a place in which we teach and study IR, the campus is international in many other aspects as well. Akin to the tours we conduct are the various other campus tours that take place here. "Campus tours" are a common ritual for universities hosting academic colleagues or delegations from other universities or during international conferences. Writing about campus tours at the University of Miami for prospective students and their parents as a ritual of higher education, Peter Magolda states, "The tour is more than an instrumental task of transporting guests around campus and conveying technical information. It is one of many formal rituals that transmit the institution's political, social, environmental, and cultural expectations and norms for prospective members" (2001, 2). Similarly, on our Mt. Scopus campus, university donors, who come mainly from international Jewish communities or the diaspora abroad (in Israel, alumnus donations are not as common as in North America), are also often taken on a campus tour organized by the university's external relations division.

These tours are focused on the early history of the university and include

50   EXPEDITION ESCAPE FROM THE CLASSROOM

a look out onto the Old City of Jerusalem from the Maiersdorf Faculty Club's balcony—a beautiful view of the golden Dome of the Rock on Temple Mount/ Haram al-Sharif (invoking the idea of "Jerusalem of Gold"). Students who worked as guides on these tours told me that they have a carefully crafted script, which does not include taking formal guests—donors, foreign diplomats, politicians, or officials from overseas universities—to view the less sublime realities or sights that can be observed from Mt. Scopus. The official university tour includes the Nobel Laureates wall,[20] the Nicanor tomb area of the botanical garden (a tomb from the Second Temple era, which corroborates a story from the Talmud), and the viewpoint from the open theater to the Moab Mountains in Jordan and the Dead Sea and the Jordan Rift Valley. The political elements in these places and points are downplayed or neutralized in the official tour. In this light, teaching the "Mt. Scopus Enclave" course is an international endeavor by definition: the course and this book based on it are about the campus as a political site, and this English-language book is meant to cross international borders and offer a more nuanced and complex picture of the campus and life in it than the one provided by the Division of External Relations.

But why is all this relevant for IR students? Even if the campus can indeed be seen as an international "object" or space of inquiry, aren't there more pressing or relevant issues to discuss in an IR course? I often hear this question/objection from students and colleagues. As discussed in the introduction, IR is after all about important or serious subjects, challenges, and phenomena: peace and war, political economy, international regimes and institutions, diplomacy, human rights, refugees, energy crises, and global warming, to name only a very few. Also, the "Mt. Scopus Enclave" course does not focus on one, singular topic, as the campus by nature is a heterotopia and an assemblage of many stories and narratives. But even though there may

---

20. This wall, which is inside the gated campus, as well as the "Founders Wall," at the Avigdor HaMeiri Square near the entry gate, feature a prominent image of Albert Einstein. Although Einstein gave only one talk (in French!) at the not-officially opened Hebrew University in 1923 and declined the offer to become a faculty member here, he bequeathed the university the rights to his image and his diaries. In recent years, the university has put this image and Einstein's name into its marketing and branding efforts. "Einstein in Gaza," for example, is an annual event in the area of Gaza Street in the Rehavia neighborhood of Jerusalem, at which Hebrew University professors give TED-like talks with an eye to recruiting new students. There was an attempt, which, thankfully, waned, to conduct an "Einstein on the Train" to Tel Aviv as well. The public relations department even distributes free Einstein WhatsApp "stickers."

be more important places or topics to study or more coherent subjects, the campus is here and easily accessible. No special arrangements are required to tour the places I take the students to, and we only need to step out of the classroom door. I'm always amazed by how simple that move is. And when we start to "dig" we always find important IR phenomena and topics to discuss— war, conflict, colonialism, imperialism, and securitization. Because they are important, they tend to be all-pervasive or omnipresent, manifested locally on the campus and its vicinities.[21]

I am reminded in this context of what "Philip Roth," the boy narrator of Philip Roth's novel *The Plot Against America*, has to say about history. In this alternate-history novel, in which Charles Lindbergh defeats Franklin D. Roosevelt in the 1939 presidential election and a pro-Nazi regime takes hold over the United States, Roth, a Jewish child from New Jersey, contemplates the true nature of history: "And as Lindbergh's election couldn't have made clearer to me, the unfolding of the unforeseen was everything. Turned wrong way round, the relentless unforeseen was what we schoolchildren studied as 'history,' where everything unexpected in its own time is chronicled on the page as inevitable. The terror of the unforeseen is what the science of history hides, turning a disaster into an epic." No wonder that further in the novel he says, "I wanted nothing to do with history. I wanted to be a boy of the smallest scale possible" (Roth 2004, 114 and 223).

Venturing out to the spaces of the campus calls into question the divisions between, on the one hand, where history/politics happens and continues to leave its mark, and on the other hand, where supposedly mundane and apolitical reality is in force. Moreover, by blurring these divisions and invoking the everyday and mundane as something worth exploring, the outings also call into question the importance of supposedly important things and people. The latter tend to consider themselves or be seen by others as important, which feeds recursion and mutual empowerment processes. The very act of doing and learning something that is not entirely, or even not at all, "important" helps to develop a more critical and ironic standpoint, perhaps even humility, among the students. So, this questioning of the boundaries between the realms, which I try to evoke during the course, is quite suitable for an IR course. As Xavier Guillaume and Jef Huysmans state,

---

21. Similarly, Anna Lowenhaupt Tsing (2015) finds evidence for the omnipresence of capitalist precarity through the stories of individuals in collecting, selling, and distributing networks of matsutake mushrooms around the world.

52 EXPEDITION ESCAPE FROM THE CLASSROOM

The international is then not a sequential history of exceptional moments and events but rather a series of personal stories of those ordinaries affected by and affecting the international, or a history of reiterative practices linked to embodied routines. By shifting the analysis from extra-ordinary politics to the ordinary, the everyday underlines a multiplicity of political temporalities and spaces as a distinct point of interest in defining what may be analytically or politically relevant and significant. (2018, 287)

But perhaps this recognition of the importance of the everyday is also a realization that can encourage the students to be more active in seeking a change in the world, understanding that there are very few "neutral" or "shielded" or "apolitical" sites or places, even within the campus. The "Mt. Scopus Enclave" course moves between the desire to have nothing to do with "history," on the one hand, and the exposing of and exposure to the historical, political, and international on campus, on the other hand. Even if this occurs in an anecdotal or incoherent manner, the result is the development of critical observation capacities *and of disillusionment*. The campus is secured—it is surrounded by high me(n)tal fences, dogs search for explosives each dawn, sophisticated sensors and cameras are mounted on the fences, armed guards are stationed at the entry gates, and backpacks are thoroughly searched upon entry. The megastructure is a solid and gloomy concrete castle "bolted" to the city of Jerusalem. But the tours reveal the following facts: as a group, we can scarcely leave the campus even to walk on Martin Buber Street or Binyamin Mazar Street, which circle the university; we cannot visit Augusta Victoria for similar reasons; the laying of the university's cornerstones in 1918 was done under the guard of British soldiers (see fig. 4). When I refer the students to this picture as we search for the lost site of the university's cornerstones (we never find the site—it was covered by concrete a long time ago), Rabin's question about the connection between soldiers, violence, and the values of the spirit becomes even more acute.

Final "Justifications" and the Influence of Michel De Certeau

A final justification for the course is related precisely to the practice of justifying. Consider how Richard Rorty thought about the emergence of new knowledge: "There is no basis for deciding what counts as knowledge and truth other than what one's peers will let one *get away with* in the open exchange of

Out of the Classroom 53

Fig. 4. Laying of the cornerstones for the Hebrew University on Mt. Scopus, July 24, 1918. (Courtesy of the Library of Congress, Prints and Photographs Division, matpc 00718, https://hdl.loc.gov/loc.pnp/matpc.00718.)

claims, counterclaims, and reasons. And this means that justification reaches bedrock when it has reached the actual practices of a particular community" (quoted in Guignon and Hiley 2003, 11; my emphasis).

We often all find ourselves having to justify the choices and content of our academic research and teaching. During the campus tours and their preparation, a former student of mine, now Dr. Yvgeny Yanovsky, acquainted me with Michel de Certeau's book *The Practice of Everyday Life* (1984). Reading the book, I found de Certeau's idea of "making do" (*perruque* in French) or "ripping off" as highly relevant for both the justification of "getting away with" my course aimed at the students and my colleagues *and* at the actual content and practice of the outings themselves. The concept of "making do" refers to the ever-fleeting ways and methods ("tactics" in de Certeau's concepts) by which ordinary "users" try to trick their way within disciplining and restricting structures ("strategies") on a daily basis. Strategies are manipulations by authorities that isolate a subject by defining a "proper place" (*pro-*

54   EXPEDITION ESCAPE FROM THE CLASSROOM

prel) where this subject must reside. There, in the proper place, the subject is administered.

In the context of the current book, the isolating strategies and the proper places I try to trick by going out on the campus tours are, first, classroom learning, and second, the academic profession and the discipline of IR within it. Not only that, but the trickery also concerns the phenomenon of international politics itself, the subject matter of the academic study. "Let us try to make a perruque in the economic system whose rules and hierarchies are repeated, as always, in scientific institutions," de Certeau advises us. "In the area of scientific research (which defines the current order of knowledge), working with its machines and making use of its scraps, *we can divert the time owed to the institution*; we can make textual objects that signify an art and solidarities . . . to make a perruque of writing itself" (1984, 27–28; italics added). Elsewhere, de Certeau explains "ripping off":

> Accused of stealing, or retrieving material for their own profit, or using the machines for their own ends, workers who "rip off" subtract time from the factory (rather than goods, for only scraps are used), with a view to work that is free, creative, and precisely without profit. In the very places where reigns the machines they must serve, they inveigle for the pleasure of inventing gratuitous products intended solely to signify their know-how by their work and to respond to the fellowship of workers with a gift. (de Certeau 1980, 3–4)

Accordingly, part of what the outings are designed to do is to creatively make these escapades from the classroom nonetheless relevant to IR—to IR-ize them, so to speak. This IR-ization is, on the one hand, a serious and honest effort to make the tours interesting and pertinent to the IR students who follow me during the campus outings and, on the other hand, a prankish/resisting act of perruque/making-do, à la de Certeau. Contrary to the conventional approach of "securitization" in IR, which is typically carried out by political and administrative-bureaucratic elites to emphasize the significance and urgency of a particular issue and prioritize it, IR-ization is a process undertaken by me, a professor/scholar, with precisely the opposite objectives. My intention is to scrutinize power dynamics, challenge the notion of "importance," and encourage an exploration beyond the confines of the classroom by engaging in campus escapades with my students. I would like to think that the campus escapades are, to a degree, de Certeau-ian acts of "ripping off" and disservice to the "machines" of academia and IR, and, with no presumption, a modest "gift" to the students who are enrolled in the course and to the readers of this book.

Hence, the outings look for the traces and marks of the international and the political on the campus and its close environment and use them as a pathway from which we can also continue to IR-ize places and things that are *imagined* by the students and me as international.[22] In this way, the tours push or stretch the limits of the academic field and discipline and question the self-importance of the "core" or "key" IR actors and phenomena and the symbiotic relations that exist between the "mainstream" of the academic discipline and the real world. This is perhaps not something new in the eyes of critical IR scholars. But for my students, the live, embodied experience of pushing or playing with the boundaries of the discipline and the world through the tours (a much more collective and vivid interaction and process than a lecture or even an open discussion within the confines of the classroom), arouses their curiosity. It is something more tangible and memorable than anything I tried with my students before. In this way, we "read" the space of the campus, not (I hope) as a social science cliché, but as de Certeau writes about the act of reading: "Readers are travelers. They move across lands belonging to someone else, like nomads *poaching* their way across fields they did not write, *despoiling* the wealth of Egypt to enjoy it themselves" (1984, 174).

I came to realize that the campus tours, which began as a coping method for my teaching anxiety (and an escape from academic boredom[23]), are also no less importantly an act of giving up on presumption and pretension while trying to connect in more meaningful ways with the students. After internalizing this, I felt I could return to autoethnography. I now have more limited goals for my teaching and writing, and instead of presuming to change the overall national "situation," I mainly harbor a hope to raise questions and curiosity and to enable smoother communication with the class. I am more realistic about the role and capabilities of the academy to effect change in such protracted conflicts as the ones in my country.

Still, I am aware that one role I can perform at least with some measure

---

22. See in this regard the various chapters in Salter (2015, 2016).

23. "The kind of boredom experienced in university departments is of a very particular kind. It is most easily identified in terms of affect: the sense that the seminar is never going to end, that the speaker will never get to the point, that the articles one is reading are proceeding at a glacial pace, that one simply cannot get into a discussion, that one dreads getting into it in the first place" (Baghdadchi 2005, 319).

of success is to open my students to concepts and discourses that show how violence and repression are not inevitable in all contingencies and that we are embedded in political power relations and fields even if they are not discernable at first glance. By going out of the classroom to tour the campus in search of the political—and of some pleasant sunshine and fresh air too—I hope that something of what I try to achieve is passed on to the students who accompany me. Patrick Thaddeus Jackson's words reflect what I feel in this context: "I count 'my' successes one student at a time, one class at a time, sometimes one class session at a time, and I put 'my' in scare-quotes because what happens to and for my students in and through my classes is something that is centrally and critically dependent on their coproduction of the space of learning" (2020: 50). I think that leaving the classroom for these campus tours helps many students to coproduce, in his words, a new space of learning.

Now, let's exit the classroom and get going!

CHAPTER 2

To the British Jerusalem War Cemetery

HETEROTOPIA AND ASSOCIATIVE ENCOUNTERS
WITH THE (FOREIGN, IMPERIAL) WAR DEAD

Introduction to the Chapter

The first field trip of the "Mt. Scopus Enclave" course is a visit to the British Jerusalem War Cemetery adjacent to the campus (see fig. 5).[1] Established in 1927, during the British Mandate in Palestine, this cemetery contains over 2,500 graves, predominantly of British, Australian, and New Zealander soldiers who lost their lives during the British conquest of Palestine from the Ottomans during World War I, between 1917 and 1918. It also serves as the resting place for some Italian, German, and Ottoman soldiers. Despite the cemetery's prominent position just beyond the pavement of Winston Churchill Avenue—the street leading up to the campus and a route students traverse daily—and the fact that its main gate is open 24/7, many students have never set foot on this site.

The visit to this British war cemetery gives us an opportunity to explore how international locations can remain inconspicuous in our everyday surroundings and to ask why most of the students have not ventured here before our visit. This tour also allows me to engage the group in discussions of Foucauldian concepts of heterotopia. Thus, I ask the students to question our current spatial and temporal context, pondering whether we find ourselves in Jerusalem or the English countryside, in the year 1927 or the 2020s. Fur-

---

1. I originally intended to insert a current picture of the area, but Google and other web services' aerial images of Israel are intentionally blurred (see the next chapter for further details on this). Nevertheless, the surprisingly high-quality photo from the 1930s, depicting the newly established Hebrew University in close proximity to the British Jerusalem War Cemetery, clearly illustrates the connections between British imperialism and the Zionist movement. This image echoes the scene from the previous chapter, where British soldiers are seen securing the perimeter while the cornerstones of the university are laid (fig. 4).

57

Fig. 5. Hebrew University, looking west along Olivet Road (1933). The war cemetery is in the distance. (Courtesy of the Library of Congress, Prints and Photographs Division, digital ID: https://hdl.loc.gov/loc.pnp/matpc.22150.)

thermore, I let them contemplate the burial of imperial and enemy soldiers within the same cemetery, prompting reflections on the blurred lines that distinguish foes in times of war and its aftermath. We also explore the broader history of military burial and the significance of the fallen soldier's body, as well as our connection as Israelis and members of the Hebrew University to these imperial soldiers interred here.

The perplexity experienced by many students during the visit arises from my deliberate blurring of the ostensibly clear distinctions between "us" (Israelis) and "them" (British), between "here" (Jerusalem) and "there" (England and Australia), and more broadly, between "enemy" and "friend." I encourage critical contemplation about the concept of the "international" as a realm defined by state borders, which, while evident in the British cemetery managed by the Commonwealth War Graves Commission (CWGC), dissolves as we recognize its integration into our own history and everyday environment. On the other hand, the fact that most students had not entered the cemetery before the tour and likely will not return afterward reinforces its foreignness and accentuates the barrier surrounding it.

As opposed to the single tour most students have here, I revisit the site annually with new groups and often come alone on other occasions. My personal connection to the site influences how I present it to the students during the visit, as many layers of meaning, memory, experience, and knowledge about the place accumulate in my mind and subjectivity. And when I sit to write the account of this tour, and recollect other tours here as well, the writing of these layers and complex connections becomes a part of my effort to reduce my teaching anxiety by bolstering the theoretical and academic legitimacy of autoethnography—goal 1 of this book. Furthermore, I show here how the process of IR-ization actually takes place in a specific location—goal 3 of the book. The detailed and sometimes evocative narrative of this experience, in turn, aspires to achieve that meaningful connection with the readers *and* the students (goal 2).

The British Jerusalem War Cemetery

Today is Monday, November 11, 2019. It is 1:05 p.m.—exactly 101 years, 2 hours, and 5 minutes since the ceasefire took effect on the Western Front in World War I, and slightly less time than that since the completion of the conquest of Palestine by the British during that war. We—me and a group of twenty-three undergraduate students from the Hebrew University—sit near the service entrance to the British Jerusalem War Cemetery at Mt. Scopus (see fig. 6). The students and I came down here on Winston Churchill Avenue, just a short walk from our campus on Mt. Scopus.[2] We are sitting close to a small office of the CWGC. The office is located today in what was originally the house of the cemetery's watchman. That house was designed by the architect of the cemetery, John Burnet, as a traditional Palestinian Arab house. Burnet designed it this way as a "courtesy" to the local environment in the 1920s. But the Cross of Sacrifice, a seven-meter-high memorial monument in the center of the cemetery, which is visible from every direction, exhibits less "courtesy" toward the environment in a land of an "other faith" (Fuchs 1996, 125 and 137). The British building of a permanent guardhouse at the time was

---

2. Churchill, a friend of Zionism, was posthumously honored in 1974 by the city of Jerusalem, and he is now commemorated here on the road to the Hebrew University, the same road he took to Mt. Scopus on his Palestine visit in 1921 as the State Secretary of Colonies. On that 1921 visit to the not-yet-inaugurated Hebrew University, see Gilbert (2007, 56–57).

Fig. 6. A view of the cemetery from the direction of the guardhouse. (Photograph by the author.)

perhaps due to the fear that prominent Christian symbols in the heart of a Muslim population might lead to vandalism.

Buried in this cemetery are 2,539 soldiers from the British Empire's Egyptian Expeditionary Force. They were killed on the battlefields near Jerusalem during the British campaign to take this land from the Ottoman Empire in the Great War. In addition to this site, several more British cemeteries in Israel and the Gaza Strip, built with almost identical design and aesthetics, contain thousands of other imperial soldiers buried during and immediately after the occupation of Ottoman Palestine (totaling about 12,000). The place is thus a mass-burial site for the dead of a long and cruel war, a space of sadness and loss. But it is designed as a beautiful, well-groomed garden with minimalist and respectful architecture—a space of tranquility and solitude within a bustling area.[3]

---

3. When in the cemetery, I am always reminded of the poem "The Soldier" by British poet Rupert Brooke:

If I should die, think only this of me:
  That there's some corner of a foreign field

First Goal: To See Human Cost of War

Our visit today has two main goals (the goals of the tours with the class are not necessarily identical to the goals of this book): First, I want the students to see with their own eyes an important aspect of the remnants of war. Various courses in the Department of International Relations discuss war, but most refrain from engaging with its direct human cost. Even though, as Israelis, we occasionally experience "outbreaks," "rounds," or "waves" of organized (and sometimes less organized) violence, the long, uniform, and regular rows of graves of British imperial soldiers that lie here, so close to our campus, clearly and uniquely illustrate the human cost of war. This is different from anything that can be learned from books or articles on the subject or even from our daily experience of a culture of violence here in Israel. Physically being in the war cemetery, so close to the graves of so many soldiers, gives a different meaning—a corporeal one—to the state-centric discourse of security studies and IR (Auchter 2016).

War, one of the fundamental phenomena of international relations, produces a large number of bodies.[4] The British Jerusalem War Cemetery is the

---

That is forever England. There shall be
  In that rich earth a richer dust concealed;
A dust whom England bore, shaped, made aware,
  Gave, once, her flowers to love, her ways to roam;
A body of England's, breathing English air,
  Washed by the rivers, blest by suns of home.

4. Hannah Arendt, in *Eichmann in Jerusalem*, presented a harsh and explicit perspective, viewing the Nazi extermination camps as corpse-making factories. The essence and style of Arendt's writing have been subject to debate. While the Nazi extermination camps had a singular and evidently irrational purpose—mass murder—Clausewitzian war, in contrast, serves multiple objectives, including occupying or defending territory, subduing opponents, and improving bargaining positions. The death of soldiers, whether enemies or allies, in war is not the primary goal but, at most, a means to achieve other aims. Therefore, the question arises, Does war genuinely "produce" bodies? In my opinion, war can, in some instances, produce bodies both as a means and as a purpose, particularly in revenge wars or prolonged conflicts without a decisive victory. For example, during the Vietnam War and several of Israel's wars against so-called "resistance organizations" like Hamas or Hezbollah, when prolonged conflict yields no clear victory, the body count of enemy fighters, and to a lesser extent, US or Israeli soldiers, becomes the central focus of media and public discussions about the war's conduct and objectives. Thus, despite the blatant term and the normative challenges of discussing war in terms of body production, to deny that the war process can take on a life of its own and become a death enterprise is also challenging. I must emphasize that when I refer to "the production of dead bodies" in this chapter, it is not meant to ridicule or show disrespect toward the deaths of

62   EXPEDITION ESCAPE FROM THE CLASSROOM

closest place to our campus I can take my students to see the results of this specific "production" of war (Zambernardi 2017).[5] This proximity to the campus allows for a quick visit without requiring special arrangements such as a shuttle bus, and the students can quickly return to campus for their next class. Over time, I learned that this element—a visit integrated into the regular and routine school day—has a considerable impact on the students: some tell me that the tour of the cemetery, so close to campus yet unfamiliar, was an experience of discovering and exposing a new area in a seemingly well-known space. As a result, they ruminated a great deal on the things we talked about during the tour.

It is not that the students never visit military cemeteries. Every year when I come here with my classes, some students will tell me that they have visited the graves of friends or relatives in the military cemeteries of Israel. But most do so on Israel's national Memorial Day—when these places are immensely crowded. This makes it difficult to pay attention to the various details of the cemetery as a unique place. In addition, Memorial Day carries a sacred and awe-inspiring atmosphere of heavy national mourning.[6] Visiting under these circumstances makes it more difficult to think critically about the space, especially when the purpose is to attend the grave of a dear one and when the visit is imbued with national and sometimes religious elements. In contrast, the British Jerusalem War Cemetery has hardly any other visitors, so we can pay much more attention to the various details. Also, it does not have the same atmosphere of sacred mourning and worship of the dead as the Israeli cemeteries. For this is a cemetery of *foreign* soldiers, who were killed in the Jerusalem area but in a war of the distant past, in which we Israelis were not

---

soldiers and the grief of their families. Instead, it serves as a cautionary statement arising from terror and profound sadness at the sight of this aspect of war.

5. As of October 2023, this 2017 article by Zambernardi had been cited only eight times, according to Google Scholar, despite the years since its publication. Other articles by Zambernardi are, in fact, widely cited, and the IPS journal has a high IF. The lack of citations of the above article may indicate a minimal research interest in military burial in the discipline.

6. The first Memorial Day in which this sacredness was breached occurred on April 24, 2023. As part of the extensive national protests against the so-called judicial reform (widely seen as an attempted forced constitutional regime change), hundreds of bereaved family members vociferously remonstrated in various military cemeteries when representatives of the Netanyahu government attempted to enter or deliver official speeches. Clashes also occurred in the cemeteries between bereaved families' supporters and objectors to the judicial coup.

To the British Jerusalem War Cemetery **63**

involved (at least not in our current form as a sovereign state). Thus, when visiting it, the students do not experience the direct feelings an Israeli military cemetery evokes, and other emotions arise.

In the context of the issue of emotions, I ask the students to reflect on their feelings about the sacrifice of these foreign soldiers. For without the British occupation of this land, the State of Israel probably would not have been established here.[7] And even though the British occupation was probably a necessary step for the establishment of the State of Israel, at least in Israel's prevailing public perception and education system, Britain introduced many obstacles to the Jewish community (the Yishuv) during its Palestine Mandate rule and even harassed Zionism (Morris 2002; Roberts 2011). In other words, what is our emotional attitude toward a rival/friend like Britain, a former imperial ruler here, in a place where Britain's sacrifice is so clearly displayed? (Bar-Yosef 2017). How can visiting here—in this sort of British extraterritorial space, a remnant of the empire that once ruled here[8]—impact students' ability and desire to empathize with the pain of another nation?

---

7. What to call this "land" is always a political question: "Eretz Yisrael" (Zionist-inclined), "Falastin" (Palestinian-Arab-inclined), "Palestina-Aye" פלשטינה-א״י (the official Hebrew name of mandatory Palestine), or simply, "the land." See, in this context, Dahamshe (2020 and 2017). Students' attitude toward the tour could easily change if I pick the "wrong" name. (Similarly, of course, the perspective of a reader of this book could also change.)

8. I examined the cadastral map of the area at the Israeli mapping service's website. While neighboring facilities and structures, such as the university's sports complex or the Hadassah Hospital, have an orderly ownership registration of their parcel and sub-parcel numbers, the British Jerusalem War Cemetery lacks such a registration. The absence of formal ownership registration raises questions about the legal status of the place. During the Mt. Scopus enclave period (1949–1967), the cemetery was part of the Israeli enclave. Yet Britain considered the cemetery as "neither Israel Government property nor Israel private property, but British property belonging to the Imperial War Graves Commission" (British Consul-General in Jerusalem to the British Foreign Office, November 11, 1956; quoted in Y. Weiss 2017b, 80). The Israelis, for their part, claimed sovereignty over the cemetery as part of the enclave. The issue was never resolved. In contrast, the other British cemeteries in Israel are registered within the Israeli land registrar's system (*tabu*) as owned by the CWGC, yet the very act of registration tacitly acknowledges the authority and sovereignty of the State of Israel over the land on which these cemeteries are built. The lack of such a registration for the Jerusalem cemetery is an exception in this regard and suggests that the conflict or disagreement regarding its status between Britain and Israel that Yfaat Weiss discusses in her article still exists today, even if dormant. I emailed the CWGC to inquire why the Jerusalem cemetery is not registered in Israel's land registrar; I did not receive an answer. I estimate that this goes back to the British refusal to recognize Israel's de jure sovereignty—as opposed to de facto control—in the Scopus enclave.

64   EXPEDITION ESCAPE FROM THE CLASSROOM

This question becomes even more intriguing when we consider that, even though this cemetery conveys a sense of foreignness, its form and planning share certain similarities with the Israeli military cemeteries. (Of course, in terms of causality, the plans of Israeli military cemeteries were inspired by the British cemeteries, and not vice versa.[9]) In addition, while the Israeli military cemeteries were based primarily on principles of British planning, certain "oddities" here raise fundamental questions about the nature of war, questions that the visitor to an Israeli military cemetery does not encounter. For example, while most of the graves here are of British and Imperial soldiers (including the Australian and New Zealand Army Corps, aka ANZAC), we also find three graves of Ottoman soldiers and sixteen of Germans—Germany was Turkey's ally in the First World War. There are also five graves of Italian soldiers (Italy was Britain's ally during that war). The design of the headstones of the foreign soldiers differs only slightly from those of the British, and they are placed at the edge of the cemetery, but not separately from the British Empire's soldiers.[10] Yet elsewhere in Jerusalem, in the Talpiot neighborhood, the British buried Hindu, Sikh, Gurka, and Muslim soldiers from the British Raj separately from the white soldiers interred in the Jerusalem War Cemetery: "The Indian soldiers were separated from the Europeans not entirely due to religious reasons" (Benvenisti 1990, 44). What can these burial practices teach us about the nature of War as a social institution and the meaning of colonial domination and imperial enmity during those times? I ask the students to think about how they would consider the burial of enemy personnel in Israeli military cemeteries or the separation of non-Jewish IDF soldiers from the Jewish ones (in fact, the latter happens routinely). Most of them are shocked merely by the question.

---

9. Israeli architect Asher Hiram, who won a governmental contest for the planning of the new state's military cemeteries in 1949, relied on the architectural conceptions of the British military cemeteries in Palestine. See Azaryahu (1995).

10. The burial of enemy soldiers in the British war cemeteries was carried out in accordance with the provisions of the Treaty of Versailles in 1919, which mandated the honorable burial of prisoners of war who died in captivity. In his article on the planning of the British cemeteries in Palestine, Ron Fuchs observes that this practice of interring enemy soldiers in these cemeteries was met with a certain degree of resentment in the British press at that time. However, apart from the obligations stipulated by the treaty, Britain also sought to maintain good relations with Turkey concerning the British cemeteries in Gallipoli. For further details, see Fuchs (1996, 118n11).

Second Goal: To Explore the Normalization and Naturalization of War Violence

The easy access to the cemetery and the relative freedom from the burden of the Israeli culture of commemoration of the war dead in Mount Herzl in Jerusalem and the other Israeli military cemeteries help to realize the second purpose of our tour here. The British Jerusalem War Cemetery allows us to explore how the horrific violence of war undergoes normalization and naturalization, and how the victims' sacrifice is given meaning.

Thus, while the nurturing, landscaping, aesthetics, and architecture of the cemetery are intended to pay homage to the dead and perhaps also to give meaning to the mass death in this war, the design and planning of the cemetery also work to strengthen nationalism and to conceal the brutal violence that produced the bodies here.[11] The horror is present but hidden under the thousands of headstones spread throughout the field. Horror is beautified by flowers, green grass lawns, and subdued, minimalist architecture. Of course, these are not new arguments or revelations in historiographical terms (Mosse 1991). Nonetheless, I feel that for most of the students, these insights are indeed unique, and their responses to these thoughts are interesting and important in themselves. The discussion of the social and historical construction of military burial is new to most of them. It illustrates the fact that researching and teaching about the dead soldier's body and that thinking about the mourning and commemorating of the war dead are often disconnected from the study of war in the academic discipline of IR (Zambernardi 2017; Sylvester 2019). In this way, the immediate experience of the tour clearly illustrates Charles Tilly's idiom, "War made the state, and state made war."[12] The visit to this war cemetery shows how military burial strengthens or at least preserves state authority. Just as the state, over the years, acquired a monopoly on the legitimate use of organized violence inside and outside its borders, the military cemetery shows us that it also acquired and operates the monopoly on the burial of those who wielded this violence on its behalf (Wagner 2013).

---

11. On the challenging emotional experience of taking care of the bodies of dead soldiers in the US military, bodies that sometimes arrive at the pre-burial care center with horrible signs of violence and corporal corruption, see Flynn, McCarroll, and Biggs (2015).

12. For a critique of this understanding of the relations between war and state, see Spruyt (2017).

66   EXPEDITION ESCAPE FROM THE CLASSROOM

The monopoly on the act of burial and the design and preservation of the burial place, in turn, has a recursive relation with the state's monopoly on the legitimate use of violence. The social construction of burial and commemoration ceremonies held on such grounds as respectful and dignified practices, as well as the constant care and preservation of military cemeteries as aesthetic spaces, have a normalizing effect on the phenomenon of war. These forms of ceremony and preservation are supposed to evoke feelings such as closure, comfort, proof of state care and responsibility, and societal recognition of the sacrifice made by the dead and their families. And this recognition might evolve into a justification of the demand that other soldiers or future generations, in turn, sacrifice their own lives for the state. The social and political readiness to sacrifice soldiers' lives during war has diminished over time, especially in liberal and democratic countries (Levy 2012). Despite this, and despite the development of various remotely controlled fighting technologies and platforms, situations still exist in which such military deaths are deemed necessary. Obviously, military burial is not the only or even the main factor in social willingness to suffer victims in war. Contemporary reality even displays a built-in paradox in this willingness: the image of caskets of dead soldiers and military funerals erodes the disposition to suffer more victims. But were it not for respectable military burial, it is doubtful whether such a readiness to sacrifice would remain at all.[13]

In my tours here with the students, I discovered that the innate contradiction of the military cemetery—on the one hand, the beautiful and well-kept garden,[14] the minimalist architecture, and the rational structure of the complex, and on the other, the thousands of headstones each marking a soldier who suffered a violent or premature death—often raises challenging questions. For example, on one tour, a student asked me in front of the group whether there was in fact a soldier buried under *every* headstone. At that moment, I perceived her question as provocative. I thought for a moment and replied that I assumed there *was*. But two years later I read an article on the history of military burial and discovered cases where, after World War I, the bodies of French soldiers that were transported from temporary mass

---

13. In this context, consider the Russian government's endeavors to hide military burials since the invasion of Ukraine in 2022, juxtaposed with the assurances made by Wagner mercenary force leaders to their ex-convict recruits of providing a proper military burial in the event of death.

14. On gardens and gardening as a means of normalizing painful history, see Callahan (2017).

graves in the battle zones to permanent military cemeteries were also buried there in mass graves. In these cemeteries, in response to the public demand in France for a respectable individual burial, rows of headstones were built above the ground to give a false impression that every soldier had their own grave. I also later heard from a former student who became a tour guide at the British Jerusalem War Cemetery that he met someone who knew a contractor who renovated many of the headstones there. According to his informant, many of the graves did not contain the remains of any soldier. Instead, soldiers were often buried together and headstones placed to commemorate them, as in the French case.[15] I also learned that in Israeli military cemeteries, coffins sometimes contain only a few remains or body tissue when little was left of the soldier's body. Such caskets and "non-bodies" are buried in ordinary or standard graves with no mention of the incomplete state of the remains beneath the headstone. The same is true in US military cemeteries (Wagner 2015; Budreau 2010). In addition, unlike in ordinary civic burial—where, in many cultures, the face of the deceased is publicly displayed at the funeral service (after embalming or preservation)—people who die in battle are almost always buried in closed coffins. This, of course, is done to maintain the dignity of the dead, but it also points to our difficulty as a society with seeing and showing the dead bodies (and also the crippled and scarred bodies of living veterans) that result from the violence of the war.[16] The life of the young soldier is cut short, and the coffin represents this separation, the border between the cause of death itself (a shot, an explosion) and the funeral.[17] And so it turns out that it is possible that under some of the headstones here there are incomplete remains—or even no remains at all.[18] But the question

---

15. Email correspondence with Avi Bladi, December 23, 2021.

16. Thus, for instance, in the Canadian War Museum, out of the 13,000 works of art housed, only 64 present dead bodies (see Shah 2017). On scars, see Steele (2013); see also Cox and Jones (2014, 308).

17. Michael Sledge writes that during the 2003 Iraq War, he served as a journalist and encountered strict prohibitions against photographing not only the remains of dead soldiers themselves but also the cases in which these remains were stored. Yet empty transfer cases were permitted to be photographed (2005, 95).

18. Fuchs (1996), in his comprehensive article on the British cemeteries in Palestine, points out that during architect Burnet's initial planning of the Jerusalem War Cemetery in the early 1920s, temporary wooden crosses were already marking the tombs of fallen soldiers on the site. Additionally, the burial of bodies continued until the end of 1920, with fallen soldiers being collected from various temporary locations in the Jerusalem region. In footnote 63, Fuchs acknowledges that "it is unclear to what degree Burnett's plan necessitated the shifting of tombs" (Fuchs 1996, 132; my

EXPEDITION ESCAPE FROM THE CLASSROOM

from that student two years ago, the ridicule it sparked among the group, and my perception that the question was teasing or too impulsive all attest to how the military cemetery, with its long rows of neat headstones and its beautiful grooming, contributes to the production of a casual or complacent attitude toward war, the state, and even history.

The headstone is equivalent to a statement of a fact by the state: here lies a dead soldier. The raising of doubt about whether there were bodies or skeletons of British soldiers under the headstones was seen by the students and me as ridiculous. And yet, under critical examination and in hindsight, the possibility that there may be no bodies is entirely feasible. The state as an institution constantly seeks to maintain and re-create certainty and lack of doubt about its actions and the narrative it presents about itself. For what are these lines of graves if not a state narrative of certainty, knowing, and closing a circle (the body was buried, it *is* here, and here it found a "peaceful resting" place).[19]

The Cemetery as a Heterotopia

These, then, are the goals that I state or plan to pursue before the visit to the British Jerusalem War Cemetery—to contemplate the human cost of war and the normalization of war. But almost always, during the tour itself, issues and aspects come up that I didn't plan to discuss. Leaving the classroom produces a more open mindset, which allows associative drifts and episodic delays, leading to diverse stories and concepts. More generally, leaving the classroom involves and even leads to an inevitable loss on my part, as a professor, of control over the content of the lesson, due to the elements of coincidence and surprise in the out-of-classroom space. This dynamic of the planned versus the sudden and the implicit versus the unspoken is of great interest to me.

---

translation). However, if there were instances of shifting of tombs, the possibility of mix-ups or confusion over soldiers' identities is plausible, and, theoretically, a headstone could stand above an empty grave.

19. "The [U.S.] Quartermaster's World War II statement in the brochure, 'Tell Me About My Boy,' that 'there is absolutely no question of the possibility [of error] of the positive identification of remains' is a goal, not a guarantee. Yet time and again, the military has shot itself in the foot by asserting something that later proved not to be the case. This is not to say that intentions were evil, only that to profess perfection in a very complicated task riddled with potential for error is asking for trouble. And the military seems at times doomed to repeat the errors of the past" (Sledge 2005, 132).

For most of the students, this is usually the first visit here—and often the last (more on avoiding the cemetery later in the chapter). But for me, the tours here with the students are recurring: I have gone on them at least twice every year for at least four years now. On each tour of the cemetery, I present the place a little differently to the group and learn to know it in different forms, and these group experiences accompany me even when I come here alone. The changing interactions with the students on each tour also build a different narrative of the place for me each time.[20] The various tours accumulate in my memory as additional layers of experience and information, of looking and feeling, thus establishing a complex connection between me and this place. This layering accompanies me when I think about the different meanings of this site.

Moreover, these layers of knowing and feeling the place and the accidental and sudden experiences and stories during the tour, along with the preconceived and planned elements, make this cemetery a heterotopia. In it, various places, times, and people reside and are narrated and experienced by me in a way that does not always make sense. The attempt to order and organize the site and its details into categories that bear apparent affinities to each other does not always succeed (Foucault 2002, xvi). The heterotopic essence of the place, which emerges and is felt during and after the tour, creates a variety of feelings and emotions for the students: wonder, intellectual satisfaction, indifference, and even anger. But for me, the associative and episodic process, which leads to the construction of the cemetery as a heterotopia, is essential in my attempt to give students a more independent and skeptical view of international politics and history. The cemetery shows a peaceful, clean, and organized representation of violent events and their outcomes (ranging from orderly maps and schemes of the major battles between the British and the Ottomans in Palestine to headstones on which the personal details of the fallen are uniformly inscribed). But on the battlefields themselves, the reality was not so orderly: obviously, there was much chaos, cruelty, absurdity, and grotesque and other, less venerable, elements that are not represented here. While the place emphasizes continuity, valor, devotion, loyalty, planning, and order, the essence of the events that led to its creation—or, more specifically, the production of the bodies here—is saturated with disarray and discontinuity, mistakes, disregard for human life, and perhaps even stupidity.[21]

---

20. On the links between teaching and research in IR, see Ettinger (2020).

21. On the tension between utopia and heterotopia in national memorial sites, see Paliewicz and Hasian (2017).

70   EXPEDITION ESCAPE FROM THE CLASSROOM

This construction of the cemetery as an other, heterotopic space is necessary for my attempt to critically teach and study war (the "Great" one and others) and its consequences. I do not know whether I would have taken my students to a British war cemetery if there was not one so close to our campus. The Talpiot neighborhood in Jerusalem has another British imperial burial site—of Indian soldiers. Mount Zion contains graves of German, Austrian, and Armenian soldiers from World War I, and near the Old City walls is a large mass grave of Ottoman soldiers and another mass grave of Jordanian soldiers from the 1967 War. But all these places are relatively far away from our campus. Visiting them requires high transport and security costs, which is a disincentive for the university administration, especially if carried on an annual basis. Given the proximity and accessibility of the British cemetery to our campus, I would say that this place calls us as students of international relations.

The Last Minutes of the Great War

I start my tour of the British Jerusalem War Cemetery today by stating the fact that the war ended at eleven o'clock and also that there were soldiers killed in the final minutes before the cease-fire took effect. The grotesque element in this story is sharpened further when I add that the cease-fire agreement was signed at 5:00 a.m., leaving six hours until the agreement went into effect. The drafters of the agreement perceived this time—the eleventh day, the eleventh month, the eleventh hour—as symbolic or symmetrical, so they chose it. The news of the signing of the agreement and its entry into force were immediately broadcast by radio to the combat units, and so the question arises: What to do in the time remaining until the official ending of the war?

As it happened, it was one of the deadliest days of the First World War. This fact raises a natural wondering at the absurdity that is sometimes embodied in symbolic dates and times (since there were no obvious military advantages to continue the war until eleven o'clock), which leads, based on Yvgeny Yanovsky's discussion of the clock as a disciplining technology, to a conversation about automatic action in war. Yanovsky argues that wristwatches or pocket watches, which were already very common among the soldiers in this war, helped create an accurate temporal framework within which precise rules and expectations about the required behavior of the soldiers materialized (Yanovsky 2015). The ability to be exact enabled the construction of strong, rigid disciplining structures (in the Foucauldian sense), which became self-evident for most soldiers, whose lives in the trenches were conducted literally minute by minute under the regime of the clock. "How many of you would have obeyed the commands and kept fighting until the last minute?" I ask the students. Some chuckle at the story and dilemma I present; some seem shocked. Four say they would have probably continued to fight; the rest claim they would have shirked or escaped.

It is hard to know what they would have done, or what I would have done, in the shoes of these soldiers in the trenches. Beyond the purely theoretical question, this is also, it seems, the first time the students have heard of this case, so perhaps their responses reflect values related to their perceptions of military service in particular (most of them were likely drafted into the Israeli mandatory military service) or, more generally, their commitment to disciplining frameworks. Those who answered they would have shirked or avoided the order to continue fighting may have said this because they thought it was what I wanted to hear. But it is evident that the thought experiment stirs some anxiety in the group—the thought of this rigidity, of ending the war at precisely eleven o'clock, while we sit at the entrance of a British military cemetery where thousands of dead soldiers from this war are buried. I recommend that the students watch Stanley Kubrick's movie *Paths of Glory*, which shows the arbitrary executions of "rebels," "defectors," or "cowards" in the French Army on the Western Front. I also mention the practice of decimation (the arbitrary execution of one in ten soldiers) by which Roman commanders punished military units under similar circumstances. The story evokes much discomfort among the students. Now, those who thought of running away seem to think again (perhaps some want to run away from this tour). One student, older than the others, who are in their mid-twenties, notes that even in the case of the "Second Lebanon War" between Israel and Hezbollah in 2006, in which he served, the cease-fire was agreed upon forty-eight hours before it took effect. During those remaining hours of the war, Israel escalated its attack, resulting in the death of seven Israeli soldiers and the wounding of many others. All this was due to the desire of the Israeli leadership to obtain a "victory image" in the time left to the ending of the war (or, perhaps, until the end of the "game"—if we apply Johan Huizinga's [2002] argument that war is a game that has its own rules and times). Luckily for him, the student adds, he was not part of the forces fighting at the front in those final hours. The arbitrariness inherent in the idea of the "last hours of the war/

72   EXPEDITION ESCAPE FROM THE CLASSROOM

game" now seems much more tangible to the group—not just a strange story about a war from the distant past but also something that we, as Israelis at this time, might have experienced ourselves.

Reluctance to Enter the War Cemetery

On this day of the tour, talking about the clock and the ending of wars takes about fourteen minutes of a ninety-minute class. The time now is 1:19 p.m. In battle, the clock is unforgiving. To a much lesser extent, of course, even in academia the clock does not always show patience (think "tenure clock"). A glance at my wristwatch raises a momentary fear that I might have spent too much time on the story and discussion of the end of the war on the Western Front. Our tour should end at 2:30, and students must return to campus for the next class, which starts at 3 p.m. Walking back to campus will only take them a few minutes, but in my experience some pressure will begin to build up toward the end of the tour, and their attention levels will decrease. This is, of course, true of almost every university class. The tyranny of the clock in war is a disturbing notion, but for better or worse the clock governs us too. While I would like to develop the temporal issues of war further, I also want to continue the tour in the cemetery without the pressure of time.

Sitting near the cemetery's office/guardhouse, we are only a few hundred meters from the main entrance to our campus. Almost anyone walking from the student dorms or arriving by car or bus to the campus, passing Haim Yaski Street or Churchill Avenue, goes by the cemetery.[22] The cemetery is highly visible—the tall Cross of Sacrifice, for example, is very noticeable from Churchill Avenue, and the green lawns and beautiful flowerbeds among the tombs can be clearly seen from the street, as can the long rows of headstones. But relatively few people look at the British cemetery for more than a few moments.

---

22. Dr. Haim Yaski, director of Hadassah Hospital on Mount Scopus, was murdered in the "Hadassah Convoy" in the Sheikh Jarrah neighborhood in Jerusalem, along with 77 other students and staff members of the Hebrew University and Hadassah Hospital, on April 13, 1948. Palestinian militants, apparently in revenge for the Deir Yassin massacre, which happened a few days earlier, fired at the convoy, stuck in Sheikh Jarrah, for about six hours. British army forces who witnessed the shootings did not intervene and refused to extricate the convoy. Thus, the war cemetery here is located at the intersection of a street that commemorates Britain's friendship with Zionism (Churchill Avenue) and a street that preserves the memory of a great tragedy that occurred during the twilight of the British rule in Palestine under the eyes of indifferent British soldiers (Yaski Street).

Fig. 7. The main gate to the cemetery. (Photograph by the author.)

One of the first questions I usually ask the students once we are inside the cemetery is how many of them had already visited here. The answers, along with observations I have made in the past at different times of the day, confirm my sense that a large majority of students avoid this place. Some avoid visiting just because they are rushing to campus. Others are reluctant to enter the cemetery as it is a space "inhabited" by thousands of dead bodies. Even though the skeletons are neatly hidden, the fact of their presence still induces feelings of fear, disgust, or aversion. Some avoid the site for Jewish religious reasons. Often religious Orthodox students tell me they are offended by the

Fig. 8. The Stone of Remembrance and the Memorial Chapel. (Photograph by the author.)

prominence of Christian symbols in the place or explain they are Kohanim and therefore prohibited from entering.[23] Some do not enter the cemetery because of the sense of foreignness it imparts, although others will say they have previously entered the place *precisely because* of the curiosity they feel due to this feeling of foreignness.

The foreignness and separation of the British cemetery from its surroundings are felt strongly here. The main entrance gate, made of wood within a stone wall, is impressive, as are other architectural elements: the Cross of Sacrifice; the Memorial Chapel for the fallen whose burial place is unknown, which includes a bronze statue of St. George, the patron of England, slaugh-

---

23. Kohanim ("Kohen" is the Hebrew word for "priest") are traditionally thought to be descended from the biblical Aaron, brother of Moses. They are prohibited from being near a corpse (except when the deceased is a member of their immediate family) to avoid becoming ritually impure. When a student informs me that they are a Kohen, I exempt them from the visit to the cemetery. Similarly, I excuse anyone else who expresses discomfort with the visit, whether due to religious or personal reasons. Instead, I request that they watch a PowerPoint presentation of the tour I have prepared.

tering the dragon; the large Stone of Remembrance, with the inscription "Their Names Liveth for Evermore" (see fig. 8). All of these create the sense of another place and space, one that a person should ask permission to enter (although admission is free for all and there is no guard at the entrance). Students tell me that visiting alone or even with a partner seems inappropriate, as if they should enter such a place only with a group or during a formal ceremony. I have no knowledge of whether they return to visit after our tour. But I suppose that the reasons that initially prevent or discourage the students from entering the cemetery before our tour also apply afterward. After the tour, they likely experience a sense of saturation, perhaps also sadness. But occasionally some tell me they do return or visit similar British and other military cemeteries elsewhere.

A Brief Interruption about Time

As I am busy with these thoughts, one student wants to say something. He is from a different faculty, not the Social Sciences, and in the two previous classes that already convened in this course this year, he has asked quite intriguing questions. He says that while I was speaking, it occurred to him that the soldiers buried here were not killed on the Western Front but in the battles between the British and the Ottomans in Palestine. He checked Wikipedia and concluded that the war did not end in as precise and uniform manner for the front in Palestine as it did for the front in the west. The fighting between the Ottomans and the British in Palestine, in what was known as the Battle of Megiddo, ended gradually, between September 18 and 25, 1918, with a decisive British military victory in several clashes. What, then, he asks, is the relevance of the eleven o'clock story to this cemetery? I think for a while and begin to feel a little anxiety creeping up on me—my breathing accelerates and my palms start to sweat. There is truth in his words. But I take a minute to calm myself down. It's not a war between him and me. There must be a good answer to his question, one that will not represent a "triumph" over him but a ground for understanding between us.

"Perhaps," I say, "I told you about the end of the war at eleven o'clock because, not only is the story important and interesting in itself, but at eleven o'clock every year on the Saturday before November 11 the memorial service run by the British Consulate in East Jerusalem takes place here." I add that British Remembrance Day, held on November 11, commemorates those killed on the Western Front and all the war dead from all the fronts, creating a general framework that consolidates the various fronts and battles in which British soldiers fought during these years and views them as a single war. This, in turn, helps to form a meaning for the mass carnage. But beyond that, the story of the the the war's ending at eleven o'clock also constructs World War I for us, as Israeli visitors to this cemetery, as a single war and connects us to events far away from us—in both time and space. The importance of the story is thus to illustrate how extensive, widespread, and great the Great War was. Besides, I ask the student, do you think the soldiers buried here would not have fought until eleven o'clock if they had been given such an order? For, beyond the particular events that occur during it, war is fundamentally the readiness, in principle and practice, of human beings to kill and be killed (Black 2007). And the thousands of graves around us here illustrate this claim most sadly.

My question remains unanswered by the student. He smiles, perhaps accepting my words, and perhaps thinking there is no point in continuing this discussion. Maybe my glance at the clock suggests that we should continue the tour. Perhaps, despite my wish to create understanding and not "victory" in our dialogue, this did not happen. The line between being able to form a deep understanding with students or creating indifference in them is sometimes very thin.

Moral Implications of Conduct in the Cemetery

On passing through the main gate, a feeling of admiration and splendor arises. The walls of the gate are engraved with the royal coat of arms of the United Kingdom and dozens of symbols of the military units whose soldiers are buried here, many containing mythical animals, such as dragons, two-headed eagles, or lions and tigers standing on their hind feet. I often ask the students to compare these symbols and coats of arms to Israeli ones in the IDF. Then we talk about the importance of heraldry in raising soldiers' pride in their units, creating solidarity and comradeship among them and garnering their willingness to risk their lives in combat.[24] A dedication in three languages (English, Arabic, and Hebrew) above the gate states, with imperial condescension or naivete (or both), "The land on which this cemetery stands is

---

24. On military heraldry, see Festus (2019) and Cusumano (2021).

the free gift of the people of Palestine for the perpetual resting place of those of the allied armies who fell in the war of 1914–1918 and are honored here." When I ask the students to read the inscription, they rarely inquire who the "people of Palestine" were that gave this field to the British occupiers to bury their dead. I typically have to introduce the question myself and develop a brief discussion on the sense of imperial mastery reflected in this wording.[25] Addressing this also opens up further discussion about our emotional attitude, as twenty-first-century Israelis, to those buried here—for without the sacrifice of these soldiers, we would probably not live in this country today, and almost certainly not under the Israeli regime that currently exists here.[26]

On the tour today, the discussion of this emotional stance comes without me bringing up the issue. As we move toward the Cross of Sacrifice in the middle of the cemetery, we see, beyond the last line of headstones, a large dog running freely on the trimmed lawn, with its owner standing some distance away. Suddenly, the dog crouches in an unmistakable position. After a few seconds, the owner whistles, and the dog starts running toward him. They turn to the service gate to leave the cemetery—without the man collecting what his dog left on the grass. My gaze follows the dog and the man; Should I say something to him? The students look at me and see the hesitation on my face. Is it my job as their professor to say something? Do they expect me, their teaching/academic authority, to be the authority for proper cemetery etiquette too?

I have in fact seen this person and his dog here several times on my past

---

25. This sense of mastery is particularly evident in the fact that landowners in Jerusalem filed lawsuits against the Imperial War Graves Commission (the original name of the CWGC) in 1929, claiming compensation for the confiscation of land to build this burial ground (Fuchs 1996, 131). Fuchs also points out, "The plaintiffs found that the commission cannot be sued because it has no legal personality, as it has never been registered as an Ottoman association. The commission, for its part, was in no hurry to register." Upon further consideration, the inscription on the gate may not only reflect naivete or mastery but could also imply imperial cunning.

26. Israeli prime minister Benjamin Netanyahu acknowledged this sacrifice and its important consequences for the history of Israel when, just weeks before our tour in the Jerusalem War Cemetery, he condemned the desecration of the British military cemetery in Haifa. Netanyahu said, "We consider the desecration of the graves of World War I heroes in Haifa as very serious. We owe them a historical debt for the country's liberation from Ottoman rule and will do everything possible to find those responsible [for the crime] and bring them to justice." See Noa Shpigel and Noa Landau, "Dozens of Headstones Were Desecrated in [British] Cemeteries in Haifa and Nof Hagalil," [in Hebrew] Haaretz, October 11, 2019. https://www.haaretz.co.il/news/law/1.7967977

78   EXPEDITION ESCAPE FROM THE CLASSROOM

visits. He is an Israeli Jew, perhaps a resident of the nearby French Hill neighborhood. Once, when I was here alone on a Friday afternoon and asked him if he thought it was a good place to allow his dog to defecate here, he said that he was not bothering anyone and that I should mind my own business. The dog, too, did not look very friendly. The man did not appear to attribute any ideological or moral significance or purpose to his actions or show any deliberate contempt for the place (but, see Saunders and Crilley 2019). It is likely simply convenient for him to come here with the dog. I now decide that this is not the right time to start another conversation with this person; he will continue to come here with his dog, regardless of what the students or I might tell him. There is no point in initiating a situation that could lead to a loud or even violent argument, especially when I am here with my class. Even if the students expect me to say something to him, I'd rather not develop the affair. We could perhaps report the matter to the local workers of the CWGC and suggest that they post signs prohibiting the entry of dogs. I share my thoughts with the group. Some shake their heads in agreement; others say we should say something to the person, but I ask them not to.

Instead, I suggest we take a moment to look at things from a historical and theoretical point of view. Why are we all angry about the act we have just observed? Some students point out that the cemetery is an eternal resting place, and even if the dead are not of our own, we should respect them and do our best to preserve their dignity as a universal moral imperative. Others also mention that without the sacrifice of these soldiers, the land would probably have still been controlled by the Ottomans and we would not have a state here. (No one considers that the Palestinian Arabs would have been able to establish a state instead of us.) "You know," I say, "that the burial of war dead in the way we see here is a very modern phenomenon, historically speaking?" In Europe, up to the mid-nineteenth century, only nobles or officers were individually buried in the wake of battle. The bodies of "ordinary" soldiers were sometimes interred in mass graves by their brothers-in-arms or even left on the battlefield without any treatment to prevent scavenging animals or human looters from defiling the bodies. Even if there were no valuables on the bodies, looters pulled out teeth for reuse as dentures or collected bones which, after grinding, were used as gardening fertilizer (Zambernardi 2017, 297). I share a few more details about the history of military burial. For example, I mention how militaries in the late nineteenth and early twentieth centuries increasingly recognized that in order to ensure the continued draft of men to war—given the growing number of casualties in armed, industrialized violent conflicts—they needed to promise some comfort to the bereaved families and dignity for the fighting soldiers in the form of respectable burial. I also mention Julia Kristeva's concepts of abjection and disgust. Against this backdrop, the acts of the dog and its owner take on historical and conceptual meaning. The man's lack of respect has to do with the fact that he has, in our eyes, desecrated a sanctified place. The introduction of the dog onto the site and the fact that its owner did not pick up its droppings are considered disgusting and despicable, precisely (in Kristeva's understanding of the abject and the revolting) because the cemetery is simply not the place for the dog and its droppings. Kristeva perceives the abject not necessarily as unclean or unhealthy. The abject, in her view, is "what does not respect borders, positions, rules. . . . Any crime, because it draws attention to the fragility of the law, is abject" (Kristeva 1982, 4).

In the past, the bodies of ordinary soldiers were left to rot and be devoured on the battlefield because these soldiers were often considered despicable or unworthy even in their lives. They were seen as an expendable resource, sometimes even considered as mere/potential criminals or mercenaries who did not belong in decent society. In their death, they were even more despicable. But, with the development of nationalism, along with liberalism and the creation of the individual as a distinct subject, death in war became an expression of the supreme sacrifice of the individual for the nation, and the bodies of the soldiers became sanctified. Alongside the consolidation of these values, the state apparatus was required to maintain soldiers' loyalty by creating and providing a growing number of honors and ceremonies that distinguish between soldiers and civilians. Modern military burial has become one of the elements in these relations between the state and the soldiers (Wasinski 2008, 117). In return for the supreme sacrifice of the soldier, the state should thus take care of the soldier's last honor.

But the honor bestowed on the dead soldier in this way—through the individual military burial commemorating the uniqueness of each soldier among the other thousands of war dead, as we see in this cemetery—also implies the creation and operation of biopolitical power in the Foucauldian sense of control of bodies. The state not only acquires a monopoly on the exercise of military force, through the bodies of living soldiers (Schrader 2014), but it also becomes the monopolist in the management and care of (what remains of) the bodies of those who exerted this power for it and were killed in the process (Wasinski 2008, 117). In this way, the military cemetery becomes a memorial site for the war dead (and, inexplicitly, a site where we see the

80 EXPEDITION ESCAPE FROM THE CLASSROOM

state's biopolitical authority) *and a space that cannot be used for any other activity*. While strolling with a dog for pleasure and enjoyment in a civil cemetery may seem acceptable (or at least somewhat less annoying or provocative) in some cultures or circumstances,[27] here the presence of the dog is challenging something sacred and violates the manifested purpose, *the only* purpose, of the place. This is why the disgusting act of not collecting the dog's droppings becomes so accentuated and makes us so angry.

"If I were writing an article about our tour here, would you suggest I refer to this incident?" I ask the students. One student replies, "Sure, but you should also talk about the 'use' of the cemetery by guys from the village of Issawiya." This student took the course last year and asked to audit this year too. Maybe he became attached to the place, and maybe he wanted to see how closely I stick to the same script or witness the differences in class interactions. He told me that he is a settler from Gush Etzion, near Jerusalem. Despite our ideological, religious, and political disparities, I appreciate his knowledge and learning skills. As a final project in the "Mt. Scopus Enclave" course last year, he submitted a paper on the conception of the members of the Jewish Yishuv (during the Mandate period) of the early Hebrew University as a secular shrine, and thanks to his paper I became more aware of the ways my idealist perception of our university was formed. I therefore treat his words seriously now. On last year's tour, we saw several beer bottles and snack wrappers discarded in the area between the Stone of Remembrance and the chapel for the fallen soldiers whose burial place is unknown. I told the students then that one of the CWGC workers, a Palestinian resident of Issawiya, a neighborhood near our campus and close to the cemetery, once told me that almost every morning, the staff at the site clears such garbage, as young people from Issawiya come here during the night to drink and smoke.[28]

Located at the foot of our campus, Issawiya is one of the poorest neighborhoods in East Jerusalem—and, in fact, in all of Israel (Isser 2016). Stones and Molotov cocktails are often thrown from the neighborhood, from the "Issawiya Bluffs," onto Highway 1 (in the Occupied Territories), leading from Jerusalem to the Dead Sea and the large settlement of Ma'ale Adumim. The Hadassah Mt. Scopus University Hospital and the Hebrew University campus

---

27. On the romantic concept of the (civilian) "park" or "garden" cemetery, see Mosse (1991, 40–44). Such cemeteries were conceived as "places of contemplation and regeneration, whether or not one looked for a particular tomb" (44).

28. On the night as an exceptional time during emergency periods, à la Agamben, see Chazkel (2020).

are also targets of attacks (even though many East Jerusalemites study at the Hebrew University or receive medical treatment in Hadassah, and the hospital is often dubbed in Arabic "Hadassah Issawiya"). A few weeks ago, a small fire broke out on the edge of the university's botanical garden because of a Molotov cocktail thrown from Issawiya. I saw the burnt land at the edge of the "plants of the Sinai Peninsula" plot. A fire-extinguisher hose was left in this area of the garden to facilitate the quick extinguishing of the fire in case of additional similar attacks. In the university archive, I discovered documents from the 1930s that indicate a conflict between residents from what was then a small village and the academic institution, as Issawatites claimed that the university's fence built around the garden intruded into their plots. The university insisted that the fence was precisely on the garden's boundary, and the British police sided with the university. The garden was initially supposed to be on the other side of Churchill Avenue, just in front of the British cemetery. But, due to the Australian government's objection to that location (as the trees might have blocked the view from the Australian monument to the Old City of Jerusalem), the garden was set where it resides today, within the campus.[29]

The Issawatites today don't consider themselves terrorists (as the Israeli police often characterizes them) but rather see their actions as stubborn and persistent resistance to the Israeli occupation. To break the will of this resistance, Israeli police have actively sought to make daily life in Issawiya very difficult for a long time now, initiating violent friction with the population (Hasson 2019). Issawiya has virtually no open green public spaces or public gardens. When I told the students in last year's tour about the garbage that youths from Issawiya supposedly leave here in the British cemetery, some seemed satisfied—as if the story confirmed for them the tendency of Issawiya residents for vandalism (especially given that the information I presented came from an Issawati Palestinian himself). Complaints are often heard from students, especially female students, about sexual harassment in the evenings on Churchill Avenue by young men from Issawiya—whistles, drawing inappropriately close, provocative statements, and even touching. At dusk, the university's security department patrols Churchill Avenue, and for a while, student vigilantes, sponsored by various right-wing organizations, also patrolled the street and even instructed students in Krav Maga. Much like in today's incident with the man and his dog, students in last year's tour

---

29. On the saga of the Botanical Garden's location, see Paz (1995).

82   EXPEDITION ESCAPE FROM THE CLASSROOM

resented the garbage in the cemetery, and most did not think that the lack of public spaces and amenities in the Palestinian neighborhood justified the misuse of the British cemetery at night.

Some of the students in today's group inquire about the auditing student's comment on Issawiya, waste, and the cemetery. I tell the story again and ask that we now move toward the Cross of Sacrifice. The students continue to discuss among themselves the cases of the dog versus the night drinking and smoking here. I leave them a few more minutes to debate whether this is also a disgusting and disgraceful practice or a constraint stemming from a discriminatory urban policy toward the Palestinian-occupied neighborhood. Perhaps next week, when we tour the university's botanical garden, I will suggest a different question: Should Palestinians, the native people that the British occupied, have to respect the graves of the conquerors? And is a military cemetery necessarily a site to be respected under all conditions?

According to Yfaat Weiss's (2017b) article on this cemetery, it is doubtful that this is what the State of Israel thought during the period from 1948 to 1967. During those years, Mt. Scopus (including the cemetery) was an Israeli enclave within the Jordanian-ruled West Bank. Israel often hindered British access to the cemetery in an effort to exert political pressure on Britain to recognize Israeli sovereignty in West Jerusalem and the enclave, and to make Jordan, Britain's ally, allow freer Israeli access to the deserted Hebrew University buildings and Hadassah Hospital. The friction between Israel and Britain in the 1950s and 1960s led to many difficulties conducting the annual memorial ceremonies in the British cemetery (Israel even challenged the British several times by conducting its own memorial services for the Jewish soldiers buried here.). Furthermore, the site was neglected because Israel encircled the compound with landmines. Photographs from the 1960s in Weiss's article show that wild vegetation grew where we now stand, and the headstones were half-hidden in the thicket.

Hobbesian "Leviathan"/Sovereign Turned Upside Down

But now—on the clean path amid the trimmed green grasses, the beautiful flowerbeds, and the pruned shrubs—we are nearing the Cross of Sacrifice. The great cross is about seven meters high and can be seen from almost anywhere in the compound. Positioned in the center of the cemetery, this Latin cross stands on an octagonal, gray, granite stone that was carved in England

Fig. 9. Inscriptions in Arabic on the outer wall of the cemetery ("Hamas," "Fatah"). (Photograph by the author.)

(Fuchs 1996, 133). A large, black, bronze crusader sword is attached to the cross at its top. The sight of the great sword affixed to the high cross with the dense rows of tombs behind it always reminds me of the well-known drawing from the frontispiece of Thomas Hobbes's book *Leviathan*. The sword resembles the one held by the King-Sovereign, whose body is made up of countless tiny figures of people who gave him their liberty in return for the security he promised to provide (Cottman 2008, chap. 4). Here, in contrast, the image reverses itself: the sword's point is aimed at the earth, not the sky, and the

Fig. 10. The Cross of Sacrifice. (Photograph by the author.)

thousands of soldiers buried here lie underground rather than making up the towering image of Hobbes's colossus sovereign. If that sovereign is the "body politic," this cemetery, with its thousands of graves, the downward pointing sword at its center, and the wall surrounding the complex, is a sort of a "political body/corpse." But while the buried soldiers are the constituents of that political corpse, when they were still alive, they were the very sword the sovereign held in his arm.

The Cross of Sacrifice, placed in British war cemeteries worldwide, was the work of architect Reginald Blomfield. He said it was "designed to symbolize 'the millions of people crucified on the battlefields,' and not necessarily their religion" (Benvenisti 1990, 41). But while the cross honors the millions who were crucified in the war, it does not explain who crucified them or why. Was it "war" itself, as a superhuman entity distinct from the acts of certain states, that crucified them as "saints"? Also, it is impossible to ignore the fact that the soldiers buried here were part of the process that "crucified" enemy soldiers, whom they certainly did not see as saints and who, in turn, did not see their "crucifiers" as such.

We now head up the moderate incline from the Cross of Sacrifice to the Stone of Remembrance. In all other the British World War I cemeteries, the Stone of Remembrance stands at the front of the complex and the headstones face it, while the Cross of Sacrifice is behind them. Here, the arrangement is reversed because of the uniqueness of the view from the cemetery—the holy city—and the religious sentiment that this setting conjured among the Christian conquerors (Fuchs 1996, 130). The students linger among the tombs and read the inscriptions on the identically designed headstones. The inscriptions are laconic and matter-of-fact: they give the first letter of the soldier's first name and surname, their military ID number, the date they were killed, their unit affiliation, and the unit's symbol. Beyond this, a short personal dedication is sometimes included, at the family's request. Meron Benvenisti, in his book *Jerusalem's City of the Dead* (telling the stories of the city's myriad cemeteries), writes of these personal dedications on the headstones, "The uniformity and military regime are disrupted, in such a British manner, with the expressions of love and sorrow of the bereaved families" (Benvenisti 1990, 42). But in these tours here every year, I feel that the inscriptions don't disrupt the "uniformity and military regime" too much. Despite the personal dimension they add, the "tone" of the inscriptions still seems to create repetition or similarity through the words designed to distinguish each fallen soldier. None of them express anger or frustration at the death of the soldiers. They reflect a degree of patriotic acceptance of these deaths, without raising any doubts.

This uniformity among the graves, along with a sense of desolation at the assimilation of the individual into the Hobbesian-Leviathanic crowd that comprises the dead colossus sovereign, so to speak, may be why students will occasionally search for the grave of the soldier Harry Potter—who, according to an "urban myth," is buried here. But Harry Potter is not in the Jerusalem War Cemetery. He is interred in the British Ramleh War Cemetery—killed in 1939 in Hebron, during the British repression of the Palestinian Arab Revolt (1936–39). Private Potter's grave is quite well-known on the internet and attracts many visitors to the Ramleh Cemetery, the central British cemetery in Palestine (where soldiers from other years of the Mandate period and World War II are interred, as opposed to the Jerusalem cemetery, which is strictly a

86   EXPEDITION ESCAPE FROM THE CLASSROOM

World War I graveyard). When students ask me if Harry Potter is buried here, in Jerusalem's cemetery, I answer that he isn't but that William Shakespeare is. A headstone with this name states that the soldier was killed on May 23, 1918, at the age of forty-one and that he served as a driver. But this year, the students do not ask me about Harry Potter or William Shakespeare. Unlike almost all other headstones, Shakespeare's headstone contains his full name, spelled out. Perhaps when the headstone was made, the stonemason noticed the unusual name and wanted to set the man's grave apart. My feeling is that through this unique treatment of Shakespeare's grave, the stonemason—or whoever gave the order to write the soldier's full name—found a certain relief from the sense of despair in the face of war's uniformity, consoled by the fact that a soldier who coincidentally had such a celebrated and famed name is buried among the large crowd of "regular" individuals.

As we move up the compound, one of the students now asks me whether, apart from the official British consulate ceremony at 11:00 a.m., family members also come to visit these graves. I answer that I occasionally see a note or a flower placed on one of the tombs, but most of the tombs are orphans because of the many years that have passed since World War I and the distance from Britain and the other origin countries. British military cemeteries were built where the battles took place. This was mainly due to the high costs of transporting so many dead bodies to Britain during the war and the desire to avoid discriminating against low-income families, who could not fund the transfer of bodies.[30] The fact that most graves do not receive visitors bothers or saddens the students. Perhaps some of them think about their visits to Israel's military cemeteries. The thought of the "deserted" tombs here is strange to the students. Later in the tour, we usually arrive at a plot of twenty-four graves of British-Jewish soldiers (a Star of David marks their

---

30. In 1928, a decade after the war, tens of thousands of veterans and widows visited the burial sites on the Western Front in Europe. These visits were organized by groups such as the British Legion, the YMCA, and the Salvation Army. A year later, thousands of Australians undertook pilgrimages to the battlefields and cemeteries of Gallipoli, although the Australian government did not provide funding for these trips. Generally, visits to cemeteries in the "East"—including Italy, Greece, Gallipoli, and Palestine—were infrequent. A report by the Thomas Cook Company for the British government even suggested that travelers to the East should be warned of "harsh conditions," which further deterred the number of visitors to Iraq and Palestine (see Lloyd 2014, 95–96). Regarding American World War I fallen soldiers, families had the option to choose between burial in the United States and burial in the battlefields of the Western Front in Europe. Approximately 30,000 American servicemen were buried in Europe. In the 1930s, the US government sponsored pilgrimage visits to the graves of these fallen soldiers for their mothers and widows (see Budreau 2010).

headstones). People leave pebbles on their headstones—a Jewish custom to note that someone had visited the grave. On a previous tour here, some students told me that a group of students from the dormitories lays these pebbles on the Jewish soldiers' graves. Are they relatives of the soldiers? I wonder. My students do not think so and believe that the dormitory students place the pebbles simply to honor the dead. Jewish religious law, Halacha, does not condone the burial of Jews in the same cemetery with non-Jews. Conceivably, Orthodox Jews could see "Jewish" tombs like those here as "orphan," even "deserted"—hence, the persistence of the dormitories' group in putting the pebbles on the headstones year after year.

Unknown Soldiers and Their Political Appropriation

I now notice a group of four students standing next to some headstones that have the inscription, "A Soldier of the Great War, Known Unto God" (see fig. 11). These stones mark the bodies of unidentified soldiers. After a few quiet moments by the tombs of the anonymous soldiers, I suggest the students also review the memorial wall—near the Stone of Remembrance and the Memorial Chapel. Engraved on the wall are the names of over 3,000 imperial soldiers killed in the battles in Sinai and Palestine who have no known graves. The tombs of the unknown soldiers and the names on the memorial wall are two aspects of the same phenomenon. They reveal how the modern state's commemorative practices, precisely because they are determined to honor each fallen soldier, also accentuate a sense of emptiness and absence: bodies buried unnamed, and names carved on the wall without graves and bodies. This sense of emptiness and absence may not have been so unusual or peculiar in the 1920s, given the immense carnage of this war, and perhaps also since such an organized and well-planned military burial as we see here was a novelty back then. Almost half of the British war dead in World War I (about 517,000) were not found and are considered to have no known grave. But the CWGC continues its attempts to identify anonymous soldiers and locate soldiers' remains in various arenas of the Great War. Once remains are found or an anonymous soldier is identified, rededication services are performed and the missing person's name is removed from the memorial boards of those with no known grave. On the board here, though, I did not notice any removal or deletion marks of any of the names.[31]

---

31. The information on the process of removing names from the memorial wall to soldiers whose graves are unknown after identifying the remains of bodies is sourced from the CWGC website. According to Margaret Cox and Peter Jones, while the British

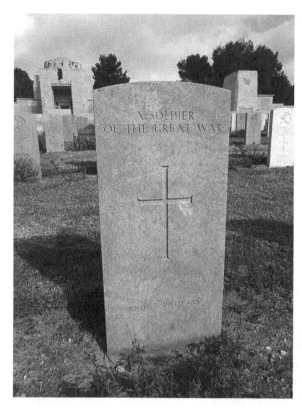

Fig. 11. "A Soldier of the Great War." (Photograph by the author.)

Government always makes an effort to identify and name the mortal remains of missing British personnel from historic cases discovered during various activities, they typically do not actively seek to locate missing soldiers from early twentieth-century conflicts with no known place of burial. The main reason for this approach is that the number of missing soldiers is often substantial, making the likelihood of identification historically very slight (Cox and Jones 2014, 296). But there have been cases where specific initiatives to search for and identify missing soldiers from historical conflicts were undertaken because local residents and communities expressed interest in the process. For instance, Cox and Jones describe a case where the initiative to search for and identify hundreds of Australian and British dead from 1916 in several mass graves at the Pheasant Wood site in Fromelles village, near Lille, France, came from local French residents and communities in Australia associated with the soldiers. As a result of public pressure and interest, the UK and Australian governments, along with the CWGC, collaborated on the project and funded the University of Glasgow's archaeological excavations and identification operations between 2009 and 2014. To aid in the identification process, potential relatives of the deceased donated DNA samples, which were used to construct family trees and to examine the remains found at the site.

To the British Jerusalem War Cemetery   **89**

Other countries, such as Israel and the United States, are also working to locate and identify missing or anonymous soldiers using advanced forensic technologies and recovery mechanisms, even decades after the fighting.[32] Moreover, the state's commitment to its dead soldiers has increased significantly since World War I, and today Western countries are unlikely to leave thousands of dead soldiers buried in the sands of faraway battlefields. Care for the dead soldier has become not only a part of the state's moral obligation to the fallen and their families but also a clear demonstration of the power, knowledge, and authority of the state. The act of finding the physical remains and identifying the fallen, sometimes through employing special forces and means across enemy lines or using various intelligence and diplomatic and economic incentives, brings closure and illustrates the scientific-intelligence superiority and sometimes the political authority of the state. The state that sent the soldiers to their violent death in war, where their traces were lost or their bodies were corrupted beyond the ability to identify them by eye, succeeds to some measure in turning back time itself. Through its forensic techniques and systems of search and retrieval, the state becomes an entity with trans-temporal powers and authority.[33] But when the search for bodies without graves fails, or when the missing soldiers are not found even after decades of searching, this creates ongoing frustration and a sense of disappointment. I ask the students to think in this regard of the famous case of missing Israeli pilot-navigator Ron Arad (whose Phantom jet was shot down over Lebanon in 1986).

One student interrupts, saying, "You don't have to look at it this way." She suggests that while it is true that a search that does not end in finding the dead can result in very harsh feelings for the families of the missing soldiers, we should also think about the values of social solidarity and comradeship (רעוּת), and the fighters' respect, their dignity, which the search reflects and emphasizes. She argues that it is not just about political interests or prestige of state and military institutions and mechanisms: "I see it as a basic responsibility of society, its dedication in return for the soldiers' ultimate commit-

---

32. In 1998, the remains of an anonymous American soldier buried in the Vietnam War Anonymous Soldier Crypt at Arlington National Cemetery were identified using innovative forensic techniques (see Wagner 2013).

33. Even today, the United States still buys remains of US troops from the Vietnam War from various ventures and private people or rewards the Vietnamese government for them in various material forms. A vibrant market for selling and foraging for such remains exists (see Wagner 2015).

EXPEDITION ESCAPE FROM THE CLASSROOM

ment." I reply to her that while I agree with her overall, my criticism stems from the fact that I know that states do not always search for the missing or identify the anonymous just because of the values she mentioned. Sometimes state institutions or regimes use the war dead to force political meaning or an anachronistic interpretation of the past, which actually harms the commemoration of the dead. I then invite the students to follow me to the graves of the Italian soldiers to show them what I mean.

The graves of the five Italian soldiers lie in the northwest wing of the cemetery. Italy was an ally of Britain during World War I, and about 500 of its soldiers joined field marshal Edmund Allenby's forces during the conquest of Jerusalem in 1917. Their role was less military and more political-religious: their responsibility was to secure the interests of the Catholic Church and the Italian clergy in the important churches of Jerusalem and Bethlehem after the occupation (Grainger 2007, 127, 149). Five of these Italian soldiers were killed in the Jerusalem area and are buried here on Mt. Scopus (one of them is an anonymous soldier). I tell the students about this history and ask them to check the graves for anything unusual about the headstones. Two students immediately note that, unlike the inscription on British soldiers' headstones, the caption here is not in English but Italian. "True," I agree, "but look at the side of the headstones for a moment." One student, who is studying in the History Department in addition to the International Relations Department, identifies it as "the fasces symbol." The other students don't know what the fasces is, and I explain that this is an ancient Roman symbol adopted by the Fascists in Italy in the 1920s (and also the origin of the word "fascism"). It depicts a bundle of wooden rods with an ax next to them (see fig. 12). In ancient Rome, the fasces was the emblem of the magisterial justice system. For the Fascists in the twentieth century, it stood for the power of the group's unity. The fasces already appeared in the heraldic designs of other states (France, the United States) before Italy's Fascist regime adopted it. Maybe that's why the symbol did not share the reputation earned by the Nazi swastika (though the swastika, too, is not a symbol that originated with the Nazis). But more important than dwelling on the history of the Fascist emblem, I want the students here to notice that the soldiers buried here were killed in 1918—a few years before Fascism took over Italy. Effectively, the headstones built on their graves in 1935[34] retroactively made these soldiers fascists. It's hard not

---

34. Email correspondence with Mr. Roy Hemington, public relations officer at CWGC. According to the CWGC records, the headstones were provided by Italian authorities in 1935, after the bodies of the Italian soldiers were brought to Jerusalem

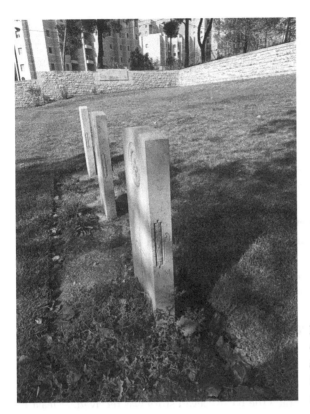

Fig. 12. The fasces on one of the Italian soldiers' headstones. (Photograph by the author.)

to see the absurdity here, and the students smile but also look surprised and disturbed by this appropriation of the dead who "turned Fascist" many years after they were killed.

But such political appropriation of dead bodies is not something that was done only by Fascist regime. I tell the students about the 1982 reinternment of bones that probably belonged to men under the command of Shimon Bar-Kosevah, leader of the Jewish revolt against the Romans in AD 132–135, after being discovered in the Judean Desert in an archeological excavation in 1960. The reburial was conducted in Nachal Chever in the Judean Desert in a full Israeli military ceremony on Lag Ba'Omer 5766 (May 11, 1982), the day associated with the Bar-Kosevah revolt. Former military chief Rabbi Shlomo Goren initiated the ceremony and presided over it, and the funeral was attended

---

War Cemetery from various sites in Palestine. The committee is unaware of other such graves (with the fasces) in its cemeteries.

92 EXPEDITION ESCAPE FROM THE CLASSROOM

by prime minister Menachem Begin and several government ministers. But absent from the funeral were the archaeologists who discovered the bones, led by Professor Yigael Yadin (a former chief of staff of the IDF). Yadin's absence was not due to his opposition to the military burial of remains found in an archeological excavation (in 1969, he attended an official Israeli funeral for body remains that he uncovered in Masada during his excavations there), but because the 1982 funeral was shrouded in religious and messianic characteristics, which Yadin highly opposed (H. Weiss 2016). Either way, Bar-Kosevah's soldiers were reburied as *Israeli* soldiers. (With the outbreak of the 1982 Lebanon War a few weeks later, there were many real Israeli soldiers to bury, I add cynically, and some students lower their gaze or look away uncomfortably.) The burial of Bar-Kosevah's men is not the same case as the Italian soldiers here who were appropriated by the Fascist state in 1935. But the pattern of forcing some symbolic meaning over the past through human remains and military burial is similar.

From Scopus to Gaza, and to Gallipoli, Canberra, and Wellington

Our tour continues for about ten minutes after the pause at the "Fascist" Italian soldiers' graves and the story of Bar-Kosevah's soldiers' reburial in an official Israeli military funeral. (The Bar-Kosevah story was received, at least by some in the group, with less good humor than the story of the Italians. Over the years, I have noticed that my students have tended to become less tolerant of a comparative-ironic view of Israel, perhaps in parallel to a strengthening of a nationalist perception of Jewish history and fate as unique and beyond any international comparisons.) We then go to the plot of British-Jewish soldiers (twenty-four in number here), where I tell the group that the British military cemetery in Gaza also contains five graves of British-Jewish soldiers and that these tombs are preserved and maintained precisely like the other thousands of tombs in that cemetery. The students are surprised to hear that Jews are buried in Gaza. The fact that Jewish graves in "enemy" territory are not protected by Israel and yet remain groomed and taken care of can be perceived by many Israelis as strange or illogical.

It also reflects a sense of blurring that has been growing over the past decades in our society between what is "Jewish" and what is "Israeli" (as the story of the Bar-Kosevah's soldiers exemplifies). After all, Israel evacuated its settlements (including cemeteries) from Gaza in the 2005 disengagement, one of the students observes. He wonders how it did it not take care of these Jewish tombs. Another student points out in response, "But these are British, not Israeli, graves." Moreover, the idea that a compound identical to the one we are currently in is located in the heart of the Gaza Strip quite astonishes the students. One of them says that it is strange for him to think that these British military cemeteries somehow connect or form parallels between Gaza and us. "You mean that these cemeteries create a kind of *parity* between us?" I ask in response. For these are unique, sacred spaces that also impose special responsibility on the state in which they are located. The fact that two such cemeteries also exist in the Gaza Strip (the other one is in Deir al-Balah), and are maintained and handled by the CWGC, perhaps reveals some humanity and civilization in the Gazan Palestinians too, which we usually cannot or do not want to see.

The students are even more surprised when I tell them that although Salafist Islamic extremists apparently corrupted the much more modest and hidden Cross of Sacrifice in the British cemetery in Deir al-Balah in the Gaza Strip, Gaza City's cemetery was far more damaged by the IDF, whose bombings on the area harmed hundreds of headstones during military operations in 2006 and 2009. Israel had to compensate the CWGC in tens of thousands of pounds sterling for rehabilitation costs. Moreover, the Gaza cemetery, like the British cemetery here, is an attraction for people who come not to visit the graves but, for example, to picnic or to play soccer in the green and well-groomed area. The keeper of the Gaza cemetery, I have learned, shoos them off (Sherwood 2013). For this guard, the Gaza cemetery is literally his personal and family life's work: Ibrahim Jareda worked there for decades as the CWGC's chief gardener and after retirement continued to work as a night watchman. His sons carry on as gardeners there (Rowley 2017). Several journalistic articles on the internet carry interviews with Jareda, including an interview on an Israeli television channel (Eldar 2011). In all these news items, he states that all wars are evil and futile and that all those killed in wars were equal human beings before God. He himself has had a good life, he says, and the dead were good companions.

We finish the tour with a look at the graves of the Ottoman and German soldiers. They are located in the northeastern section of the cemetery. But the design of the headstones is very similar to that of the British, and their surroundings are well maintained and preserved. These graves seem to illus-

94 EXPEDITION ESCAPE FROM THE CLASSROOM

trate a British commitment to the Treaty of Versailles and an attempt to win the goodwill of the Turks in places like Gallipoli, where tens of thousands of British and ANZAC soldiers are buried on Turkish soil (Yilmaz 2014). But they could also express an ethic of mutual respect between militaries and perhaps even a desire for reconciliation and a hope of overcoming enmity. I recall the following words, attributed to Ataturk from 1934, which appear on a memorial in one of Gallipoli's British cemeteries, and then I read them to the students from my cell phone screen:

> Those heroes who shed their blood and lost their lives, . . . you are now lying in the soil of a friendly country. Therefore, rest in peace. There is no difference between the Johnnies and the Mehmets to us where they lie side by side here in this country of ours. . . . You, the mothers who sent their sons from faraway countries, wipe away your tears; your sons are now lying in our bosom and are at peace. After losing their lives on this land they have become our sons as well.

These words have been cited several times by Australian prime ministers over the years, as well as in the Australian press. Two identical memorial plaques with this caption are also found in Canberra and Wellington: in Canberra, the memorial plaque is in a garden dedicated to the valor of ANZAC soldiers *and* Turkish soldiers. Yet, most probably, Ataturk did not say these words. The text is apparently a liberal and very expansive translation by an Australian veteran of words delivered in 1938 *on behalf* of Ataturk by a Turkish minister close to him. Ataturk's alleged words may have brought some comfort to bereaved families in New Zealand and Australia and contributed to political reconciliation with Turkey. Inscribed on identical memorials on three continents, they also reinforced the national myth around ANZAC in Australia and New Zealand. They touched the hearts of tens of thousands of tourists visiting ANZAC memorial sites in Gallipoli and Australia (Daley 2015). But do these words indeed honor the memory of ANZAC soldiers, who were sent as invaders to Gallipoli by a neglecting British command, and the memory of the Ottoman soldiers that Ataturk sent in human "waves" to repel the invaders (with close to 57,000 of the Ottomans killed)? It is doubtful whether the "Johnnies" or "Mehmets" saw each other as brothers or whether the "Johnnies" would have liked to be remembered as the "sons" of the Turks, whose capital, Istanbul, they were supposed to conquer in the same campaign on the Gallipoli Peninsula.

Final Thoughts on the Way Back to Campus

I leave the students pondering this, and our tour ends. In a few minutes, we will all be back on the Mt. Scopus campus. I will return to the British Jerusalem War Cemetery with the next class in the next semester. The students who visited with me here today can choose to write about this tour in their take-home exam at the end of the course. Readings for this tour include articles by Ron Fuchs, Yfaat Weiss, Haim Weiss, George Mosse, and Lorenzo Zambernardi, who discuss the history of British cemeteries in general (Fuchs 1996), the story of this particular cemetery (Y. Weiss 2017b), and the issue of military burial (Mosse 1991; Zambernardi 2017; H. Weiss 2016). These five articles provide an excellent basis for understanding military burial and the history of the place we were touring today. But they are written in a formal academic manner that keeps an analytical-theoretical distance from the research subject. In contrast, I seek in this tour to highlight the emotional and psychological dimensions and the personal and everyday, seemingly banal dimensions of the visit here. It is important for me to share with the students the personal connection I have to this place and to create a living memory of the tour here. My intention is not necessarily to create an emotional connection with the memory of the particular soldiers buried here or even to generate sympathy toward the institution of British military cemeteries worldwide. Of course, I want the students to look respectfully and empathically at the pain of the British, the Turks, and the other peoples who lost so many lives during the conquest of our country and the First World War in general. But the more significant lesson I hope students will take from the tour is that it is worth looking more skeptically at the state's demand—perhaps any state, but especially our state—that its soldiers and civilians be willing to sacrifice their lives for it. I also want to highlight the importance of questioning the claims, imposed by the state, of "lack of choice" and necessity when turning to using violent force and killing others. I hope that the rows of orderly graves here and the sense of despair that lies hidden behind their stoic façade, as well as the stories of abusing the war dead's memory to further political needs, convey my intention clearly.

As I walk up Churchill Avenue and am about to enter the fortified campus and pass the security checks, I think that while the cemetery remains almost unchanged since its official opening in 1927, our campus has undergone a dramatic transformation. It is unrecognizable from its early days as a small and relatively open campus (look again at figure 5 opening this chapter). It

EXPEDITION ESCAPE FROM THE CLASSROOM

has now been transformed into a fortified, gated megastructure, its towering presence and stringent security measures reflecting the ever-present reality of violent conflict in our country. But even in its nascent years, the university's existence relied on the support of British military power, and so foundational relations between the campus and the cemetery were established.

Within the confines of the British cemetery, time seems to have frozen in 1918, when the production of dead bodies during World War I concluded, and in 1927, the year of cemetery's official dedication. Unfortunately, many other wars, both here and in different parts of the world, have erupted since then and are likely to continue in the future. Military cemeteries continue to witness the creation of new graves, while countless other bodies of those killed in war remain unburied in any dignified manner. Within the specific visit to the British Jerusalem War Cemetery, I brought my students here to reflect on war in a broader sense, the price of conflict, and the enduring emotional scars war leaves behind, as well as how these scars get camouflaged and normalized. Moreover, I aimed to expose the students to the heterotopic elements present in this place, to encourage them to think critically about the notion of strict boundaries in IR—both as an academic discipline and as a real-world practice. I sought to provoke them to ask questions during our tour: Where are we? When are we? And what do we feel in this segment of space and time that seemed properly defined and bounded when we entered (namely, a British World War I cemetery) but had become fuzzier by the time we left?

As the security guard checks my university employee card and then my backpack before letting me in the campus, I wonder whether the ironic or indignant tone I sometimes speak with during the tour keeps students from learning the things I want them to learn here. Listeners can accept or tolerate a certain degree of irony and anger, especially when dealing with fundamental issues of our political subjectivity as human beings. I try to identify this threshold during each tour and not cross it. I harbor much anger and resentment toward the institution of war and militarism, and I have an ironic view of the conduct of states and political actors. I also feel frustration and fear in the face of the long rows of headstones here—and in some ways I express these feelings. But it is always a subtle art not to let my irony, anger, fear, and frustration distance some students from the lessons I want to teach or the questions I want to present (while others open up to my concerns *thanks* to such an approach). I hope that the measured exposure of my feelings during the tour encourages students to at least wonder why I am expressing my feelings on these issues and why it was important to me to bring them here.

Beyond a certain dimension of performance on my part as instructor, which occurs in almost every interaction in a tour like this, I hope the students experience my feelings as *authentic* (Willis 2014). From my perspective, I want students to express their feelings as well—both during the tour, in subsequent classes, and in the reflexive writing task of the take-home exam at the end of the course, which doesn't necessarily have a "correct" answer. In this way, I hope to convey to students that their knowledge and sentiments on these issues are important and that I consider them partners in creating a more nuanced understanding of politics (Ettinger 2020). It is precisely this sense or degree of partnership, arising from the tour, that enables me to return with the next class to this complex and sad place.

CHAPTER 3

Looking for Roots in the Mt. Scopus Botanical Garden

IDEOLOGICAL FLORA, BUFFER ZONES, AND SEEING/IGNORING

> "For we are like tree trunks in the snow. In appearance they lie sleekly and a little push should be enough to set them rolling. No, it can't be done, for they are firmly wedded to the ground. But see, even that is only appearance."
> —FRANZ KAFKA, "THE TREES"

> "Mr. Dizengoff, without roots, it won't work; without roots—there is no future."
> —WINSTON CHURCHILL[1]

Introduction to the Chapter

I open this chapter by providing context about the situation and time of its writing, which was during the third COVID-19 lockdown in Israel, in December 2020. In preparation for a virtual tour of the Mt. Scopus Botanical Garden conducted on Zoom—a tour that leverages platforms such as Google Street View and Google Earth to explore the garden—I reflect on my experiences with virtual teaching and compare it to in-person instruction. Certain challenges and consequences came from transitioning to remote teaching, including the impact on the overall experience of a course—like this one—that is

---

1. On March 30, 1921, the British Colonial Secretary, Winston Churchill, visited the recently established city of Tel Aviv. Prior to his arrival, municipal workers were tasked with swiftly bringing plant cuttings and tree branches from the surrounding area to be planted along Rothschild Boulevard, ensuring the street looked as verdant as possible. But as the entourage proceeded down the boulevard, led by Churchill and Mayor Meir Dizengoff, a civilian accidentally leaned on one of the tree branches, causing it to collapse with a loud noise. The anecdote recounts that Churchill turned to his host, Mr. Dizengoff, and remarked: "Mr. Dizengoff, without roots it won't work; without roots—there is no future." See Rapp (2002).

based on the notion of escape from the classroom. Using web imagery services to conduct campus "outings" during the lockdown had advantages and disadvantages. These platforms have become for me an essential part of the virtual learning environment in the pandemic and might become relevant again in the developing reality of climate change, since very high temperatures here in Jerusalem in the afternoon hours limit the ability to be out of an air-conditioned environment for long periods. Yet beyond such constraints, the use of services like Google Earth in this course inevitably raises an interesting aspect of IR-ization—being the third goal of this book. This is because the low resolution and outdated imagery of Israel available on such international web platforms necessitates a discussion about the politics of digitally obscuring certain areas and how this impacts transparency and our ability to know the spaces we occupy.

Following this, I focus on the relations between place and identity. The pandemic has altered my perceptions of place and personal identity, and virtual teaching has played a role in shaping these changes. The pandemic influenced my relationships with physical spaces, such as the Mt. Scopus campus, making them more volatile. Within this framework of evanescent and volatile places, I delve into the distinct essence and complexities of the botanical garden, emphasizing the limitations of a remote setting compared to an in-person visit. The computer-guided tour lacks the multidimensional sensory experience of being in the garden, such as the feel of the wind, the scents of plants, and the captivating view of the Dead Sea and Judean Desert. But, of course, this is not merely a botanical or scenery tour: the focus is on the interwovenness and separation between the botanical garden and the Palestinian neighborhood of Issawiya beyond the garden's fences.

The favela-like Palestinian neighborhood is clearly visible through the green foliage of the garden, but almost all the students in my course barely turn their gaze toward it before our tour. In this respect, the tour aims to further IR-ize the garden: to illustrate that its seemingly secure, ordered, green space cannot truly be separated from Issawiya, a neighborhood where people live in poverty and face regular police interventions and harassment. The black clouds of smoke from garbage burning in Issawiya are carried to the garden on the wind, and the alarming gunshots and stun-grenade explosions frequently heard from the neighborhood disrupt the garden's tranquility. These two places reflect and project upon each other, highlighting their entwined nature, despite the fencing of the garden.

This reflection and projection, which can even be observed during the vir-

100 EXPEDITION ESCAPE FROM THE CLASSROOM

tual tour, underscore the complexities and contradictions between certitude and illusion, security and danger, and presence and absence embodied by the garden. My preparatory physical garden visit before the Zoom class becomes a tour of a frontier space, a geography of danger in the present and past. It prompts me to consider how to convey these aspects to the students, helping them perceive the garden as a site that raises challenging questions about political and disciplinary boundaries, authenticity, and belonging. I also think about the possibility of a shared vision of our field of study, enviously comparing my experience with IR students to the bond between the early botanists of the Hebrew University and their students. This aligns with goal 1 of this book: discussing the anxiety of teaching the political.

During my preparatory garden tour, I also reflect on the concepts of rooting and uprooting as laid out by Simone Weil in her book *The Need for Roots*. Weil emphasizes the significance of being rooted, connecting it to empathy and resistance against violence and uprooting. I contemplate my own rootedness in the garden, campus, and country, while I also acknowledge the systemic discrimination and oppression faced by nearby Palestinians. I grapple with Weil's call to resist oppression, which presents a moral and practical challenge. I wonder if my students will be able to understand my dilemma. My reflections on the botanical garden and my positionality illustrate the site's complex nature, pushing me to present the situation thoughtfully. This autoethnographic account prompts readers to consider themes of rootedness, empathy, resistance, and ethical dilemmas within a place of beauty and scientific dedication that is situated in a context of conflict, domination, and violence, thus matching with goal 2 of the book: creating meaningful connection through autoethnography.

The chapter concludes with an incidental encounter with an East Jerusalemite Palestinian student from my course who happened to be on campus that day. Despite the period of social distancing, we are happy to meet in the physical world. I invite him to join me in observing the copy of the Lachish Relief at the university's institute of archaeology. I encourage the readers to imagine what happened on our joint physical tour to the institute of archaeology before the virtual Zoom class (Park-Kang 2015).

Virtual "Pilgrimage" to the Mt. Scopus Botanical Garden

Today is December 27, 2020; it is noon. In five hours, the third COVID-19 lockdown in Israel will enter into force. My ninety-minute class for the "Mt. Scopus Enclave" course will begin before that, at 2:30 p.m. I am on campus and leaving my office in the Social Sciences section of the megastructure to take a walk in the botanical garden, right across the inner-campus road—Defenders of the Mountain Road.[2] The 25-dunam (6.17-acre) garden is the largest open space on campus. Today, I will teach a class on the botanical garden and the "ideological flora" on campus from my office using the Zoom app. Because of the pandemic, all the courses in the university have been taught on Zoom since March 2020.

In today's class, we'll explore the garden using the Google Street View and Google Earth platforms and the Survey of Israel maps website. We have already done this in previous virtual tours this year: to the British Jerusalem War Cemetery and the "Founders Wall" at the entrance to campus (during a class on the origins of the Hebrew University). Something about this way of teaching reminds me of the option available to medieval pilgrims to tour holy places not by physically making a pilgrimage to the site but by guided observation of large paintings of the seven great churches of Rome, prepared with the permission of the Catholic Church. This virtual pilgrimage earned the believers an absolution from the church, like the one they would have received if they had visited Rome itself (Ehrenschwendtner 2009; Power et al. 2013; Luque-Ayala and Neves Maia 2019). Similarly, the virtual tour of the botanical garden could earn my students points on the course's take-home exam if they choose to answer the question about this site (:

On the Politics of Low-Resolution Imagery

While Google Street View gives a good representation of the surface, and one can virtually "walk" on many parts of the campus (the botanical garden included) and observe numerous details, the images are from December 2011, when Google's team last surveyed the campus (and many other parts of Jerusalem and other Israeli cities and towns too, as well as several Palestinian cities in the West Bank). Much has changed on the campus since then. In this sense, using this application has an "archaeological" element. It also has ben-

---

2. This inner-campus road commemorates the military unit Matzof 247, which guarded Mt. Scopus during the enclave period of 1948 to 1967. Nowadays, hardly anyone at the university is aware of the road's designated name as the Defenders of the Mountain, perhaps because there is no street sign indicating it. I stumbled upon the name only thanks to Google Maps while preparing course materials for the enclave classes during the COVID-19 pandemic.

efits—to ponder the meaning of "walking" in a time capsule while learning about a current site. Conceptual questions become more salient, such as to what extent we can know a place from afar (or know a place at all).[3]

For now, at any rate, the COVID-19 crisis has frozen almost everything, and we have to make do with a combination of images from different sources to "see" the campus. Notably, some of the students in the course have studied only one semester so far on the campus, and they barely remember it as a physical place. The satellite images of Google Earth are from 2016, somewhat newer than Google Street View's. But the resolution of the images is not sharp enough (see fig. 13). This is a deliberate blurring, and it is not a local initiative of the Hebrew University—the entire area of the State of Israel, including the occupied territories (West Bank, Gaza Strip, and Golan Heights), is presented in a relatively crude resolution of 2 meters per pixel (the smaller the number, the higher the resolution). The reason for this is an American legislation from 1997—the Kyl-Bingaman Amendment (Zerbini and Fradley 2018). The current image resolution of Israel that the US government allows is 0.4 meters per pixel (US National Oceanic and Atmospheric Administration 2020), after US authorities were recently shown that such imagery from non-US sources is available for purchase online (University of Oxford 2020). But Google and other American online providers of free satellite images (e.g., Microsoft's Bing) still adhere to the blurred 2 meters per pixel limit for unknown reasons (pressure from the Israeli government? technical/financial issues? See Sharf 2022). The Survey of Israel aerial photographs offer a slightly better resolution than Google Earth. Still, the maximal magnification is 1:1250—you can clearly see cars in the street, for example, but cannot zoom in more than that to see what make they are.

Thus, the option of adding satellite/aerial images to the campus tour so that we can instantly alternate between surface images and satellite/aerial ones in the Zoom app adds an interesting spatial dimension to the course.[4] But at the same time, as long as the satellite imagery remains relatively blurred and the maximal magnification in the aerial photos does not show subtle details on

---

3. See Dening (1980). Dening tells about the shock of realizing how little he understood the place he had studied in detail for years from written historical sources before actually visiting there.

4. Indeed, we can also watch satellite images when we are out in the field with smartphones. But for some reason, I didn't think of this before the COVID-19 crisis— we were so much "in" the experience of the tours that this did not come to mind. Perhaps in the future I will implement this option for the in-person tours as well.

the ground, the main lesson we can draw from these images is not so much about the features of the areas we study but about why these features are hidden. In a recent class, several students said that the blurring must be to hide the bases of the IDF and other sensitive security installations. I responded by showing them, on Google Earth, the top secret Dimona nuclear reactor: the location is easily found after typing the name of that "holy of holies'" in the search box. We also managed to see many of the site's outlines, including the nuclear reactor's shimmering dome, which glitters even with the current blurring of 2 meters per pixel. We were able to locate other military and security sites similarly—IDF headquarters in Tel Aviv, various airstrips, and the entrance to the government's nuclear-proof bunker in Jerusalem (though some of these sites are blanked out on the Survey of Israel website).

But if the reason for blurring is to protect security-related sites, why is the rest of the country also blurred? I find it hard to believe that the enemies of Israel do not already possess detailed and high-resolution images of the entire (small) country. Additionally, areas and locations that are not under Israel's formal sovereignty, such as the West Bank and, more than that, the entire Gaza Strip, which Israel claims to have withdrawn from in 2005 (but keeps under tight aerial, maritime, and land control/siege), are also blurred. This might be related to an interest in hiding the spatial outcomes of the occupation, I suggested to the class—for instance, house demolitions, environmental degradation and unregulated exploitation of the environment, the establishment of small military outposts, the exact route of the separation fence, and the expansion of Israeli settlements (Agha 2020). "Hide this from whom?" one student asked, somewhat agitated. I responded almost automatically, "Well, from civil society groups, environmentalists, academic researchers, human rights organizations, and the news media." Another student interjected, "To hide it from us, regular Israelis, who never visited or served in the territories."

How right she was, I thought. No precise data exists as to the number of Israelis who visit the West Bank,[5] but even those who visit or live there hardly notice the physical manifestations of the occupation thanks to various mechanisms and methods of directing the gaze off it (Záhora 2018). The Mt. Scopus campus is not within the occupied territories (it's a pre-1967 Israeli enclave within occupied East Jerusalem). But the realization that we

---

5. A 2017 survey estimated that between 30 and 42 percent of Israelis never visited the West Bank. "When Did You Visit the West Bank?" *Walla News*, May 28, 2017 [in Hebrew], https://news.walla.co.il/item/3067529

Fig. 13. The botanical garden in low resolution, as viewable on Google Earth. (Image courtesy of Google Earth.)

still cannot observe our campus in high-resolution satellite imagery partially because of the occupation and partially because of Israel-US understandings was a reminder that even though this is a course about a university campus—a relatively small and bounded civilian location—we cannot evade the broader politics of the conflict in Israel/Palestine and Israel's international relations. There are no enclaves of high-resolution satellite imagery in this country. Even through the little Zoom windows on my computer's screen, I saw the disappointment on some students' faces when they realized that I "managed" to throw the conflict into a course they assumed, or hoped, would not mention it.[6]

The Dissolution of the Real during the COVID-19 Pandemic

On day of this tour, December 27, 2020, we are in the second semester that the Hebrew University has been using Zoom to teach. In previous semester (March–June 2020), during the first lockdown (March–April 2020), when Israelis didn't venture out of the 100-meter-from-home perimeter decreed by the government, I taught from my living room. Now, after another lock-

---

6. On the effort not to mention problematic history and contentious political issues, see Barak (2007).

Looking for Roots in the Mt. Scopus Botanical Garden **105**

down (which was much less restrictive and ended in mid-October), the campus is open most of the time. I occasionally leave home and ride my bicycle here to teach from my office. Riding to campus provides me with a sense of freedom and control (but in other senses, keeps me "within" my previous book, *The Politics of the Trail*). Although the campus is fairly deserted, it is still good to "come to work." But "work" in these times is a strange place—for even if I teach from my campus office, the students are not here, and we meet on Zoom. The botanical garden is so close to my office, just across the Defenders of the Mountain Road, and yet on the Google Earth app it seems far away and blurred. So before I start the botanical garden Zoom tour today, I'm visiting the garden physically. I want to contemplate what I'll say to the students, to construct a narrative of the garden by walking in it. But creating such a narrative exposes the fractures in my own identity, the inherent difficulty I find in providing a decisive and coherent depiction of the place, thus revealing my simultaneous connection and estrangement from it.

I find it hard to tell a linear and uninterrupted narrative of most of the campus sites I take the students to visit, and this always confuses some students. Even though I devote the first classes of the course to talking about narrative as a "bumpy" and unsmooth mode of description and analysis, a nonlinear and not necessarily consistent understanding of the world, and even though I read with them from de Certeau's writings about "making do," students still seek clarity and continuity. They want a single meaning that they will be able to carry from the classes. I, on the other hand, emphasize that places are not static and comprehensible entities but rather ever-changing and imbued with the histories and memories of their pasts. This makes them more than just physical locations. They are also deeply interconnected with human experiences and emotions: places are "haunted" by "fragmentary and inward-turning histories" (de Certeau 1984, 108). Thus, the class often "digresses" into a rhizome of narratives and stories, and some students get frustrated (yet others, I see, enjoy it, or at least try to figure out how to find meaning). So, it is always an act of balancing between keeping a purposeful academic discussion, on the one hand, and talking about places as a de Certeau-ian network of stories and emotions, on the other.[7] My visiting

---

7. I am reminded of these memory fragments from *The Practice of Everyday Life*: "'Here, there used to be a bakery.' 'That's where old lady Dupuis used to live'" (1984, 108). With these fragments, De Certeau is referring to the strong links between presence and absence in the formation of the meaning of places.

106   EXPEDITION ESCAPE FROM THE CLASSROOM

the botanical garden before the class starts today is an opportunity to weigh these aspects in my mind.

But my purpose in going out to the garden now is not only for a get-ready-to-class stroll (I also want to take a few up-to-date pictures from the garden to show the students). This short excursion to the garden is also a reality check: strangely, I need to see that the garden is still there. More precisely: I want to ensure that *I* am still rooted in it. I sense that something fundamental has changed in the passing year. Something in my—in our (societal)—experience of the real has altered. As a technological solution to the threat of the pandemic, as an immediate adaptive emergency response, the virtual platforms of Moodle and Zoom are indeed very convenient. They have several technical advantages, such as the "share screen" option or the ability to teach asynchronously (to upload a video with the lecture part of the class and then use the actual class time itself for discussion and Q&A). And, of course, home is safer than campus when it comes to the virus threat.[8] But the longer I have stayed at home this year, the easier it has been to get along in this new virtual reality without the routines and practices I deemed constitutive to my identity. The computer tours in this course, with all their limitations, keep the concept of the campus alive, to a certain extent, for the students and for me. But they also highlight that while tangible-physical places and the practices we perform in them are (still) integral and necessary for the possibility of human experience and identity (Malpas 2018), places are also, in turn, a memory or even an illusion. They are fluid and transient to an extent I never thought they could be or never was willing to accept.[9] This contradiction—between the tangibility and certitude of the campus as a physical place for meeting, wandering, staying, teaching, and learning, on the one hand, and the swift disappearance of campus during this period, on the other hand—really startled me.

Certain changes signified a personal and institutional positive adaptability at a time of a severe health crisis: for example, the speed with which all teaching (and much of the interaction among the faculty) in the university was literally dis/re-placed into Zoom meetings. I managed quite easily with the

---

8. But, on home as a site of inbuilt dangers, inequalities, and cruelty, see Kay (2020).

9. In this context, the attitudes and practices the community of the Hebrew University developed during the exile from the campus of Mt. Scopus after the 1948 war are relevant, as they also exemplify coping with abandoning the campus. See Paz (2017).

Looking for Roots in the Mt. Scopus Botanical Garden

use of online technologies of remote sensing and some PowerPoint presentations to convert this course into a functioning virtual one.[10] I also enjoyed the convenience of teaching from home without the effort of toiling on the roads to campus, and I discovered I could "ghost out" from boring departmental meetings and seminars so much more quickly than in the physical world. But such understandings and changes also raised questions about critical decisions I made in my life and doubts about the connections between place and personal identity that informed my decisions.

Most notably, I asked myself, If the Hebrew University is such a central element of my personal and professional identity, and the Hebrew University is for me an idea(l) and concept *adjoined* to a specific physical locale here on Mt. Scopus,[11] what does it mean that at a stroke of a virus, so to speak, it dissolved one day as a real place—it became a danger zone, a potential site of infection—and that *nevertheless* I could go on with my life quite comfortably at home, separated from what had always been my "second home"? What does this abrupt change tell me about my identity as a scholar who writes about places, a person who thinks he is constructed by places, situated and grounded in them, and committed to them?

Being on the Campus and Away from It

Of course, this is not the first time I have been absent from the Mt. Scopus campus for an extended period, and I do not mean to say that I am a rigid person who cannot change location and identity or adapt to changing circumstances. After completing my PhD here in 2001, I spent two highly intellectually stimulating years at the University of Toronto as a post-doctoral fellow. And between 2011 and 2013, I was on a sabbatical leave at the University of Victoria, Vancouver Island, British Columbia. I developed deep emotional

---

10. My score in the teaching survey last year, when the course became virtual, was even better than the pre-COVID course in 2019: 7.12/10 in June 2019 and 8.43/10 in June 2020 (and 8.35/10 in February 2021). In the June 2020 and February 2021 surveys, students wrote that even though the course was virtual, the campus tours felt real, and they could experience the various places through the computer.

11. "The identity of people is inextricably bound to place, and not merely to place in some general, abstract sense (which would be meaningless), but also, as a consequence, to those *particular* places, multiple and complex though they may be, in and through a person's life is lived" (Malpas 2018, 11). This is what Malpas calls the "Proust Principle."

EXPEDITION ESCAPE FROM THE CLASSROOM

connections to (the city and university of) Toronto and to Vancouver Island. If I could, I would have stayed longer in both places and explored them further. Yet these connections to other places did not threaten my stable attachment to the Scopus campus and the sense of security I felt regarding it. What I'm trying to say is that I knew, ontologically speaking, that the Mt. Scopus campus was there and that I would return at some time to Jerusalem: as a postdoc in Toronto, my entire plan was to get a position in the IR department at the Hebrew University (and this indeed happened), and during the sabbatical at Victoria, while I could envision myself living on the island in the future, I also knew that my position in Jerusalem is an anchorage (it was a year or two after receiving tenure), a stable basis from which I can set out and always return (Zweig 1964, 160). In other words, there was an element of privileged *choice* in the decision of whether or when to return to Mt. Scopus from Canada. Now, with the COVID-19 crisis and the *forced* shutdown of (teaching on) campus, my choice of where to *be physically* was much reduced and dictated by external forces. Moreover, where to be and how to teach were not only personal questions for me—the entire institution and its community went virtual. Even today, in December 2020, when teaching from my office at Mt. Scopus, the class will be virtual.

The virus will be eliminated or controlled soon—vaccines are arriving shortly, and other factors (medications) and developments ("herd" immunity) will hopefully eventually restrain it. But I feel that the element of choice I was talking about and the ontological certainty regarding the physicality and stability of places will not be fully restored to their previous condition. In other words, the COVID-19 pandemic indicated to me that places are tangible but also volatile and dreamlike. The securitization and criminalization of the virus-containment effort, which included severe restrictions on the freedom of mobility, various surveillance methods implemented by the government to locate "suspected" (why not "possible"?) carriers of the virus, an electronic health declaration one had to show upon entering into many places (and the assumption that almost everybody carries a smartphone), the lockdowns and the police checkpoints, the risk to health in just going out, the quarantines, all these clarified to me how easily places can evaporate.

I also started to understand what it might feel like to be a Palestinian, whose freedom of movement is even more restricted with no foreseeable hope for improvement. And, along with all that *and despite all that*, an element of convenience accompanied some of these changes (think, almost-empty roads, no crowds anywhere, teaching from one's home or office). This combination of evaporation/disappearance of places and the accompanying conveniences are among the effects on place-making and movement in space that will remain in various forms and ways even after the pandemic.

The move to remote teaching also eroded a significant part of the "trickster/idler/slacker" component of this course and defeated much of the original purpose I had in mind for this endeavor. Namely, the escape from the confines of the classroom to the open air, the sensation of a mini-expedition, and the random (and not always course-related) conversations among the students and me that can occur while walking to the tour area or during the tour itself, the flâneurist component of the tour—all these are gone or considerably changed in Zoom teaching. Over Zoom, the tour starts almost as soon as the class begins, and I need to cut to the chase quite quickly. I also need to organize the Zoom class more systematically than the semi-spontaneous, in-person getaway from the classroom on campus. Students also suffer from "Zoom fatigue" and are even less open to stories or conversations that are not directly related to the subject of the class. Also, the element of surprise caused by accidental encounters or unexpected occurrences in the field is absent from the virtual tour. All these components of the tour help to create an experience of place-making among the students on the physical tour, and for me too. Even though their satisfaction with the course as a "product" (at least as measured in the teaching surveys) is higher in the last two (virtual) runs of the course, I feel they learn less than in the physical version.

Interwovenness and Separation in the Garden

Especially in the case of the botanical garden, the computer tour lacks many dimensions of the unique essence of the site. Students cannot feel the winds blowing in the garden (Eig 1938, 106)—planted on the summit of Mt. Scopus and the watershed of the Jerusalem hills—through remote sensing platforms, nor can they smell the pleasant scents of the plants and flowers. The captivating view of the Dead Sea, that waning blue spot (the saline lake's level decreases by more than a meter per year), and the glimmering whiteness of the hills of the Judean Desert seen from the garden are small images on students' computer screens (and even smaller on their cellphones). The deep shade of the oaks and the magnitude of the old pine trees planted here in the 1930s are lost on the computer-guided tour. The students cannot feel with their fingers the softness and elegance, along with the vulnerability, of a

Fig. 14. In the oak grove, within the garden. (Photograph by the author.)

new, shining, green leaf; they cannot pick fruits or leaves from the plants in the garden and taste them. This season, red, sweet, and juicy fruits of arbutus still hang on the garden trees, and one can also chew the leaves of the Mediterranean saltbush that grows in the Judean Desert plot in the garden and taste their delicate saltiness, or enjoy the sourness of Bermuda buttercups, an aggressively invasive species from South Africa that grows everywhere among the rocks here. Usually, when I encourage the students to chew or taste something here, some hesitate and genuinely fear that the fruits or leaves might be poisonous (even though signs next to all the garden plants indicate whether they are edible). This leads to a funny discussion about my botanical authority (I have none—nevertheless I have never caused any student to be poisoned!).

Likewise, it is impossible to hear the muezzins calling from the mosques of the Palestinian neighborhood Issawiya, which closely borders the garden—just across Martin Buber Street, which encircles the campus from the outside. You can neither see nor smell the black pillars of smoke billowing almost every

Fig. 15. Black smoke from burning waste in Issawiya, as seen from the botanical garden. (Photograph by the author.)

day over this neighborhood and over the adjacent Shuafat Refugee Camp,[12] a Palestinian community that is disconnected from the rest of the city by the concrete separation wall. (Issawiya, on the other hand, is "within" the wall—that is, its residents do not need to pass through a fixed Israeli checkpoint on their way to and from home. Nonetheless, ad-hoc checkpoints often pop up.) This is smoke from garbage burning, which the residents of these neighborhoods, favelas, and camps burn because of the unpredictable and insufficient waste removal services of the Jerusalem Municipality in their area (Stamatopoulou-Robbins 2019).[13] And it is also impossible in the virtual tour to perceive the alarm when gunshots and explosions from Issawiya (police shooting "rubber bullets" and stun grenades, or sometimes local youths shooting fireworks directly at the police, or criminals within the neighbor-

---

12. On the sensory dimensions of the occupation in East Jerusalem, see: Shalhoub-Kevorkian (2017).

13. Stamatopoulou-Robbins conceptualizes waste in the West Bank as matter that has no place to go, cannot be discarded, and is often burnt outside homes or at the edges of residential areas. See also Abu Hatoum (2021). Notably, the Jerusalem Municipality garbage-removal service in these places is unpredictable also because the garbage trucks are sometime stoned by locals.

112   EXPEDITION ESCAPE FROM THE CLASSROOM

hood shooting at each other) suddenly disrupt the garden's tranquility—such abrupt occurrences that nonetheless happen regularly.

The botanical garden and Issawiya, while they are two distinct and separate(d) spaces, project and mirror each other. Thus, for example, the garden is at the top of the mountain and is the boundary of the campus (Sheridan 2016), and Issawiya is on the slope and in the valley, both watched over by the garden and looking up at the garden. The garden, as part of the entire campus, is surrounded by security fences and electronic monitoring devices, patrolled each morning by the security department's explosive-sniffing dogs. Despite its proximity to Issawiya, the garden can be visited only by entering the campus, after a fairly rigorous security check. In contrast, the Israeli police and paramilitary forces of Magav (border police) enter Issawiya daily. The sounds and smells from Issawiya leak into or penetrate the garden and disturb its serenity, while the greenness and sense of spaciousness of the garden are watched enviously by residents of the village that has turned into a favela (I know this from conversations with Issawiya residents).

This interwovenness/separation is essential to the garden visit experience that I try to convey to the students. For this is not a botanical tour per se (even though we discuss many historical and cultural aspects related to plants), but a tour of a liminal space and a heterotopic site, through which I ask the students to think about issues such as political and disciplinary boundaries, authenticity and belonging, as well as seeing and ignoring. For me, it is also a place that represents paradoxes and contradictions of certitude versus illusion, of the permanent versus the ephemeral. It is a place of security and order and danger and anxiety. Finally, it is a place of a vocation and of lack and absence.

Entering through the "Roots Tunnel"

It is getting cold now at the entrance to the garden. To realize and materialize the botanical garden, to belong in it and perform it (Dening 2002), I enter the garden. The main entrance is a twenty-four-meter-long, box-like concrete tunnel that rises at a very moderate incline. Along the tunnel's walls, water rushes down loudly in two open streams. Yellow electrical lights shine upward from the margins of these conduits, making the water streams murky, while only dimly illuminating the tunnel's earth-colored mortar walls. On the walls and the tunnel's ceiling above are detailed and botanically accurate brown

Fig. 16. Issawiya, from within the botanical garden. (Photograph by the author.)

frescos of the root systems of *Pistacia*, oak, almond, cypress, fig, olive, pine, and other trees that grow on the grounds above the tunnel. All of these are native trees of the "Land of Israel."

The garden, since its dedication in 1932, has been devoted only to the local and indigenous flora of this land (according to the different phytogeographical regions and floral societies)—a unique concept for a botanical garden in Israel, and probably in the world too, and decades ahead of its time. Yet the names of the tree species, engraved below the representations of their root systems, are in Latin, according to the Linnean system of classification of species: *Olea Europaea*, *Amygdalus communis*, *Quercus calliprinos*, etc. The plants are local, but the language of their names, at least here at the entrance tunnel, is foreign. This is a university botanical garden, and so this "scientification" by Latin nomenclature is not entirely surprising. But the Latin monopoly on naming here at the entrance tunnel, along with the partial darkness that engulfs you once entering it, the specters of the roots, the water's murkiness, and the feeling of coolness and dampness, create a sense of strangeness, of entering into an other space, an underworld.

Why enter a garden, an open green space, through such a strange and dark

114   EXPEDITION ESCAPE FROM THE CLASSROOM

underground passage? In fact, I hardly thought about this until two years ago when I heard Ran Morin, the landscape architect of the garden, talk about his inspiration when renovating this tunnel and the garden in general in 2008.[14] On hearing Morin, my initial thought was that I had not earlier considered "the question of the tunnel," perhaps because so many other parts of the campus are so bunker-like that this tunnel never seemed unusual to me.[15] But it turns out that this entrance tunnel, unlike other parts of the campus that were indeed purposefully designed to look like a fortress and its components, was not a part of such a layout.

The reason why the entrance to the garden is through a concrete tunnel and the fact that the garden level is above entering visitors is simply that Mt. Scopus's southern side was lowered by about five meters after construction work began on the new campus in the 1970s, with the university returning to the compound when the area was reconnected to Israeli Jerusalem after the 1967 War. Thus, a height gap was created between the botanical garden, originally planted on the northern side of the summit of Mt. Scopus, and the new, lowered campus on the southern slope. The botanical garden was left as an enclave within an enclave, above the artificially lowered grounds of the new fortified megastructure. The tunnel solves the problem of this height gap and connects the garden to the campus (Morin 2019). In fact, it was not even built principally as a main entrance to the garden but was rather a corridor for pipes to the campus from the central air-conditioning unit that was placed in the 1970s at the border of the garden. In this sense, the tunnel tells a story of how the garden was left over, almost forgotten, after 1967 and how, nonetheless, it struggles to remain a part of the campus today. The garden has a few other entrances, but this tunnel is the main one, the closest one to the center of the campus, the indoor forum. Perhaps the tunnel's dark and eerie ambiance is one of the reasons why the garden remains unknown or remote to many of the campus dwellers.

Simone Weil and Rootedness and Uprootedness in the Garden

In a documentary film about the garden (U. Rosenberg 2016), Ran Morin, the garden's landscape architect, relates (beginning at 43:00 in the film) that the

---

14. Ran Morin's words in *The People of the Garden*, beginning at minute 43:00 (see U. Rosenberg 2016).

15. On the fortified architecture of Israel, see Weizman (2012).

Fig. 17. Two views of the roots tunnel. (Photographs by the author.)

inspiration to chart the root frescos on the walls of the tunnel came to him parallel to a surprising, in hindsight perhaps even mystical, discovery of the elaborate roots system of a fig tree in one of the burial chambers from the Second Temple period that is within the garden (the Cave of Nicanor). He realized then that the central theme of his renovation here should be roots and rooting, emphasizing the garden's value as a unique heritage site. He then read a line from Simone Weil's book *The Need for Roots* (1949), stating that rooting is perhaps the most important but the least acknowledged need of the human soul. Thus, the air-conditioning tunnel was turned into the "roots tunnel."

Following Morin's words, I went (before the COVID-19 pandemic) to see the fig roots in the burial cave within the garden. For me, it was an uncanny experience: the soft, chalk cave was full of large, buzzing flies, the air was dense and heavy, and the fig's roots, which run on the floor of the burial chamber and its walls, looked like tentacles or spreading hair, reminding me again of Julia Kristeva's concept of the abject as something that is discardable or disposable, something that sheds off from the "other" but engulfs and swallows the "self" (Kristeva 1982, 9). Morin probably saw life, continuity, and tenacity in the fig's root system in the burial cave. I saw death, excess, and

EXPEDITION ESCAPE FROM THE CLASSROOM

chaos (embodied in the countless flies). I'll "take" the class to see that cave in the virtual tour today, thankfully from the outside only, using the Google Street View platform, and we could talk about how a single place can invoke inspiration or horror and repulsion in different people. I will also mention Simone Weil's *The Need for Roots*, along with her essay the "Iliad, or the Poem of Force," two texts I read recently and that left a strong impression on me.

Weil, a Jewish-descended French philosopher and social activist (who adamantly rejected Judaism and was eventually baptized into Christianity), wrote *The Need for Roots* as a program of regeneration for France after the end of the German occupation, at the request of the French Resistance. But it is much more than a recovery program. It is a manifesto for all humanity on how to live in a free society by respecting and protecting people's dignity and material and spiritual needs (Linklater 2007). Weil writes about roots and rooting as an essential requirement for the human soul, basically as a need for genuine physical and spiritual connection to place, history, and community. She also emphasizes the danger of uprootedness, mainly due to the pursuit of money in urban life or caused by regimes of occupation and military dispossession and systems of lying and misinformation. She saw uprootedness as the most dangerous situation for human societies, for the lack of roots is a pervasive and contagious phenomenon: rootless individuals and societies tend to conquer others, abolishing and trampling the dignity and freedom of the conquered. The Romans, the ancient Hebrews, the Germans after the First World War, the Spaniards and the English since the sixteenth century, and the French after 1870 are all, for Weil, examples of conquerors who expanded due to detachment, an uprootedness from their rooted environment and historical continuum: "Whoever is uprooted himself uproots others. Whoever is rooted himself does not uproot others" (Weil 2005, 45). She found a direct correspondence between Germany's occupation of Paris in 1870 and the consequent drive of France toward colonialism to compensate for that humiliation. She mourned the corruption of France's very soul and vocation of liberty, equality, and fraternity, which were "the one true source of strength from which to challenge Hitler" (Kinsella 2021, 79).

In Weil's thinking, the idea of rootedness is strongly connected to empathy and even identification with the suffering of the oppressed and those treated by the powerful as "things." She argued that violent force was the means, and sometimes the end, by which people were stripped of their humanity and turned into things. Her first lines from the essay "Iliad, or the Poem of Force" are remarkable in their ability to capture the meaning of violence: "The true hero, the true subject, the center of the *Iliad* is force. Force employed by man, force that enslaves man, force before which man's flesh shrinks away. In this work [the *Iliad*], at all times, the human spirit is shown as modified by its relations with force, as swept away, blinded, by the very force it imagined it could handle, as deformed by the weight of the force it submits to" (Weil 1945). Weil's identification with those who suffer from violence and her understanding of obligation as accompanying rootedness is epitomized in her death: she probably starved herself to death in 1943 due to her refusal, while admitted with tuberculosis to a sanitarium in England, to eat more than the food rations that she believed people in occupied France received.

Weil's idea of rootedness speaks to my heart, as does her understanding of violent force and imperialism as self-corrupting and self-consuming. Yet, while I appreciate these aspects of her writing, I am also deterred by her stern and unforgiving understanding of the concept of duty, as revealed by her self-starvation. Naturally, as T. S. Eliot writes in his introduction to *The Need for Roots*, it is not helpful to be distracted, tempting as that may be, by considering how far, and at what points, one agrees or disagrees with her. "We must simply expose ourselves to the personality of a woman of genius, of a kind of genius akin to that of the saints" (quoted in Weil 2005, vii). Nevertheless, and despite Eliot's advice not to enter into a debate with Weil, I feel now, upon entering the garden through the roots tunnel, that the strict and absolute obligation to resist oppression and uprooting that she stresses in her words—and more so, in her deeds as a thinker and in her death—is a heavy moral onus that reading her ideas imposes on me. Her writing does penetrate the heart, and she is indeed akin to the genius of the saints, as Eliot notes. Yet not everybody can reach that spiritual level. Also, perhaps not everybody *wants* to be a saint.

For the garden now presents to me this question: To what degree am I rooted in these places—the garden, the university campus, the city, the country—and to what extent do I accept the Weilian idea that rootedness also means empathizing with those turned into "things" by violent force *and* acting to resist this force.[16] How can I reconcile my rootedness here with the

---

16. Similarly, this is also the question of nativity that Meron Benvenisti, one of the wisest and most profound Israeli intellectuals I read and met, raises in *The Son of the Cypresses* (2007). For Benvenisti, a native understands the pain of all the inhabitants of the land, Jews and Palestinians, and this *public* understanding and empathy in itself is a political act, for it entails, à la Benvenisti, a historian's elaborate resistance, in writing, to the deletion of the Palestinian history and landscape. See also his *Sacred Landscape* (2002).

118 EXPEDITION ESCAPE FROM THE CLASSROOM

daily systematic discrimination and oppression of Palestinians, so close to the garden, and how can I cope with the violence that is also a part of my constitution and identity as a member of the more powerful side in this ethnic, political, national, class, religious, and gendered conflict system, a structure that entails so many policies and practices of uprooting the weak? How can I keep myself safe but also resist a system of oppression that increasingly does not tolerate even being watched while it performs its domination? Are my students in this class a part of this oppressive system, or will they be willing at least to hear about my dilemma? Over the years, I feel that they have less and less tolerance.

Nonetheless, if I do talk with my students about Weil, I want to include the story of a visit I made to Issawiya. In November 2019, I joined Israeli activists who perform "police watch" walks in Issawiya. This was following a public event in the university, at the Mandel School for Advanced Studies in the Humanities (located at the edge of the botanical garden). A few hundred students and faculty attended, and they came to hear residents from Issawiya talk about police brutality and harassment in their neighborhood. The residents asked the members of the university community to come down to Issawiya, to walk and follow the riot police units that patrol the neighborhood, and thus, hopefully, not only witness the violence wielded by them but also ameliorate it by their very presence. It was an intense experience: I saw how the police harassed, for no apparent reason, the neighborhood as a collective. They placed a temporary blockade in the middle of the main street for no clear purpose but to create traffic jams. They did not even check drivers' licenses, but just blocked the road for ten minutes, on and off, standing in the middle of the street and gazing with blank faces at the drivers and passersby. The resultant traffic jams, in turn, provoked youths to throw stones at the police. Consequently, they had a justifiable reason to retaliate by shooting rubber bullets and other "nonlethal" ammunition (which sometimes does cause lethal injuries nonetheless).

The senior officer of the police force threatened us, the group of six Israeli "watchers," not to follow his men or he would detain us for "disturbing a police officer in performing his duties." We kept a distance. After several such walks in Issawiya, I realized it was too dangerous: I could not risk getting arrested or beaten by the police or (accidentally?) stoned by the locals. I stopped taking part in these activities. But I continued to come to the botanical garden, in part to watch Issawiya from here and also to show the neighborhood to my students, many of whom will be seeing this area for the first time (many also don't even know the name of the neighborhood). In previous, in-person, visits here, we watched the neighborhood from the viewpoint circle at the western end of the garden. Now, when preparing for the Zoom class, I suddenly realize that we can also use the Google Street View application to virtually "visit" Issawiya itself (several of its streets were surveyed in 2011).[17] This way, we won't risk being shot at or having stones thrown at us.

A Fenced-Off, Atypical Colonial Garden

My thoughts go back and forth between what can be seen *in* the garden and what can be observed *from* it. It is a puzzling place, this garden: it was established as a scientific garden for the study of the native flora of Palestine ("Palestine" in the British Mandate administrative and geographical sense of the term, that is) in order to reconstruct and preserve the land's "authentic"/authentic[18] forests and plant societies. But despite this strong element of locality in the garden, its intellectual origins and some of its historical beginnings go back directly to European colonialism and imperialism. Nonetheless, this is not a botanical garden that was meant to serve colonial and imperial interests by acclimatizing various beneficial plants from different parts of the empire (think, the rubber tree or the bread tree). Nor was it meant to present the exotic magnificence of the empire at the metropolitan center, as many late nineteenth-century and early twentieth-century botanical gardens were cultivated for.[19] Yet it was planted and maintained as part of the effort to colonize Palestine by the Zionists (Paz 1995; Leimkugel 2005), and this colonization involved establishing a settler society that is still based on structural

---

17. For an interesting perspective on a walk in Issawiya using the Pokémon Go game/app, see Cristiano and Distretti (2017).

18. I will return to this distinction between "authentic" and authentic further below. For now, it is sufficient to say that Palestine surely had an ancient floral system that was highly influenced and changed by human habitation and exploitation over the millennia. One of the major aims of the founders of the garden was to reconstruct the vegetation of "pluvial Palestine" and to reintroduce the forests that covered the land in previous eras. On the forests of ancient Palestine, see Liphschitz (2007).

19. "Acclimatization is intimately entwined with the rise of modern imperialism and with the marginalization and alteration of indigenous ecosystems and peoples. . . . Naturalists formed acclimatization societies to promote the rational exchange of aesthetically pleasing and 'useful' flora and fauna, . . . attempting to Europeanize the tropics and simultaneously render Europe more exotic and cosmopolitan" (Osborne 2000, 135–36). On gardens and power, see also Callahan (2017).

120   EXPEDITION ESCAPE FROM THE CLASSROOM

violence.[20] Related to this is the fact that since its opening, the garden has been a target for attacks and sabotage by residents of Issawiya, who claim that parts of their land were illegally confiscated or unfairly purchased from them by the Mandate government and the Hebrew University, respectively. I did not find indications for the validity of this claim in the archive of the Hebrew University, but since the 1930s, and this is recorded in the archive, various frictions with Issawiya residents along the fences of the garden have occurred. Today, Issawiya is boxed in on all its sides by Israeli neighborhoods, roads, and the Hebrew University.

The garden presents local and indigenous vegetation and trees, but it is somewhat sadly cut off from its immediate environment: almost since its formation, the garden has been fenced off, first to prevent goats from "the village at the lower end of the garden" (Issawiya) from eating its plants (Warburg 1931; Schlesinger 1934),[21] then to stop the villagers from cutting the garden's trees (Ben Menachem 1938), to hold them off from cultivating plots in the garden that they claimed were theirs (Arnon-Ohana 2008: 52), and currently, to make it more difficult for them to throw Molotov cocktails into the garden with the intent of setting it on fire. In addition, the fences are meant to impede or prevent terrorists from entering the campus through the garden (Cohen 2007: 50).[22] The garden is green and now, at winter's apex, even lush. It has an artificial system of streams and pools to demonstrate wetland and riparian vegetation. But outside the garden, the Palestinian space is dusty, dry, pale, and congested.

Religious and Secular Temples

I reach the end of the roots tunnel and emerge into a small courtyard. Along its perimeter is a circular pool or canal of aquatic plants, from which flow the

---

20. Nowhere is this better expressed than in Lieutenant General Moshe Dayan's obituary for Roee Rothberg, a youth who was killed along the Gaza border in 1956: "We are a generation of settlers, and without the steel helmet and the gun muzzle, we will not be able to plant a tree and build a house" (quoted in Löwenheim 2014, 137).

21. Schlesinger (1934) writes that the garden was meant to show also "how the high forest is attacked by other trees in addition to the attack by man and *beast*" (emphasis added).

22. The perpetrator of the Frank Sinatra Cafeteria bombing at the Hebrew University on July 31, 2002, used an explosive device concealed within a backpack. It is suspected that the backpack was thrown over the garden fence and subsequently retrieved by the bomber within the campus.

streams running inside the tunnel. Various ferns and mosses grow on the walls between the schist slates. Although the walls are about three meters high and surround the visitor, I can see the garden above, where fig, arbutus, and oak trees grow, and the sky is visible. The square evokes no sense of closure—on the contrary, the moist greenness of the ferns and mosses on the walls and the canopy of trees above, together with the peaceful circular pool and the water dripping from the walls into it, give this entrance courtyard a quiet, magical character.

Today the garden no longer serves as a scientific site for botanical experiments and research. After 1948, the botanical department of the university (now called Plant Sciences) moved to the newly built campus of Giv'at Ram, at the center of West Jerusalem. A new botanical garden was planted on that campus, a much larger one, with plots of plants from all over the world. The Scopus Garden survived the enclave years (1948–1967) mainly because its plants are native to the land and need little treatment or cultivation. It was a space of military action in those years, as the "defenders of the mountain" IDF unit exercised "sovereignty patrols" in it, and mines were placed among the trees. Some skirmishes between Israeli and Jordanian forces took place here then, claiming the lives of several soldiers and UN personnel (Theobald 2006).

After 1967 and the return of the Human Sciences to the Mt. Scopus campus, the botanical garden endured here as part of the original campus from before 1948—an original campus that was engulfed by a newly constructed megastructure (Selzer and Paz 2009). Now the garden is a site for recreation for campus occupants who stroll along its paths and sit on wooden benches for an out-of-office lunch; a place for students' romantic encounters (increasingly, between East Jerusalem Palestinian students, who have enrolled in in higher numbers in the Hebrew University in recent years); a space for environmental education for primary-school students; a location for preservation of endangered plant species; a Jewish and Zionist historical heritage site; a post-trauma permaculture rehabilitation volunteer site for a group of IDF soldiers from the 1973 war; an urban sanctuary for butterflies; and, finally a setting for a tour in my course, "The Mt. Scopus Enclave."

From this entry courtyard, two more short tunnels diverge: to the right, toward the plot of the Cave of Nicanor, and to the left, toward the main path that crosses the garden and watches over Issawiya and Shuafat Refugee Camp. The official tour of the University's External Relations Department, which presents the campus to donors and guests from abroad, turns right to the Nicanor plot. Now I, too, turn right.

EXPEDITION ESCAPE FROM THE CLASSROOM

Fig. 18. The Nicanor burial cave plot. (Photograph by the author.)

"Nicanor" is probably Nicanor of Alexandria, a Jewish philanthropist who donated the copper doors to the Second Temple and is mentioned in the Talmud and by the Jewish-Roman historian Flavius Josephus. The burial cave of the Nicanor family, discovered in 1902 in what is now the heart of the botanical garden, was then located on a plot purchased by Liverpool's Sir John Gray Hill to expand his estate on Mt. Scopus, in which he and his wife Caroline spent the winters and springs in the late nineteenth and early twentieth centuries, out of a romantic-orientalist impulse and love for desert and Bedouin life (Gray Hill 1891). Eventually, and due to Gray Hill's crystalizing sympathy for the Zionist idea of a Jewish university, he sold the estate in 1914 to the Zionist Organization. Its buildings and territory formed the basis for the Mt. Scopus campus (Wahrman 1997). One of the ossuaries found in the burial cave in 1902 bear the following words, inscribed in Greek: "Bones of those [i.e., of the house or family] of Nicanor of Alexandria, he who made the gates. Nknor Alexa." Gray Hill, who was a board member of the Palestine Exploration Fund, transferred the ossuary to the foundation, which donated it to the British Museum in London. It remains there to this day. Its importance hinges on its archaeological confirmation of cultural and historical sources: the Talmud and the writings of Josephus.[23]

This confirmation of the ancient Jewish sources is the main reason the university's External Relations Department also includes the Nicanor tomb as part of its tour. The tomb plot underwent an impressive restoration during the renovation of the garden in 2008 and also includes the burial cave of Menachem Ussishkin (head of the Jewish National Fund, who died in 1941) and Yehudah Leib Pinsker (a prominent Polish/Ukrainian–Jewish Zionist, who died in 1891). Two of my previous students who worked as tour guides in the External Relations Department told me that, while guiding donors and eminent visitors in the garden, they were asked to relate a narrative that presented an implicit comparison between Nicanor and present-day donors. The story of Nicanor's tomb often plucks on the heartstrings of many of my students too.[24]

I, on the other hand, am a little less excited by the story of Nicanor and the doors of the Temple, even if it is a historical testimony or confirmation of ancient Jewish sources. I have no longing for the Temple, especially after reading a few years ago the new Hebrew translation of Josephus's *The Jewish War*. The Temple and everything associated with it mainly repulses me (with its clerical corruption and constant animal butchering). But it also frightens me, mostly due to the growing tendency among messianic right-wing circles, Jews, and evangelical Christians, in Israel and the United States, to

---

23. For a strong rebuttal of the claim that the inscription was a forgery, see Macalister (1905).

24. The students are very surprised to hear that Pinsker, who was among the inspirational sources for the "Territorial" faction in Zionism in the early twentieth century, and who is also buried in the Nicanor plot, wrote the following words in his 1882 *Autoemancipation:* "We must not attach ourselves to the place where our political life was once violently interrupted and destroyed. The goal of our present endeavors must be not the 'Holy Land,' but a land of our own" (Pinsker 2007). Pinsker's position served later as one of the bases of the Territorialist movement in Zionism (mainly during 1905–25), which sought other territorial options for a Jewish state apart from Palestine. Yet eventually, Pinsker was (re)buried here on Mt. Scopus, in 1934, after his body was taken out of the grave in Odessa and brought to British-ruled Palestine at the request of Ussishkin. The latter, who could not think of any other place for the establishment of a Jewish state but Palestine and devised the idea of a National Pantheon on Mt. Scopus and asked to be buried in the Nicanor plot, was cut off from the State of Israel in 1948 when Mt. Scopus became an Israeli enclave within the Jordanian-ruled West Bank after the first Arab-Israeli war. Access to this pantheon-of-two was very limited between 1948 and the 1967 War.

124   EXPEDITION ESCAPE FROM THE CLASSROOM

link the memory of the Temple to practical intentions to rebuild it on Temple Mount—a move that will undoubtedly involve terrible violence, the destruction of the mosques of Haram al-Sharif, and possibly even worldwide chaos.[25] The yearning for the symbolic or historical place of the temple as a spiritual idea is replaced by practical plans and a desire to materialize them in the form of rebuilding the center for ritualist Judaism. Furthermore, many in the wider, and not necessarily messianic, Jewish public are increasingly sympathetic toward this trend (Persico 2017). This reawakening of the holy and the temple saddens and scares me, for in religious holiness I see something stern and unforgiving, necessary and arbitrary, veiled, irrational and unexplained, and absolute. Hence, it holds a high potential for righteous violence and no space for compromise.[26] In the case of the Jewish temple, this rigidity means that in today's Judaism the temple can reside or be rebuilt only on Jerusalem's Temple Mount. (Although, in the past, other Jewish temples existed apart from Jerusalem's, like the one on the island of Elephantine in the Nile River in Egypt [S. Rosenberg 2004]. More recently, in 2014, in São Paulo, Brazil, the evangelical Universal Church of the Kingdom of God opened a giant replica complex of Solomon's Temple that serves as a church.)

Standing now in front of the Nicanor burial plot and thinking about the concept of the holy, I suddenly recall the cover image of Diana Dolev's 2016 book on the architectural design of the early Mt. Scopus campus in the days of the British Mandate: a plaster cast model of Mt. Scopus and the campus on it, installed on a wheeled base, thus driven to be presented at the Levant Fair in Tel Aviv in 1936. The model is very detailed and accurate, and even the botanical garden appears in it.[27] The Hebrew University was seen then in the Yishuv as a secular and scientific temple of learning, with much of the

---

25. For an excellent literary representation and criticism of this commitment, see Chabon (2008). However, Esther Zandberg, in a review article of Diana Dolev's book on the planning of the Hebrew University, offers some consolation: she writes that if the planning process of the Third Temple has to go through just some of the lengthy crises (financial, personal, architectural) that the planners of the Hebrew University's campus had to endure, then we can breathe easy—"[the temple] will never be erected." See Esther Zandberg, "A New Book Reveals the Controversies behind the Construction of the Hebrew University," *Haaretz*, March 30, 2016 [in Hebrew], https://www.haaretz.co.il/gallery/architecture/environment/.premium-1.2899122

26. On the other hand, Rudolf Otto (1936) understands the holy as an elation and strong emotional connection to a metaphysical reality that cannot be achieved in words and logic alone.

27. On the role of models of the Jewish temple in the reawakening of the Third Temple movement, see Padan (2019).

self-importance adjoined to such a view.[28] But unlike the Jewish temple on Temple Mount, the Hebrew University exists today on several sites and campuses. These are "temples" too: thus, three cedar trees were planted near the entrance to the Giv'at Ram campus. The cedars "symbolize the university's mission to serve as a 'temple' of secular and pluralistic education" (Yuval and Tal 2012, 5).

Mt. Scopus's Garden and Zionist Nation-Building

Yet even if both of the two main campuses, Mt. Scopus and Giva't Ram, were seen as "secular temples," they are very different from each other in many other respects. The difference is starkly evident in the botanical gardens of the two campuses. The Giv'at Ram garden was privatized some two decades ago, and visitors must pay an entrance fee. The garden has been fenced off from the rest of the campus, making it essentially a separate unit/area. Here at Mt. Scopus, you can visit free of charge, and the garden is connected to the campus (although entry to the campus is strictly regulated by security). At Giv'at Ram, in addition to various plots of plants from different regions of the world, the garden has a restaurant, a greenhouse, a visitor center, and numerous installations for children's play and enjoyment. Although renovated in 2008, Mt. Scopus's garden has stayed much more basic, almost frugal. Botanist Dr. Michael Zohary wrote of the Scopus Garden in 1938, "The botanical garden needs to be a central place of knowing the homeland for the teacher, the student, and the researcher, and therefore the flora of the homeland should be represented in the garden with meticulous faithfulness, those little bushes and shrubs that are not always spectacular are the crucial elements in the structure of the floral formation presented" (Zohary 1938).

Indeed, the garden has remained very loyal to how its founders envisioned it in the late 1920s and early 1930s. There is no fanciful or exotic element here (think, giant cactuses); the beauty of the garden is simple and quiet.[29] Twenty-seven plots show various plant societies according to their geographical distribution in the country.[30] A system of small ponds and a stream

---

28. An ironical perspective on university life and professors' self-importance in Jerusalem in the 1930s can be found in Shmuel Yosef Agnon's novel *Shira* (1989).

29. On the fanciful element in urban botanical gardens, see Neves (2009, 146).

30. See the map of the garden here: https://botanic-garden.huji.ac.il/book/botanical-garden-map

126   EXPEDITION ESCAPE FROM THE CLASSROOM

between them simulate aquatic and riparian vegetation, beyond which the garden's landscape changes into the Jerusalem hills forests and shrubland. The garden has a geophyte plot, a Negev desert habitat of saltbushes and acacias, and even a section of the plants of the Sinai Peninsula, which is no longer under Israeli control but for some reason stayed in the garden and was not returned to Egypt in the 1979 peace accord (Should we alert the Egyptian government? I often ask the students.) Even though various types of soil were brought mainly during the 1970s and 1980s to these different plant plots (sand, clay, and even granite rocks from Eilat) to allow the plants to grow in their natural conditions, the greater part of the garden is Mediterranean maquis, batha (shrubland), and garigue vegetation—namely, Jerusalem pines, Palestine oaks, *Pistacia* shrubs, figs, and arbutus trees. This is the "regular" floral formation of many of the hilly areas of the land—the Judean and Samarian Mountains and the Galilee. The garden has no distinct tourist attraction besides, perhaps, the Cave of Nicanor's tomb system. Visibility and extravagance, which dominated European and North American botanical gardens in the nineteenth century, are absent here.[31] This is not a garden that intends to present a monarch's or an empire's riches and power (Spary 2000, 23). Nor is it a garden that attempts to assimilate an occupied colonial population into the culture and aesthetic order of the imperial conquerors—if anything, quite the opposite.[32]

Rather, the Scopus Botanical Garden was meant to demonstrate the different plant societies and regions of Palestine (Zohary and Feinbrun-Dotan 1966–1978) first and foremost to the Zionist settlers, the newcomers to the land—the scientists/botanists, their students, and the broader public—thus constructing a coherent and distinct notion of a "land," at least from the botanical perspective.[33] Classifying and collecting the land's plants and dis-

---

31. "The 'useful' and the 'curious' have been the two guiding categories of collecting plant specimens and conducting botanical research [during the 19th century]" (Carroll 2018, 310). For drawings of famous historical botanical gardens, see Hill (1915, 224ff.).

32. On Japan's effort to educate and acculturate occupied Koreans in Japanese "taste" and culture through the Seoul botanical garden, see Kim and Zoh (2017). See also Besky and Padwe (2016, 18).

33. In a letter addressed to the management of the Hebrew University on July 16, 1937, Dr. Alexander Eig, from the university's botany department and the founder of the botanical garden, expressed his thoughts as follows: "[Apart from the teaching needs of the Department of Botany], the botanical garden can serve as a first-class instrument for propaganda in favor of the university, focusing on promoting certain highly beneficial and positive aspects for the Yishuv. . . . (a) We can transform the

Looking for Roots in the Mt. Scopus Botanical Garden

tinguishing between different botanical regions in the country, beyond the mere scientific and agricultural/agronomical value of the project,[34] created the garden as an assemblage that became a part of the nation-building process of the Zionist movement. In a parallel movement, it disregarded and even deleted the Palestinian Arab landscape and nature, often due to perceiving that landscape as a product of Palestinian neglect and rootlessness (Marnin-Distelfeld and Gorney 2019; Kushnir 1949, 46).

I leave the Cave of Nicanor now and return to the entrance courtyard to take a picture of the phytosociological map of Palestine prepared in 1938 by Dr. Alexander Eig of the Hebrew University's botany department (see fig. 19). Eig, along with Prof. Otto Warburg, was the founder of the botanical garden, and it was he who struggled daily against many financial and administrative obstacles and challenges to establish the garden and keep it thriving (Warburg mainly stayed in Germany, while Eig was based here in Jerusalem). The vision of a garden that would present only the local and native plants of Palestine was Eig and Warburg's; the latter even considered such a botanical garden as the only viable option for botanical gardens outside Europe in the colonial world. I recall Warburg's strong words in this context: "Everything that cannot adapt dies."[35]

---

garden into a top-notch nature teaching facility for the young generation in the land, particularly for elementary and high school students in Jerusalem and beyond. Given its wholly 'Eretz Yisraeli' character, this is of utmost importance. My plan involves organizing pre-arranged visits to the garden for Jerusalem school students, three to four times a year. For students from other locations, we can arrange an annual visit program. (b) We can establish a dedicated 'tree and forest day,' attracting thousands of visitors to the garden. This event would offer a tangible representation of the floral situation in the country, its current state, and what can be achieved through dedicated efforts. (c) We can also make the garden a center for university visits. Within a few months, the area by the pool will likely become the most beautiful spot in the university. With suitable arrangements, visitors should find comfortable resting spots in the shade, while also satisfying their curiosity about the nature of the country to the fullest extent of the concept" (Hebrew University Central Archive, Botanical Garden file 2350/14580; original text in Hebrew).

34. On the technocratic element in Zionist science in the early twentieth century, see Penslar (1990). See also Davidovitch and Zalashik (2010).

35. Warburg, a "practical Zionist" and a respected authority in German colonial botany, wrote in the context of local botanical gardens in the tropical colonies, "To be of use to science, a botanical garden like that of Buitenzorg [Indonesia] has to fulfill certain conditions that are few, but absolutely necessary. Most of all, it is not feasible, like, for example, our European gardens of Kew, Paris, or Berlin, to unite samples from all over the world in order to cultivate them under artificial conditions, or rather, letting [the plants naturally] vegetate. No, the tropical garden is first and foremost a

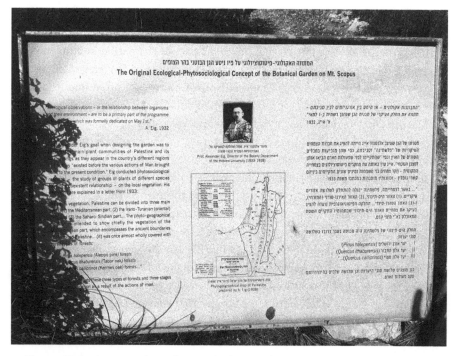

Fig. 19. Eig's phytosociological map of Palestine, located in the botanical garden. (Photograph by the author.)

Desolation and Resilience in the Garden

Initially, the garden was to be planted on land donated to the university by New York's Solomon Lamport to commemorate his son, Montague, who died while saving four girls from drowning in Bell Harbor, Long Island, New York (today, in a strange twist, the Hebrew University's Scopus swimming pool, which opened in 2003, is located there). The Lamport plot is just below the

> local garden that only aspires to unite samples of the tropical and subtropical flora, so that they, in their natural cultivated conditions of existence, [present] students and scholars . . . nature as it is and lives, not in the abnormal conditions of our glass houses or in the poor form of our herbaria. No glass houses, no cold halls, at most open canopies; no precautionary measures to keep the plants alive outside their natural habitat. . . . *Everything that cannot adapt dies*." (O. Warburg, "Der botanische Garten von Buitenzorg—ein Vorbild für unsere tropischen Versuchsstationen," *Tropenpflanzer* 2 (1898): 329–34, quoted in Leimkugel [2005, 239]. Italics added; translated from the German).

British Jerusalem War Cemetery, and the Australian government objected in the late 1920s to the botanical garden being planted in that location. The Australians worried that the garden's trees might block the view of the holy city of Jerusalem from their monument in the war cemetery (Paz 1995, 448). After many frustrating and prolonged discussions between the university, the Mandate government, and the Australian government, the garden was planted on the current plot, at the summit of Mt. Scopus, on land that already belonged to the university (about 700 meters up the hill from the original Lamport plot). The original Lamport field was turned in the 1940s into a general-systematical botanical research plot with no high trees to block the view from the war cemetery to Jerusalem. The establishment of the garden here on top of Mt. Scopus, I tell the students every year, is another outcome of World War I.

At first, I used to refer to World War I in this respect half-jokingly, to IRize the botanical garden (namely, that it is in this current location directly because of a world war—but so are many other sites and institutions in this country). But I also wanted to link the war cemetery tour we had done previously in the course to the botanical garden visit in order to create a continuous narrative and thus allude to a meaning that I hope emerges from these tours as a whole. I even planned this morning to start today's class by telling about the dispute over the Lamport plot. But now, as I stand in the garden, contemplating the adaptability and resilience of the local flora—the key criterion envisioned by the garden's founders, Warburg and Eig, in selecting the plants to inhabit this space—I am reminded of their initial skepticism about the chances of this particular site becoming a thriving botanical garden.

The quality of the soil and the microclimate in the original Lamport plot, below the British Jerusalem War Cemetery, were much better than the current plot's. Eig characterized the soil in the Scopus summit's location as "meagre and not deep," highly saturated with calcium carbonate, strewn with "Nari" limestone, and exposed to violent cold and hot winds in winter and spring (Eig 1938, 108). Nonetheless, many of the trees and shrubs Eig and his students had planted here took root and survived the decades, including the violent enclave years. There is something consoling and encouraging in the endurance of these original parts of the garden, a recognition of life's resilience but also of the dedication of the garden's caretakers to this project. Perhaps this is a better lesson or point to start the class with, not necessarily to focus on the dispute with the Australians.

Truly, the perseverance of the garden and its caretakers is inspiring, and

130 EXPEDITION ESCAPE FROM THE CLASSROOM

personally it serves as a profound reason for my deep connection to this place. Spending countless hours at the Hebrew University's archive, researching and preparing this class on the garden, I have come across many letters Eig sent to the institution's management, begging for financial support, personnel, and land. Delving into the historical efforts required to navigate British mandatory officials and overseas donors, I have witnessed the immense physical and intellectual dedication of Eig and his students in establishing and maintaining this garden.

Walking among the trees today, knowing that some were personally planted by Eig and his students, fills me with awe, relief, and pride. Despite facing unfavorable conditions on the challenging terrain of Mt. Scopus, these trees, plant formations, and societies envisioned by Eig managed to take root and thrive. Even during the demanding nineteen years of the enclave, when the garden went uncultivated and lacked proper care, it survived, remarkably. Such resilience and success against the odds remind me of the determined spirit that sustains this garden. The dedication and hard work of those who nurtured it resonate deeply, and I find myself connected to this place, a witness to its enduring legacy. Like the students and donors who feel connected to the garden and the university when hearing the story of Nicanor's donation of the doors of the temple—for me, knowing that I walk here in a garden that was so important and dear to this visionary and relentless scientist generates a feeling of belonging and attachment because I can feel and appreciate the sense of vocation, steadfastness, and commitment embodied here. Moreover, I envy the strong bond between Eig and the biology and botany students and their devotion to a common cause. I admire their way of studying by touring the land and its neighboring countries (Lebanon, Syria, Transjordan, Turkey) to bring specimens to the garden (Frumin, Frumin, and Weiss 2019). How I wish I had such a bond with my students, such a shared commitment and basic understanding of what the purpose of our profession is, what we should study and how.

When I walk in the garden, I feel that a considerable part of Eig's project of knowing, presenting, and protecting the land's flora continues to exist here today. I admire Eig, his colleagues, and students for leaving something beautiful, material, and helpful in this world, something that can benefit anyone who comes to visit here. And this includes schoolchildren from Issawiya, who, until the COVID-19 crisis, came on a biweekly basis to the campus for a tutoring program administered by the Mandel School. At the same time, it is so hard and frustrating, and also frightening and sad, to watch the Palestinian neighborhoods below the garden and to recognize—and empathize with—the hardship and duress of the residents that entail such daily "uprooting" practices (à la Simone Weil).

What is this garden, then? A beautiful and "natural" green space at the edge of the campus, or a buffer zone between the campus and the violence that resides outside it? And is the violence indeed being "buffered" at the fence of the garden, or is it inherent, structurally speaking, within the garden and the campus, more generally? I know what my answer to this question would be if I were a Palestinian. Is there another answer, a *valid* one, for me, as an Israeli?

Moreover, despite the garden's resilience and perseverance over the years, and perhaps precisely *because* of this resilience and perseverance, when visiting here I often also think about the desolation and neglect that reigned in the garden during the 1948–67 period. In those years, the botanical garden was strewn with landmines, and the undergrowth among the trees spread uncontrolled. The formerly beautiful garden disappeared and was unrecognizable (Gilat 1969), perhaps similarly to the neglect that spread during that time in the British Jerusalem War Cemetery, also because of landmines around the site. The botanical garden visit, hence, brings to my mind thoughts about toughness and rootedness, but also the specter of desertion, withdrawal and siege, and the invasion of the violent, wild, and disorderly into the rational and protected world of the botanical garden—*of the university campus*. Gardens, it is so clear here, are constantly spaces that are "both ruled and always at risk of becoming unruly" (Besky and Padwe 2016, 17).

But even without being sieged or mined, neglected, and deserted, the garden constantly represents the contradiction between being ruled and becoming unruly, between serving a clear purpose and acquiring many other functions and roles that took over its initial rationale. In its appearance and order, it is a place of knowledge and regularity through scientific classification, on the one hand, and a site in which the forces of ambiguity, chance, and disorder work, on the other hand. Yes, the plants are each marked with an identification sign that mentions the plant's classification and name in Hebrew, Latin (Linnean classification), and often, but not always, in Arabic.[36] The sign also

---

36. According to the garden director, Dr. Meni Neuman, and Hebrew University's botanist Professor Avi Shmida, not all plants have Arabic names from the outset. Whenever possible, the name of the plant will appear in Arabic as well, they told me. Interestingly, there is no parallel or similar Palestinian-Arab "Flora Palaestina" project. Nonetheless, in some cases the same plant has several Arabic names, according

132   EXPEDITION ESCAPE FROM THE CLASSROOM

notes whether the plant is edible or medicinal and its conservation status. This meticulous systemization, collection, and presentation of the flora of the (then new and unexplored) land was in the 1930s and 1940s a proclamation of Zionist custodianship, if not ownership, over the land through botanically/scientifically knowing it (Marnin-Distelfeld and Gorney 2019, 66; Sheffi and First 2019, 200; McOuat 1996). For example, in the 1930s, the garden joined the international exchange network of botanical gardens worldwide (on this network, see Spary 2000, chap. 2). Eig noted in a letter to the president of the Hebrew University, Dr. Judah L. Magnes, that such an exchange of seeds and bulbs could help "us" very much, since many botanists abroad had an interest in the flora of Palestine and its neighboring countries, due to their "holiness" and "historical fame" (Eig 1929a). Supplying bulbs and seeds in this manner involved a claim of authority over the land and its flora. But at present, the garden's display of systematic botanical knowledge is less a learned claim over the land (the garden is after all a botanical "mini-Israel," and the land was already claimed) but more a reminder of the *absence* or leaving of the natural sciences from this campus and the ongoing scientific isolation of this garden.

Indeed, the garden is no longer under military siege, yet it is much forgotten. In the 1970s, soon after the reconnection of Scopus to Jerusalem, the garden was renovated for the first time (and again in 2008), and many new plots were created in it. One of the aims of the renovated 1970s garden was to supply natural and reproductive materials for research in the university's Institute of Life Sciences and other scientific units.[37] But currently, only one scientific research project is conducted here.[38] And concerning the international exchange of seeds and bulbs, this activity hardly takes place in our garden, or in any other botanical garden in Israel, anymore. Instead, such exchange happens through the Israel Plant Gene Bank at the Ministry of Agriculture (but see O'Donnell and Sharock 2017). Thus, even though the garden is now well-maintained and is beautiful and alive, it was left behind as a site for doing science for most of its existence.

---

to how it's known in various parts of the country. See also Bernhardt (2008, xi): "Traditional cultures often fail to name plants that have no immediate use." In contrast, plant names that have been given by traditional cultures can teach a lot about the use of a particular plant or tree. It is important to note that as part of the colonization process, the traditional plant names of many cultures and peoples occupied by European powers were erased or disappeared (see Martin 1995).

37. Program of the botanical garden of Mt. Scopus (Library of the Mt. Scopus Botanical Garden, 1971), 1.

38. Correspondence with Dr. Meni Neuman, the garden director, December 21, 2020.

The disparity between the supposed scientific appearance and original designation of the garden and its continuous reality as a space that ranges between being an effective "buffer zone" between Issawiya and the main campus, a Zionist and archaeological heritage site, and a semi-secret green lung is utterly confusing to me. The place's past lingers so much in its present, and these are often contradictory or divergent realities. After all, it turns out that I, too, look for a continuous narrative and a clear lesson that can be learned here, while I keep discovering these are not possible. How then can I complain about my students' search for consistency and order?

"Everything That Cannot Adapt" Doesn't Always Die: Foreign Cedars in the Garden

Having taken a picture of Eig's map of Palestine's three phytogeographical regions, I sit on a woo)den bench beneath an old pine tree close to the garden's main path. The garden, says Eig in the plaque on which the map is drawn, presents the land's three types of forests and "three stages in their degradation as a result of the actions of man." This design of the garden carries an element of knowledgeable and authoritative *accusation* or scolding (Which "man" is responsible for this degradation of the land's forests? Ottoman? Palestinian Arab? Bedouin?[39]). But the garden was not only a botanical instrument of accusation or a means of scolding. It was also a utopian site for reforestation and, in effect, terraforming.

Eig, a Jewish immigrant from Belarus, who arrived in Palestine on his own at the age of fifteen in 1909, was an autodidact who eventually completed a PhD in botany (1931, Montpellier). Already in the mid-1920s, he was celebrated in the botanical community in Palestine, and Otto Warburg, the leading Jewish botanist of the time and the founder of the Hebrew University's botany department, took him as his protégé. Significant, too, was Eig's connection with Nikolaï Vavilov, the great Russian geneticist, agronomist, and botanist. Vavilov, who was among the preeminent founders of the scientific research of food security and who was eventually executed by Stalin by means of starvation in 1943, visited Palestine in 1926 and was highly impressed with Eig, who wasn't yet a faculty member at the Hebrew University then.[40] Vavi-

---

39. Surely not the British, thought Eig. On the reforestation activities initiated by the British, see Tal (2013, chap. 3).

40. Vavilov, eventually, was among the recommenders for Eig for the faculty position here (see Frumin, Frumin, and Weiss 2019, 15).

134   EXPEDITION ESCAPE FROM THE CLASSROOM

lov was a great botanical explorer and adventurer who traveled the globe in search of the origins of cultivated food plants, to find resilient and durable crops that could help in the fight against famine (Vavilov 1997). Vavilov's explorations motivated Eig to adopt the same practice in his cataloging and systematization of Palestine's flora. In this way, one of the most important research trips Eig took with several of his students was in the summer of 1931, when they traveled to Lebanon, Syria, and southern Turkey to document what they believed was the original form of the forests in Palestine. Among the rich botanical materials they brought back from that trip were 350 seedlings and many more seeds of Lebanese cedar (Eig 1931).

The cedar, it was known already then, is not a native tree of the "Land of Israel" and cannot grow here without support and cultivation during its first years (Boneh et al. 2014). Nonetheless, Eig made an exception and planted these cedars in a special section at the northern corner of the garden (Eig 1938). As far as I know, these were the only acclimatized "emigrant" or "introduced" species in the garden.[41] This was due to the cedar's important place in Jewish culture and lore and in Zionist history. In terms of the former, Solomon's Temple in Jerusalem was said to be built from cedars sent to him from Lebanon, and the cedar is the single most mentioned tree by its name in the Old Testament. In terms of the latter, Theodor Herzl planted a cedar close to Jerusalem in his single visit in Palestine in 1898 (the "cedar" turned out to be a cypress, though, and was cut down by unknown persons in 1917).[42]

Now I reach the northwestern point of the garden, close to where Eig's *Cedrus libani* grove once grew. The main pedestrian entrance gate to the campus and the Faculty of Social Sciences is at the foot of the hill that I'm standing on, as well as the "Eig Gate" of the botanical garden. The cedar grove, which took root and survived the enclave years,[43] eventually succumbed to

---

41. According to historical phytogeographical studies, the Muslim conquerors brought crops such as bananas, sugar cane, mulberries, and citrus to Palestine. The Crusader conquerors spread seeds of various plants from the western Mediterranean throughout their conquests, with concentrations of aromatic oil plants they brought from Europe (*Artemisia arborescens L.*) near the ruins of their forts, such as Monfort Fortress. In fact, some argue that the paths of the Frankish Crusaders can be traced by following the distribution of certain plant species (see Dudai and Amar 2017).

42. The cedars of Lebanon are perhaps the oldest botanical cultural symbol, as they already appear in the epic of Gilgamesh (see Starkey 2018, 251). On Herzl's "cedar," see Mishory (2019, 259).

43. In 1965, M. Bolotin of the afforestation section of the Jewish National Fund wrote in an article titled "A Cedars Survey in the Jerusalem Area" that in the Scopus grove, out of the 200 cedars planted by professor Eig in 1934, about 150 survived.

Looking for Roots in the Mt. Scopus Botanical Garden **135**

air pollution from the nearby Hadassah Hospital's chimneys in the 1970s and 1980s, which killed many of the trees (Balivis and Peleg 1981). The trees that survived fell victim to the demand for a parking lot for the university's growing student body. The last cedars were cut down in 1993. In one cut trunk from before that (1974), a slice of which somehow found its way to the municipal museum of the town of Kfar Saba, the lack of cultivation during the 1948–1967 period left a clear mark in the form of reduced annual growth rings. Then, after 1967, the tree returned to normal growth, probably thanks to irrigation and cultivation, until it died in a fire that broke out in the garden in 1974 and was cut down.[44] There was something very sad in the image of that slice of the trunk—it showed how dependent the tree was on human support and cultivation, as a vulnerable living organism that was taken out of its natural habitat and brought here to this dry and rocky summit, and how, eventually, it died in a fire and was cut down.

Eig always dreamt of a campus immersed in greenery and groves. He wrote to the university's management in 1929 that such groves could help alleviate the "evil" of heat waves so typical of the summer here by creating a more moderate microclimate. Trees could also break the harsh winter winds on the summit of this mountain, beautify the campus, and make it into the healthiest place in Jerusalem (Eig 1929a). His love of trees and yearning for the tall and thick European forests of his childhood prompted him to plant the cedar grove here despite the species' foreignness to the land, hoping that the little seedlings would grow into mighty cedars, as described in the Hebrew Bible. He disregarded Warburg's words: "everything that cannot adapt dies."

Precisely because of their mightiness, in the ancient Mesopotamian *Epic of Gilgamesh*, the hero, Gilgamesh the king of Uruk, seeks to make a name for himself and transcend human mortality by cutting down the massive cedars of the Cedars of God Forest and killing Humbaba, the guardian ogre of the forest. Gilgamesh and his friend Enkidu then used the cedars to build the great temple door in Nippur. In succeeding Mesopotamian myths and literature, cutting down cedars was a form of exhibiting a king's prowess and sovereignty (Shaffer 1983). In the book of Isaiah, Sennacherib, king of Assyria, boasts that he had cut down, by himself, the high cedars in the inner mountains of Lebanon. Many others came after him and cut down most of those forests in Lebanon, causing the cedars to almost disappear from that

---

44. "Archaeo-botany," item no. 84, Kfar Saba Museum, available at https://kfar-sa ba-museum.org

Fig. 20. Relocation of a cedar from Eig's cedar grove in 1993. (Courtesy of the Library of the Scopus Botanical Garden.)

country.[45] (In current times, trees in Israel and Palestine are often subject to violence related to the conflict between the two rival communities; see Braverman 2009.[46])

Here, in the Mt. Scopus Botanical Garden, before the cedar grove was eliminated, a few trees were dug out with their roots and surrounding soil and moved to other locations in Jerusalem. Two were replanted inside the Mt. Scopus campus, near the university's Faculty of Law. I decide to go and see them now. I exit the garden through the Eig Gate, and as I cross the Defend-

---

45. According to 2014 data, *Cedrus Libani* forests in Lebanon spread over 17 square kilometers, standing for 0.7 percent of the country's total forest land (Boneh et al. 2014, 6).

46. It should be noted that many of the pine forests in Israel were planted by the Jewish National Fund in the 1950s on the ruins of demolished Palestinian villages, whose inhabitants were driven off or escaped during the Nakba. Such forests were planted to prevent the return of refugees to their villages and lands, and also to serve as means for military camouflage. See Kliot (2004). See also Eitan Bronstein Aparicio, "Most JNF-KKL Forests and Sites Are Located on the Ruins of Palestinian Villages," *Zochrot*, April 2014, https://www.zochrot.org/publication_articles/view/55963/en?Most_JNF__KKL_forests_and_sites_are_located_on_the_ruins_of_Palestinian_villages

ers of the Mountain Road, I pass what I had previously believed to be "Churchill's palm," planted during his visit here in 1921 (however, I now know that this palm is not the same one). Moving on, I reach the entrance to the Senate Building, traverse the desolate indoor forum of the megastructure, and take a brief walk through the narrow inner garden flanked by the Faculty of Humanities and the administration building. Finally, I arrive at the two replanted cedars. Both trees were successfully established in their new location and grew to a height of at least five stories (they are irrigated and cultivated). I look upward, appreciate their size, and then get closer and try to hug each of their trunks, but my arms cannot encircle them completely—they are so large. I feel happy and thankful that these trees, "foreigners" as they are, were saved and that they now thrive here, inside the protected campus.

Reconnecting to Myself, to the Course, to the World

While hugging one of the cedars, I suddenly hear someone calling me—"Dr. Oded, is that you?" I look over, surprised, and see someone sitting not far away from the cedars on a picnic table. He looks familiar. "Do I know you?" I ask. "I'm Ra'ed, from the 'Mt. Scopus Enclave' course," he replies, smiling. Neither of us is wearing a face mask. Suddenly, everything looks so familiar and real, so in existence, so in its place. The mature cedars seem formidable— even Gilgamesh, Enkidu, or Sennacherib would not be able to cut them down. They took root here; they're safe. I look at my watch. "Class starts soon; I guess I'll see you in Zoom, right?" I tell Ra'ed, smiling too. Then I suddenly add, "You know, I need to go to the Institute of Archaeology here before that. I want to take a picture of the Lachish reliefs—they have a copy there and I want to show it today to the group." "The Lachish relief . . . ?" he says, somewhat puzzled. "Come with me; I'll show you," I say, and we both hurry to the Institute of Archaeology.

CHAPTER 4

The Enigma of Portrait Busts

EXPLORING POWER, ART, AND HISTORY IN HONORIFIC SCULPTING ON CAMPUS AND BEYOND

Introduction to the Chapter

In this chapter, I probe into the bust sculptures on the Mt. Scopus campus, and broaden the scope to include fictional representations of this art form, such as busts depicted in paintings or literature. By incorporating insights from a variety of knowledge fields, I amalgamate my observations on the campus sculptures with discussions on renowned busts from around the world. In doing so, I map out the domain of what I term "bust-ology."[1] These sculptures, whether they depict iconic historical figures or lean on conventions to present lesser-known personalities, such as second-rank politicians or bankers, aim to invoke feelings of wisdom, honor, authority, and power. Yet, alongside my acknowledgment of these dimensions, I'm equally captivated by the busts' absurd, eerie, and spectral characteristics. Their handless, armless forms, coupled with vacant stares, lend them an uncanny aura, challenging the conventional boundaries of the human figure. This duality in my perception—simultaneously harboring reverence for their historical and political significance (and, in some cases, for their artistic qualities) while maintaining a sense of irony toward their potential over-glorification or selective memorialization—forms a core aspect of my exploration.

Then, reflecting on an incident of public disrespect during a campus tour toward the bust of Professor Norman Bentwich, I tell how I was confronted with the echoes of those very challenges that busts represent. A student's

---

1. Much like Anna Lowenhaupt Tsing uses diagrams in a playful and self-consciously joking manner in her *Friction: An Ethnography of Global Connection* (2005) while keeping a "serious attempt to focus attention on the specificity and process of articulation" (60), I hold onto my position and occasionally mock the formal academic or analytical approach, but I also see its value and don't outright reject it (I thank Patrick Thaddeus Jackson for this observation).

The Enigma of Portrait Busts 139

seemingly playful act of lifting the bust in the air underscored not only the boundaries of decorum but also the tension that lies within my subjectivity between tradition and rebellion. This experience not only emphasized the duality in my perception of these sculptures but also highlighted the fine line between jest and disrespect. It reinforced my evolving perspective as an educator, reminding me of the delicate balance of power and authority, not only in the classroom but also outside it, thus aligning with goal 1 of this book: reflecting on and discussing my teaching anxiety.

I also reflect on the paradoxical combination of accessibility and distance from power that busts offer and/or evoke, and consider how these artifacts symbolize authority, intellect, and social status. Drawing inspiration from the bust of Louis XIV, sculpted by Bernini and exhibited in Versailles, I engage with the enigmatic nature of art, political power, and sovereignty. The Louis bust embodies both the legitimate exercise of power and the original violence that underpins its legitimacy. Jacques Derrida's interpretation of Walter Benjamin's essay "Zur Kritik der Gewalt" ("Toward the Critique of Violence") offers further insight into the enigma of sovereign power.

I then consider the theme of missing or stolen busts, such as Edgar Allan Poe's bust stolen from a museum in Richmond, Virginia, or the busts of Lt. Gen. Moshe Dayan or Elisabeth, Queen of the Belgians, which both mysteriously disappeared from our campus. Similarly, I explore Arthur Conan Doyle's fascination with Napoleon busts in the Sherlock Holmes short story "The Adventure of the Six Napoleons," interpreting the busts of the emperor as cultural artifacts that continue the legacy of the Napoleonic Wars. Throughout these discussions, I show how this engagement in bust-ology sparked my curiosity to explore various fields of knowledge beyond International Relations but at the same time provided ways to IR-ize these artifacts. This matches with goal 3 of this book: to inculcate critical thinking and expand the customary boundaries of the discipline, sometimes through de Certeau-ian tricks and "making do"/"ripping off."

As the chapter continues, I talk about a bust of Rabindranath Tagore, a renowned Bengali poet and Nobel laureate (1913), sculpted by Ramkinkar Baij in 1940. A bronze cast of this bust is positioned in the courtyard of the Faculty of Humanities on our campus and was presented to the university by the government of India. Tagore's bust, depicting an old man with a pensive expression, captures the tumultuous times of World War II and British colonial rule in India. The bust's unique impact and artful qualities spurred me to learn about Tagore's vision for international cultural dialogue and India's

140   EXPEDITION ESCAPE FROM THE CLASSROOM

international "bust diplomacy" campaign, disseminating replicas of his bust worldwide. This IR-ized bust of Tagore thus became a destination for me and my students when we "escaped" the classroom, reflecting goals 3 and 1 of the book, respectively.

Overall, the field of bust-ology becomes an exploration of artistic expression, representations of power and authority, and the human experience, leaving me to ponder questions of meaning in the context of my academic journey. Just as the busts (attempt to) symbolize wisdom, authority, and power while embodying an enigmatic and absurd quality, my teaching anxiety represents an underlying cause of vulnerability and doubt. My struggles with anxiety in teaching and research mirror the partiality of the busts, as they problematize not only the boundaries of the human body but also those of academic life and the expectations placed upon scholars. This aligns with goal 2 of the book: to foster empathy within IR and reach out to readers, trying to establish a meaningful connection.

Literary Inspiration: Exploring "The Raven" and Its Resonance

My interest in portrait busts—sculpted figures showing a person's head and neck and sometimes varying portions of the shoulders and chest—likely stems from my fascination with Edgar Allan Poe's poem "The Raven." I first read the poem many years ago in a side-by-side Hebrew-English bilingual booklet (which also contained Poe's "Annabel Lee"). I am still thrilled when the raven bursts into the chamber of the narrator, who sits there pondering, "weak and weary / Over many a quaint and curious volume of forgotten lore." He seeks to borrow from his books "surcease of sorrow—sorrow for the lost Lenore." The raven's dramatic entrance into the chamber leads me to reflect on the invasion of the unexpected and unruly element into the life of a scholar (see also chapter 3, on how gardens are always in the liminal zone between the orderly and the unruly). But after bursting in, the raven simply perches on the bust of Pallas, the Greek goddess of wisdom, which is positioned just above the chamber door (see fig. 21), and responds to all the narrator's deep and painful questions with the repeated sardonic word: "Nevermore"—or "al ad ëin dor" אל עד אין דור, in the beautiful Hebrew translation by Vladimir Ze'ev Jabotinsky (literally, "never there is a generation").

The poem's gloomy gothic atmosphere and unique alliteration serves its central theme well—the eternal devotion of the lover to his dead loved one. There is something enchanting in this poem, and Jabotinsky's skillful trans-

Fig. 21. The raven perching on the bust of Pallas Athena. (Illustration by Gustave Dore, 1884. Image courtesy of Wikimedia commons.)

lation reinforces this sublimity, so much so that even David Ben-Gurion, Jabotinsky's harsh adversary in Zionist politics, was very impressed by this translation, telling him, "The Hebrew is very elegant and noble, but also natural.... You translate with supreme grace." The two had met in London in 1934 to discuss a peace agreement between their two rival Zionist factions when Jabotinsky recited his translation to Ben-Gurion (at least, as depicted in A. B. Yehoshua's play *Can Two Walk Together?* [Yehoshua 2012, 31–35. The meeting did occur in reality, but the dialogue between the two is fictionalized]).

While the bust of the goddess symbolizes wisdom and enlightenment, the raven signifies the specter of unruliness, death, and helplessness—answering every question of the narrator in the same obscure and eerie way. It remains perched on the bust of Pallas to the end of the poem, leaving the narrator's

142 EXPEDITION ESCAPE FROM THE CLASSROOM

soul forever in the black shadow of his inability to forget his dead lover yet doubting the possibility of ever uniting with her in the next world. "The Raven" also speaks about the constant contradiction between the learned person's desire for knowledge and meaning, their yearning to decipher the mysteries of life and death, and, at the same time, their ingrained inability to achieve this understanding in full. "Leave my loneliness unbroken!—quit the bust above my door! / Take thy beak from out my heart, and take thy form from off my door! / Quoth the Raven, 'Nevermore.'" Indeed, Pallas should have had an owl and not a raven as her tutelary bird (Merivale 1974, 960). Still, it is the raven that remains perched on her portrait bust.

Perhaps it was the mixture of sublime atmosphere and gothic sentiment in "The Raven," in combination with my grappling with teaching anxiety and a sense of lack of meaning and agency in my academic profession, that allowed me to see the various portrait busts scattered on the Mt. Scopus campus as artifacts that share similar attributes with Poe's bust of Pallas. Ever searching for purpose and wisdom in academic knowledge but painfully aware of the ephemeral nature of such knowledge (Weber 1958), I started to see the campus busts as potential landing spots for ravens who croak, dauntingly and spitefully, "nevermore"/ אל עד אין דור.

About thirty such busts are presented in various locations on the Mt. Scopus campus, with quite a few more in several university warehouses. Many more are exhibited on the Giva't Ram campus. They often depict illustrious men (only three busts on campus are of women)—poets and writers (e.g., Sholem Asch), humanitarians (Oscar Schindler), scientists (Albert Einstein), musicians (Leonard Bernstein), philosophers (Martin Buber), leaders (Harry S. Truman), judges (Louis Brandeis), prominent figures from Hebrew University's history (Judah L. Magnes), and notable donors to the institution (Felix Warburg). As such, each bust in its way is reminiscent of the hope/pride and, at the same time, the despair/absurdity embodied in the statue of Pallas in "The Raven." As representations of people of fame, authority, and power, the busts are meant to commemorate them, impart gratitude and even reverence, and perhaps raise inspiration (Gell 1999; Jones 1991, 14–15).[2] In addition, the busts symbolize, by their very presence in the public spaces of the university, a respectability of the institution itself, which purportedly shares with them their outstanding features—qualities for which they were presented as

---

2. Jones (1991) mentions how he was inspired by two busts of Voltaire at the Taylor Institution at Oxford.

Fig. 22. Author Sholem Asch, by Sir Jacob Epstein, in the foyer of the Senate Hall, Hebrew University of Jerusalem. Note how the sculpture is made of two separate parts, the head and the right hand (only). (Photograph by the author.)

head sculptures in the first place (in a nice loop of mutual empowerment). Yet there is also something inherently absurd and melancholic about the busts.

For they are just *head* sculptures, albeit sometimes with a part of the torso. They are only a piece of the whole human being; the rest of the body is missing. Importantly, busts are almost always armless and handless (see fig. 22 for an interesting artistic engagement with this convention). The hands are what make us distinctive as a species (Tallis 2003), or even, some argue, capable of language (McGinn 2015); they are the tools through which we act in and upon the world (think, the hands of the sovereign depicted on the frontispieces of Hobbes' *Leviathan*: he carries a scepter and a sword, the symbols

144   EXPEDITION ESCAPE FROM THE CLASSROOM

and instruments of government). Busts are handless not due to intentional damage or the ravages of time (as in the Venus de Milo statue, whose arms were broken). Instead, this is the essence of this form. Had Pallas had hands, she could have flung the raven away. But Poe's narrator *does* have hands, and yet he doesn't toss anything at the intruding raven to expel it—he wants it to leave, *demands* that it leave, but is enchanted by the raven's presence and keeps asking it unanswerable questions. The material representation of Pallas, the ideal/idol of wisdom and knowledge, is awakened to life by the raven landing on top of it. But all we get from this new hybrid creature (of which the narrator perhaps also becomes a part) is the repeated, meaningless cry "nevermore," and the paralysis of the narrator, who uses only words in his attempts to understand and then exorcise the raven.

Similarly "stuck" or paralyzed like Poe's narrator, I realized at some stage that taking action about my teaching anxiety was the key to ameliorating it. Escaping the classroom with the students and exploring the campus on my own in search of something to teach outside the usual setting was one of the ways I addressed this impasse. The campus busts captured my attention as fascinating artifacts that could become the subject of an engaging campus tour. To make this idea a reality, I needed to first develop an "introduction to bust-ology" and find interesting ways to IR-ize these artifacts. In what follows here, I elaborate not just on the material mechanics of "bust-ology" but also on the deeper implications of these artifacts. As we navigate between enchantment and cynicism, I invite readers to explore with me my ideas about busts and their role as a metaphor for authority.

Introduction to Bust-ology: Touching the Past and the Fascination and Uncanniness of Busts

Unlike Poe's narrator, I am not expecting any answers from portrait busts.[3] Nor from ravens. And I know that busts lack limbs because this form of por-

---

3. In Rembrandt's *Aristotle Contemplating a Bust of Homer*, "Aristotle yearns, we may imagine, for an essence somewhere beyond the portrait bust. *Theoria* is the Greek word for the rapt gaze that is here lost in space. But Homer defeats him, with what is perhaps the most magical element of the painting: a marble that has begun to take on the colors of flesh. Not just more philosophical than any possible history, poetry is likewise more historical than any possible philosophy. Its silent voice puts philosophy's theorizing generalization into question. Unsettling our expectations, it moves us into time" (Brown 1992, 15).

Fig. 23. US Senator Edward Kennedy presenting a bust of his late brother John F. Kennedy to Prime Minister Yitzhak Shamir at his office in Jerusalem, December 11, 1986. Note the amused expression on the faces of the staff present in the room. (Photograph by Herman Chanania. Courtesy of the State of Israel—National Photos Collection, Governmental Press Bureau, picture #D180-050.)

traiture is meant to represent and commemorate the spiritual and cerebral elements of the subject, hence the focus on the head along with the absence of most of the rest of the body. Originally, busts evolved in ancient Rome from death masks into sculpted three-dimensional portraits of the heads of the dead placed on tombs or as effigies of the ancestors of noble families presented in the atrium of the house (Evald 2008; Belting 2011, 116–17). In the Middle Ages, they were also used as reliquaries. As a form of commemoration, perhaps even of art, they might have become popular because it is often cheaper or quicker to produce a bust as a partial sculpture than a whole-body one. Busts are also more easily stored, showcased, or given as a present (see fig. 23—literally, an IR-ization of a JFK bust in action) because they occupy less space and are more portable.

Even considering all these points, it never stopped surprising and sometimes amusing me how these separate(d) heads or pieces of the upper body have become normalized and even popularized as a form of art and commemoration. In paintings or photograph portraits of the head or the upper body,

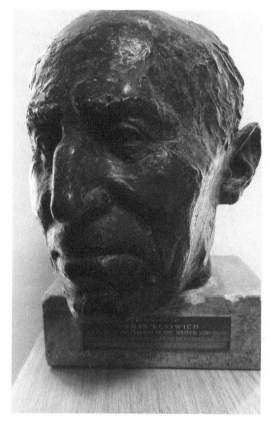

Fig. 24. The head sculpture of Professor Norman Bentwich, at the Faculty of Law. (Photograph by the author.)

viewers know (or reasonably assume) that the rest of the body is not severed from the head even though they don't see it. Perhaps this is the effect of the frame or margins of the canvas operating as a sort of a window or a border through which we observe and access the sitter. Unlike paintings or photograph portraits, sculpted busts are more direct and present. They are the complete object—nothing hides beyond a frame; and they are three-dimensional, touchable artifacts (Onol 2011). In Rembrandt's painting *Aristotle Contemplating a Bust of Homer*, Aristotle's right hand rests on the bust of Homer. I have noticed a similar need to touch busts in many other cases too. For instance, during the campus bust tour when I introduce students to the head sculpture of Prof. Norman Bentwich, the inaugural chair of International Peace Law studies at the Hebrew University (appointed in 1932), many students instinctively touch it. While its distinct detachment can be unsettling to some, it captures the fascination of others.

Fig. 25. Prime Minister Ehud Olmert with the Bonds delegation at the Knesset, Jerusalem, May 5, 2008. The prime minister (*second from the left*) and Knesset speaker Dalia Itzik (*on the right*) observe and touch a bust of David Ben-Gurion. At the left is finance minister Roni Baron. (Photograph by Amos Ben Gershom. Courtesy of State of Israel—National Photos Collection, Governmental Press Bureau, picture #D1019-043.)

Over the years, having observed students repeatedly touch these artifacts and noting similar patterns in various photographs, I have come to believe that this urge to touch—often accompanied by an amused expression—stems from a desire to reconcile the uncanny nature of these items. Touching provides a sense of control, linking the detached head to the toucher's own body. Thus, in my experience of them, busts problematize the boundaries of the human body by omitting from the sculpture most of the sitter's figure.

Despite being separated from the rest of the body, however, the busts usually have expressions that are serene, solemn, or slightly wry (the bust of Voltaire by Houdon has beautiful smirk[4]). The subject of a bust is rarely portrayed as being horrified by its disconnection from the rest of its body. A clear exception in this regard is Pedro de Mena's bust *Saint Acisclus* (ca. 1680): "Acisclus seems not to have a large following or much of a story—he

---

4. See the image of this bust at https://www.nga.gov/collection/art-object-page.46715.html#history. The magnification option is superb.

Fig. 26. Rembrandt, *Aristotle Contemplating a Bust of Homer* (1653). (Image courtesy of Wikimedia commons.)

was beheaded in Córdoba, in 312 A.D., is about all we know—but Mena has made him unforgettable. For one thing, the guy's a dreamboat: flawless skin, soulful eyes, meticulously tousled hair. But what stops you is his expression: hurt, uncertain, unbrave, *and the thin red thin line across his neck that explains it*" (Cotter 2021; italics added). Yet even this bust is not entirely self-aware (metaphorically speaking, of course): below the cut in his neck appears, as in many other specimens of this form, a portion of his upper chest and shoulders (wearing Roman body armor). So, is he horrified by the cutting of his neck or the severed upper torso? Marshall Brown writes that in Rembrandt's depiction of the bust of Homer (see fig. 26), we can observe the artist's awareness of the unnatural, separated essence of busts: "Remote from conventional experience, hardened into stone, *cut off from its limbs*, devoid of distinguishing tokens, its blind eyes cast into the shadows, the bust nevertheless rests on the most vibrantly colored human artifact of the painting, a table of rich red. *Rendering visible the truncated body's lifeblood, Rembrandt turns the world inside out*" (Brown 1992; italics added).

Busts' defining partiality as being only a piece of the body is compensated by the fact that they represent mainly the head. The head, and the face on it, is the most common symbol of a person's humanity, wisdom, and authority. In portrait busts, the face becomes a moral beacon of intellect and social status worthy of appreciation and admiration (Kohl 2013, 60). Decapitated human heads have recently gained high visibility in popular culture thanks to television shows like *Game of Thrones* or *Westworld* or because of the horrible practice of the terrorist group ISIS in the mid-2010s. Unlike these heads, portrait busts highlight how political, cultural, scholarly, scientific, or even financial power stems from the mind; that power *is* the head. As Cecelia Tichi writes, "The heads [of US presidents] at Mt. Rushmore, of course, are not to be experienced as severed from their bodies. The presidential heads, on the contrary, *are* the bodies, brain feeders every one" (Tichi 2001, 31).

Decapitation is a theatrical expression of the abolition of this sublime power—representing the dissolution of the human image by degrading the face and head into a bleeding trophy (Brilliant 2007, 91) that is hoisted in front of an enthusiastic mob or stuck on a roadside spear. But portrait busts, even though they isolate the head from the rest (or most) of the body and place it on a pedestal, typically maintain a calm and dignified expression.[5] Busts almost always concur with the decorum of the sitter (Randolph 2014, 28). The head sculptures are meant to elevate and glorify the person.[6] Casting

---

5. The bust of the assassinated mayor of San Francisco, George Moscone, sculpted by Robert Arneson, is a fascinating example of how the pedestal can significantly influence the reception of the artwork. Arneson's head sculpture depicted the mayor as warm and smiling, but the engraved pedestal showcased various events from his life and the violent events surrounding his assassination. The combination of the bust and the elaborate pedestal caused a scandal, leading the municipality to reject the piece. Currently on display at the San Francisco Museum of Modern Art, the controversial sculpture serves as a thought-provoking reminder of the intricate relationship between art and public memory. See it at https://www.youtube.com/watch?v=cpkoc-J5kbEY

6. In 1956, during the Hungarian Revolution, an eight-meter-high statue of Stalin in Budapest was torn down by the crowd. The demonstrators then cut the statute into pieces and severed the head from the torso with oxyacetylene torches, effective-

150   EXPEDITION ESCAPE FROM THE CLASSROOM

the bust as a bronze figure or carving it in marble confers on the sitter's head an element of trans-historicity, eternity, or superhumanity, yet also an eerie and ghostly quality. Busts capture life and death simultaneously. They do this through being designed as more beautiful, or at least more noble, than the sitter's living figure (the elevation effect), on the one hand, and through the unique contour of blank, rigid, sometimes cold bronze or marble (the eerie effect), on the other.[7]

Perhaps due to these reflections on barbaric decapitation and head-hoisting in contrast to the cerebral authority emphasized by busts, I once reprimanded a student who actually lifted the Bentwich bust from its pedestal during a campus tour. This reaction came after I had recounted to the class how in 1932 a group from the Alliance of the Hoodlums—an ultranationalist Jewish faction from the early 1930s—disrupted Bentwich's inaugural lecture. The Hoodlums jeered at Bentwich, shouting "Go to the Mufti," in reference to Haj Amin al-Husseini, the then leader of the Palestinian national movement. Dr. Magnes, the university's president, summoned the British police, who forcefully removed the demonstrators, restoring order to the lecture hall.[8]

The student's act of lifting the head, combined with his self-satisfied smile and the overtly amused giggles from the group, suddenly struck me as eerily reminiscent of the 1932 Hoodlums disturbance. Even though he probably just meant to get a laugh, I got angry. Busts, of course, cannot feel or sense anything, and I did not perceive any physical danger to the artifact. Additionally, I confess that I, too, occasionally felt compelled to lift this bust and observe it at eye level, although I resisted the urge. There is something about these sculpted heads that almost irresistibly draws one to do so, much like Hamlet when he lifts up Yorick's skull and contemplates death and the nature of existence. But because Norman Bentwich was basically the first IR professor at the university, and because I could see how the "comic" lifting of the bust transmitted not only disrespect for the memory of Bentwich but also for the

---

ly making it into a bust. The face, of course, remained the same as before, but the unintended bust was a symbol of everything opposite to respect and decorum. See the image at https://en.wikipedia.org/wiki/Stalin_Monument_(Budapest)#/media/File:1956_a_budapesti_Szt%C3%A1lin-szobor_elgurult_feje_fortepan_93004.jpg. See also Végső (2013, 51).

7. When thinking about the inherent *strangeness* of busts, I was very surprised to learn that in antiquity and classical times, marble sculptures were vividly painted to make their appearance more human. Bronze statues were also decorated in color (mainly gold) and precious stones. Mattusch (2015).

8. "Brats Disturb Bentwich's Lecture," *Davar*, February 11 1932 [in Hebrew].

academic profession in general (already before this tour I perceived that student as a "wisecracker"), I took it personally. In the iciest tone I've ever mustered in this course, I ordered, "Put it down." Taken aback, the student quickly returned the head to its place. The remainder of the tour proceeded under a cloud of tension.

After the class ended, I felt I had been too harsh with him. He was merely jesting, and perhaps he had imbibed some of my own rebellious spirit, evident not just in that outing but others too. Was I the only one permitted to challenge the discipline's boundaries? Was I alone in my entitlement to display irony or cynicism about the objects or places we explored? Clearly not. My irritation highlighted to me that even outside the classroom, the inherent hierarchy between instructor and student isn't fully dissolved. Sometimes, the mere perception of this hierarchy's dissolution can, paradoxically, cause me to emphasize it even more. Additionally, my reaction underscored my deep emotional connection to the academic discipline of IR. Even if I sometimes diverge from its mainstream, it remains integral to my identity. I recognized a dichotomy in my professional self: while I sometimes diverge from my discipline's norm, I am still very much shaped by it and harbor deep respect for it. Initially, I saw this as a flaw, viewing myself as indecisive. Now, I take a lighter and more forgiving view. And if another student were to lift the bust in the future, I doubt I would react with the same severity—unless there's clear intent to damage the piece. To make a long story short: not every jester is a "hoodlum."

Bridging Sovereign Power with Bernini's Louis XIV

Not every bust is accessible for direct physical contact or touching (for instance, in museums or galleries). But by allowing the spectator to come near to the representation of the powerful or important person's head, busts also make that person more knowable to the spectator. At the same time, though, the idealized and intrinsically uncanny nature of the sculpted figure somehow disassociates the bust from the viewer, creating a confusing sense of proximity to and distance from power. An example of this is Bernini's Louis XIV bust, from 1665, one of the most famous busts in history (see fig. 27). The sculpture's artistic perfection and detail are clear evidence of the twenty-seven-year-old king's political power, which can be felt intensely by the viewers but never fully understood or accessed. Alfred Gell notes,

Fig. 27. Bernini's bust of Louis XIV (at age 27), displayed at Versailles Palace. (Image courtesy of Coyau / Wikimedia Commons / CC BY-SA 3.0.)

"The court sculptor, by means of his magical power over marble, provides a physical analogue for the less easily realized power wielded by the king, and thereby enhances the king's authority. What Bernini can do to marble (and one does not know quite what or how), Louis XIV can do to you (by means which are equally outside your grasp)" (Gell 1999, 173).

Gell's comment stayed with me for several years as I was thinking and reading about busts. I felt that Gell really *saw* the fundamental nature of this bust. He captured not only something related to Bernini's Louis XIV bust but also an important essence of sovereign power itself: this kind of power is concrete, observable, and potentially lethal, yet it is also enigmatic, strange, and not entirely intelligible.

I once quoted Gell's observation in correspondence with a colleague, a political theorist. I asked him whether he knew any political thinkers who conceive of sovereign power as mysterious in this manner. My colleague was not as impressed by Gell's formulation as I was. He said that he was unaware of such understanding of power in political philosophy, that he read only "boring" analytical philosophers, and that he didn't think Louis XIV was so powerful. After this conversation, I considered that perhaps Louis was not that formidable. After all, he himself admitted that he "lost more of France

The Enigma of Portrait Busts   **153**

to the astronomers than to his enemies." He supposedly said this in 1684, after receiving, from astronomer G. D. Cassini, the first scientific map of the coast of France, which showed a much smaller country than was believed to be ruled by the Sun King (Murdin 2009, 30).[9] Before handing the new map to the monarch, Cassini had been terrified, fearing how the king would receive his kingdom's downsizing. He was relieved when the sovereign responded with good humor. I wonder if my political theorist friend would have been brave enough, as Cassini was, to bestow such a map on Louis. I am unsure whether I would have been able to tell such a truth to power.

For especially in the case of absolute rulers like Louis, but in all other forms of sovereign power too, a fundamental contradiction lies between the exercise of force by legitimate and just law and the fact that such law is always founded on original violence that fashioned this legitimacy and was not authorized by any anterior legitimacy. Following up on my colleague's statement that he didn't know any political theorist who writes about the mystery of political power and sovereignty, I found Jacques Derrida's discussion of the mystical foundation of the power of law. According to Derrida's reading of Walter Benjamin's "Zur Kritik der Gewalt," where "Gewalt" is both legitimate power and violence (Derrida 1992), the mysterious element in sovereignty is this possibility of oscillation between legitimate law and its enforcement, on the one hand, and the original unauthorized, sometimes unpredictable, violence that still lurks at the foundation of the law, on the other hand. The prospect is that the law will give way to the state of exception or that it might recede in other ways, allowing the foundational violence to reappear.

And this is exactly what Gell sees in the bust of Louis XIV: the mystery, weirdness, and lethality of sovereign power. "What Bernini can do to marble (*and one does not know quite what or how*), Louis XIV can do to you (*by means which are equally outside your grasp*)" (italics added). The purpose of our work as political scientists, IR scholars included, is to do the best to reduce this movement into the state of exception, to highlight how dangerous the mystical/mysterious element of the sovereign's power is, to diminish the ability of the Louis XIVs of the world to do to us what Bernini can do to marble.

---

9. Note that the words of Louis about the astronomers are often cited in discussions about the history of cartography and the role of science in the shaping of political territories. However, the quote's veracity and origin are somewhat dubious, as it appears to be more a historical legend than a well-documented quote.

154   EXPEDITION ESCAPE FROM THE CLASSROOM

Mysteries, Misadventures, and Mundanities:
The Life of Busts beyond Their Pedestals

The busts on our campus rarely inspire the awe and mystery that Bernini's Louis XIV evoked in Gell. As I guide the group around campus, searching for busts that might spark feelings similar to those Gell felt observing Louis XIV's portrait, students often point out the apparent pretentiousness and self-importance of some subjects, sculptors, and even the university showcasing them. Admittedly, few busts here even approach the intricate marble craftsmanship of Bernini. While observing one of our less captivating busts, and discussing Louis's as a prime example of this art form (students access an image of the Louis bust on their phones), I once mentioned its popularity during Louis's era and the many copies made then (E. Levy 2011, 247). "Imagine if we had one of those copies," I said. Such a piece would serve as a powerful learning tool, allowing us to grasp the allure of power while also critically examining it.

When students suggested that I ask the university to acquire a Louis copy, I recounted my conversation with the institution's curator of art. She told me the university only accepts donated art and doesn't purchase it. In jest, I suggested acquiring instead cheap plaster casts of Napoleon Bonaparte to break.[10] This suggestion puzzled the curator (and, later, the students). Seeing the students' confusion, I explained, "While Napoleon and Louis are both renowned French rulers, Arthur Conan Doyle's 'The Adventure of the Six Napoleons' can tie into Gell's fascination with Bernini's Louis, but from a different angle."

In this story, which takes place in 1904, detective Sherlock Holmes is called by Scotland Yard to help solve a mystery: someone has been smashing plaster-cast busts of Napoleon around London—in private homes, offices, doctors' clinics, and antique shops. Why would anyone want to destroy Napoleon busts? Is this a hate crime (a term not yet coined in Holmes' time)? Holmes eventually discovers the more mundane reason: a certain criminal has hidden

---

10. The distinction between my humorous suggestion of purchasing Napoleons to shatter and the student's playful act of lifting the Bentwich bust lies in mine being merely a hypothetical suggestion, posing no risk to any object, and referencing a work of fiction (Arthur Conan Doyle's "The Adventure of the Six Napoleons"). Furthermore, Napoleon does not carry the same ideological and historical significance here (i.e., at the Hebrew University campus) as Bentwich does. I brought my suggestion to the curator up to the students as a transition into discussing the lessons to be drawn from the Holmes story.

The Enigma of Portrait Busts **155**

a rare black pearl stolen from Italy in one of these replicas. The thief cannot remember in which of the identical busts he hid the pearl, and in his search for it, smashes these representations of the head of the French emperor, one after another.

Conan Doyle's plot is interesting enough, but the important question, politically, as Simon Bainbridge (2015) argues, is what exactly all these busts of Napoleon are doing in the British capital, almost a century after the end of the Napoleonic Wars. How did Napoleon, one of Britain's greatest enemies, turn into a cultural artifact in early twentieth-century London? The sculptures, says Bainbridge, are in fact a continuation of the Napoleonic Wars by other means, thus reminiscent of Foucault's well-known saying in *Society Must Be Defended* that politics is a continuation of war by other means (unlike Clausewitz, who believed that war is a continuation of politics by other means). Napoleon's busts, which were probably quite common in Britain at the time, were a means of repeatedly defeating Napoleon by his very domestication and reproduction and turning him into a mass cultural artifact, robbed of his aura (à la Walter Benjamin), placed in various everyday spaces and sites in London. This deprived Napoleon of his uniqueness as a one-time military genius, and he was finally defeated (Bainbridge 2015).[11]

Lastly, while the Hebrew University has no shattered busts, we seem to have had at least two busts stolen or lost—one of Moshe Dayan, the famous Israeli general and politician, and another of Elisabeth, Queen of the Belgians (see figs. 28 and 29). We were unable to locate these in any of my bust survey expeditions, university archives visits, or campus field trips with the students. A worker in the Institute of Archaeology (where the bust of Elisabeth was once displayed in the foyer) told the class and me, when we were searching the institute for "Elisabeth," that she believes the bronze bust was stolen by metal smugglers before the Beijing Olympics in 2008. The smugglers, she continued, probably planned to sell it to China as part of that state's so-called "metal hunger" of that time. This perhaps revealed common notions and prejudices about China as a state that does not always respect legitimate international trade practices and that deals with illegal traders. In response, one of the students, who told me during the search that he once participated

---

11. It should be interesting to explore whether this theory could also be employed in the modern television series *Sherlock*'s episode "The Six Thatchers," in which Holmes pursues a similar case in our time. Still, the busts are of Margaret Thatcher, not Napoleon. The criminal who smashes the Thatcher busts is not looking for a pearl, but for a memory key that stores important national security information.

Fig. 28. Elisabeth, Queen of the Belgians, appreciates her portrait bust during the inauguration ceremony of the Institute of Archaeology's new building in Giv'at Ram Campus, 1958. The bust disappeared; only the pedestal is still in place today on the Mount Scopus campus. Queen Elisabeth was herself a sculptor. Perhaps this is why she seems amused in this picture. (Photograph by Werner Braun. Courtesy of the Hebrew University Photo Archives.)

in a reenactment of the Battle of Hattin of 1175 (in which the forces of Saladin vanquished the armies of the Crusader states close to the Sea of Galilee), said that China was "hungry" for steel, not bronze. I guess he knew what he was talking about—he said he has an interest in ancient weapons, smelting, and metallurgy. Besides, he added, if it was the Chinese or their illegal suppliers, they wouldn't have stolen only one bust. The fate of Dayan's (marble) bust was even less clear than what we managed to gather about "Elisabeth."

But to encourage the students, when they return without any information from the search mission for the lost or stolen busts, I tell them the story of the theft—and strange return—of Edgar Allan Poe's own bust from the Poe Museum in Richmond, Virginia, in October 1987. No one noticed the disappearance of the highly acclaimed bust (sculpted by Edmond Thomas Quinn in 1908) from the museum's courtyard until a caller demanded that the museum's director read to him Poe's poem "The Spirits of the Dead" in return for information about the location of the bust. When the director unenthusiastically complied with the caller's strange request, the voice said "It's at the

Fig. 29. The bust of Moshe Dayan (*upper-middle right section*), showing Maurice B. Hexter, the sculptor, at the Harry S. Truman Research Institute for the Advancement of Peace at the Hebrew University, April 2, 1976. Dayan's bust is no longer to be found on the Mt. Scopus campus. Also shown (*lower left corner*) is another bust by Hexter, of Golda Meir (which is still present at the institute today). (Photograph by Werner Braun. Courtesy of the Hebrew University Photo Archives.)

Raven Inn" and hung up. Meanwhile, across town, a man entered the Raven Inn, put the bust on the counter, and asked the bartender to pour a beer for him and his "body here." When the bartender turned to pour the beer, the person disappeared, and the bust remained to wait. It was later returned to the museum by the police. Some suspected that the thief was a writer with writer's block (Matthews 1994). The bust was afterward moved to a secure location within the museum.

"Strange Attractors" in the Campus Landscape and Disciplinary Border Crossings

So it seems that the Mt. Scopus Campus does not have any awe-inspiring sovereigns like Louis XIV or smashed, mass-produced plaster-cast Napoleons,

158   EXPEDITION ESCAPE FROM THE CLASSROOM

nor a kidnapped Edgar Allan Poe returned for a literary ransom (what a fantastic concept, a literary ransom! The whole affair connotes the allure of art theft in popular imagination, as seen in literature and film). Perhaps someone stole Moshe Dayan's figure (a fate befitting the antique robber Dayan was) or Elisabeth's bust was indeed melted for the bronze it contained (unlikely, as bronze is much more easily acquired today than in antiquity, when sculptures were indeed melted for their metal [Mattusch 1988]).[12] Most of the busts here attract little attention. They are more banal, and even "transparent" elements in the eyes of most passersby, and only a few people stop to appreciate them or are even aware of their existence.

I have often found during my campus wanderings that the busts, instead of being appreciated, become "strange attractors." I once saw a plastic "marking tape," one of those used to delineate construction sites or crime scenes, wrapped around the bust of Nobel laureate (1913), Bengali poet, author, educator, and playwright Rabindranath Tagore in the courtyard of the Humanities Faculty. In another case, a long-empty disposable coffee cup was left for several days on the pedestal of the bust of Chaim Weizmann, the first president of the State of Israel and the influential chairman of the Hebrew University's board of governors for many years, in the university's main administrative building. Trash bags are routinely placed at the foot of the pedestal of the statue of Theodor Herzl, "visionary of the State of Israel," at the entrance to the Faculty of Law building, waiting for custodial workers to take them to the garbage. I don't think anyone intentionally intended to damage or degrade the busts in any of these cases, or to challenge or defy Zionism by "humiliating" the sculptures of Herzl and Weizmann, or even Tagore's, who passionately supported Zionism (as a national-cultural ideology and program of Jewish rejuvenation, not so much as an exclusionary political movement[13]). The busts simply became prosaic elements in the campus environment, banal artifacts, and objects that lost their original ceremonial meaning (perhaps the finest hour of many busts is, indeed, their dedication ceremony).

---

12. Mattusch (1988, 2) notes that many Roman marble statutes were copies or adaptations of original Greek bronze works that were lost throughout the ages due to melting and recycling of the metal.

13. In a meeting between the two in 1926 in Prague, Tagore told Martin Buber that he was concerned by the possibility that "after becoming autonomous, [the Jewish people] will adapt to the petty-minded nationalism and soulless pan-technism of the Western peoples, to be able to exist in this land, which is a challenging geopolitical point." See Löw (2015, 44). On Tagore's concept of love and consequent rejection of hyper-nationalism, see Hartnett (2022).

Fig. 30. The busts of Tagore (*left*), Weizmann (*right*), and Herzl (*bottom*) turned into "strange attractors." (Photographs by the author.)

180   EXPEDITION ESCAPE FROM THE CLASSROOM

While not offended or angry for the busts themselves (again, one can't seriously feel such emotions for pieces of bronze per se), I found such treatment as placing garbage bags near Herzl or wrapping tape around Tagore regrettable. I became increasingly intrigued and enchanted by the *idea* of the bust, as manifested in Poe's Pallas, Rembrandt's Homer, or Houdon's Voltaire: weird, severed artifacts that combine the sublime and the absurd. Moreover, the stories I read about busts introduced me to histories and concepts I would not have known otherwise, and some of these histories touched on sensitive areas of my identity. These included Derrida's idea about the mystical element in the law; Bainbridge's reference to Foucault's concept of politics as the continuation of war; and Brown's almost tactile description of Homer's limbless bust in Rembrandt's painting. The way Aristotle longingly places his hand on the head of the poet prompted me to think more about the centrality of the human hand, not only in art but in philosophy and politics too. I started noticing what a repeating and prominent image the human hand is on IR book covers, which led me to read—and to try to write something—on the paratext (Genette 1997) of the discipline: what can be learned about the imagination of the field through the images on the covers of the discipline's books. (Many IR book covers feature the human hand—hands clenched, shaking, protesting, concealing something, holding weapons, moving chess pieces, to name a few repeating motifs. Very few hands caressing or as part of an embrace, though.) These aspects have exposed not only the emotional element in politics, which I have long been aware of and accustomed to, but also the mystical and mysterious dimensions. Despite my openness to what can be broadly termed "non-positivist" approaches to International Relations, this aspect still unnerves me.

Likewise, I learned from reading about the Herzl bust on our campus why Herzl grew a beard. While in Vienna, Herzl wore sideburns that were notably fashioned after those of Emperor Franz Joseph, but during his stay in Paris (1891–96) he abandoned his sideburns and grew a long, black, Assyrian beard, a look that evoked ancient Jewish origins that had gained popularity amidst the Orientalism trend. This fascination with the East was fueled by archaeological discoveries at that time in the Middle East, particularly images of Assyrian rulers. His oversized beard in this sculpture and other artistic Zionist representations of him at the turn of the twentieth century shows how Orientalism, interpreted through aesthetic and historical lenses, played a crucial role in shaping secular Jewish identity at the time (Kamczycki 2013). As a secular Jewish Israeli, having read Herzl's diaries and his novel *Altneu-*

land, I often grapple with questions surrounding my own national and personal identity, as well as notions of "proper" masculinity and body image. In this context, the bust, distinguished by its pronounced Assyrian beard, holds significance for me.

The engagement with busts thus led me to trespass on other fields of knowledge, to become a nomad and traveler who moves across lands belonging to someone else, who "poaches" and "despoils," à la de Certeau, the wealth of "Egypt" to enjoy it myself.[14] In other words, this form of sculpting gave me meaning by introducing me to specific artifacts, their creators and subjects, and some of the cultural and historical contexts in which they were made and presented. A sweet and exhilarating sense of wandering off from IR accompanied these explorations in foreign lands (along with the constant, sometimes irksome, and at other times enjoyable need to IR-ize what I discovered). But in fact, isn't this the essence of IR—to cross borders, to problematize the concept of the border itself?

"Tagore's" Pensive Gaze: A Tangible Link to Colonialism

It was in early 2016 that I discovered the bust of Rabindranath Tagore, the first Nobel laureate from India (1913, literature), in the inner court of the Faculty of the Humanities—with the marking tape around it. Tagore was a world traveler who crossed many state and cultural borders in his efforts to abolish colonialism and bridge, through literature and art, the divisions between what he saw as the "material West" and the "spiritual East" (Richardson 2019). Tagore's vision was one of a nonhierarchical international and cultural dialogue that would not eliminate difference but would enable change and growth (R. Kumar 1999, 17). The bust that depicts him, first created in cement in 1940 by Modernist Bengali artist Ramkinkar Baij (the original is in the National Gallery of Modern Art in New Delhi), shows Tagore as an old man, one year before his death. His head is bowed toward his chest, and his face is solemn and sad, perhaps reflecting this internationalist and humanist's stress from the violence of World War II that had just erupted then and the continuation of the British colonial smothering of India.[15] This expression could also be due to his growing frustration over the rejection of his political ideas of anti-

---

14. This is how de Certeau understands the practice of reading (1984, 174).

15. These themes appear in Tagore's last public address, "Crisis in Civilization." See Dutta and Robinson (1995, 363–65).

162   EXPEDITION ESCAPE FROM THE CLASSROOM

imperialism in the West but also in Japan and China, and the breakdown of his vision of an "Asian way" (Datta Gupta 2020, 284–85).

As opposed to some other nondescript busts I have seen on our campus, Baij's Tagore is clearly a work of art; it contains something mysterious and enchanting, something intense that hints at a depth to the sitter's personality and inner world. The fact that the bust was used by the workers who renovated the nearby student union offices as an "anchor" for their marking tape reminded me strongly of the raven perching on Pallas's head in Poe's poem. After seeing the bust for the first time, its intriguing uniqueness led me to spend several weeks reading some of Tagore's literary works. I also read *about* Tagore and Baij, and through them I became acquainted with a fraction of India's history and culture—about which, I am ashamed to say as an IR scholar, I knew almost nothing before.

As my research progressed, the carelessness and apathy manifested in the use of the Tagore bust as an anchoring point for marking tape during the renovation of the student union offices became increasingly clear. The plastic tape on the figure's neck was a disregard or ignorance of the bust's artistic value. I at first thought that the bust, donated by the Ministry of Culture of the Government of India to the Hebrew University in 2012, was a unique gift that reflected the very favorable approach of Tagore toward the Jews and the Zionist movement.[16] I also recalled there is a Tagore Street in Tel Aviv, which intersects with Einstein Street near the university there. The two men, I learned later, met at least five times in Germany and the United States. They discussed issues of epistemology and metaphysics (Singer 2001), expressed their worries at the spread of hyper-nationalism, and called for the protection of human rights and creative freedom in the cause of world peace (Ghose 2020, 342). Yet after researching more on Tagore, I learned that the government of India presented similar busts of Tagore, who is in many respects an Indian national cultural icon (despite his adamant rejection of nationalism as "mental slavery" and a "machine of power" [Tagore 1916, 38–39][17]), to various

---

16. The bust was given to the Hebrew University as a symbol of Indian culture and history. The plaque on the pedestal notes that the bust was donated by the Ministry of Culture, Government of India, 2012, on the 150th anniversary of Tagore's birth.

17. Yogita Goyal (2019, 56) writes in this context, "He was frequently criticized in India for being too cosmopolitan and friendly to the imperialist West, and insufficiently nationalist or Bengali, though the postcolonial state has successfully elided the memory of his fierce anti-nationalism and invented him into a nationalist icon." Yet "although he is most often read as a Bengali poet, the 'geographical diminution' of Tagore as a 'parochial possession' of Bengal overlooks his travels to Europe, North and

The Enigma of Portrait Busts **163**

academic and cultural institutions and installed the busts in several locations around the world, especially in 2011–12, the 150th anniversary of Tagore's birth. This included in London, Seoul, Sydney, Bogota, Vancouver, Lausanne, Dublin, Maribor, Beijing, Shanghai, Colombo, Prague, and Borobudur temple (Indonesia).

A replica of Baij's bust of Tagore identical to the one we have here was presented by the Indian embassy in Sweden to Upsala University in 2014.[18] Another replica of Baij's Tagore bust had already been placed in 1984 in Balatonfüred, Hungary, at a cardiologic sanitarium by Lake Balaton, where Tagore recuperated for ten days in 1926 after a long and exhausting celebrity tour in Europe. But this bust was replaced in 2005 by the Indian government with a more "standard" bust of Tagore (namely, one that idealizes and beautifies the sitter), as an increasing number of Indian politicians and other Tagore admirers who visited the sanitarium and the Tagore promenade there complained that Baij's sculpture did not represent an "authentic" image of the sage-like poet. The "sad" bust of Tagore was moved into the room where he stayed during his healing in the sanitarium (Pisharoty 2017; Basu 2021). The specific bust the Hebrew University received, then, was a part of a worldwide Tagore "bust diplomacy" campaign, directed at supporting Indian studies in various countries (Sengupta 2012).

The realization that such a bust campaign existed and that our Tagore is one of a few replicas of the distinctive "sad" bust of him increased my curiosity and led me to read more. I started to come and observe the bust almost daily, trying to "figure it out," to decipher its mystery, and perhaps also to amend and "repent" for the construction department's disrespectful improvisation and use of the bust. But to own the truth, my preoccupation began to be less about the staff's disregard for Baij's art or India's national pride than about seeing the tape around the neck of Tagore as tied around my own neck too. For Tagore's expression is so human, reflecting the many travails and pains he had experienced and witnessed during his lifetime (even though he descended from a privileged and wealthy landowning family in Bengal). Baij

---

South America, China, Japan, Iran, and Indo-China. His university, 'Visva-Bharati,' translates as 'India in the World' or 'The World in India,' signalling his insistence that India 'was and must remain a land without a center,' a land of confluences of cultures and religions."

18. See "Spectacular Rabindranath Tagore Programme at Uppsala University," SASNET, https://web.archive.org/web/20141219133535/http://www.sasnet.lu.se/content/rabindranath-tagore-statue-be-raised-uppsala-university

184   EXPEDITION ESCAPE FROM THE CLASSROOM

tried not to idealize his image. "Listen," Baij recalls that Tagore told him while working on the sketches for this bust, "when you observe something, grab it like a tiger by the nape of the neck and then don't look back" (Ghatak 1975, beginning at 17:54). Unlike those who demanded the removal of the Balatonfüred "Tagore" replica, saying that the bust did not reflect the authentic Tagore, I thought that Baij did indeed manage to grab that "something" in this sculpture. The bust tells the viewer a great deal about the sitter, enabling us to empathize with him.

While Baij made the sketches for the bust, Tagore was preparing an obituary for his longtime friend, Anglican priest and anticolonial educationist C. F. Andrews, and he himself was unwell (Chaudhuri 2021). Tagore's lowered and mournful look, his sunken eyes, and the irregularities in the unpolished bronze of the sculpture create a representation of Tagore as a vulnerable man who has almost given up hope.[19] Moreover, as opposed to many other busts, in which the torso is smoothed where the arms should have connected to the shoulders, the rough surface of Tagore's bust creates an impression that the arms were torn off from the sculpture. The greenish corrosion patina of the bronze adds to the strong impact on the viewer. This is not the heroic and flawless representation of a wise Eastern seer, as he was perceived and depicted in many countries during the 1920s and 1930s, when he essentially was an international celebrity. Instead, he is a man who has lived since birth under colonial rule and who has come to the end of his life with little hope of seeing the British leave and India turn into a unified and strong country. He worked and yearned for the end of the British Raj, yet it outlived him, and when it finally ended, terrible communal violence between Hindus and Muslims erupted. Jawaharlal Nehru, in his prison diary, wrote, "Perhaps it is as well that [Tagore] died now and did not see the many horrors that are likely to descend in increasing measure on the world and on India. He had seen enough, and he was infinitely sad and unhappy" (Quoted in Sen, n.d.).

Moreover, Tagore was very concerned throughout his lifetime, especially during his last years, about the vast numbers of illiterate people in India and the horrible living conditions of the Indian masses, which he saw as purposefully perpetuated by the British to prolong their grip over India. On his deathbed in the summer of 1941, he wrote the following, in response to Ms. Eleanor

---

19. Toward the end of his life, Tagore grew more and more disturbed by the rising conflicts between Muslims and Hindus and the strategy of *swadeshi*, self-reliance, and boycotting foreign goods adopted by the National Congress led by Gandhi in its dealings with the British. See Datta Gupta (2020, 290). See also Tagore (1939).

The Enigma of Portrait Busts **165**

Rathbone's "open letter to an Indian friend." Rathbone, a former British MP and feminist, had scolded the Indians for their lack of cooperation with the British in the war. Tagore responded,

> It is sheer insolent self-complacence on the part of our so-called English friends to assume that had they not "taught" us, we would still have remained in the Dark Ages. Through the official British channels of education in India have flowed to our children in schools not the best of English thought but its refuse, which has only deprived them of a wholesome repast at the table of their own culture. . . . Our people have been deliberately disarmed and emasculated in order to keep them perpetually cowed and at the mercy of their armed [British] masters. (Tagore 2006, 851–52)

The plaque on the bust's pedestal also contributes to the impression of vulnerability and loneliness that one feels from the sculpture itself. But despite its somberness, it inspires some hope. It features a section from one of Tagore's last poems (written on his last birthday) in three languages: Hebrew, Bengali, and English. The following is the English version of this poem as it appears on the plaque:[20]

> My bag is empty today:
> I have given away
> all there was to give.
> If something comes in return—
> some love, some forgiveness—
> I shall take them with me
> when I set sail in my raft
> towards that silent festival
> of the end.

In this poem and in many of Tagore's other poems, I saw his preoccupation with the question of loneliness and belonging. Beyond articulating these existential aspects in his art, he was determined to take some practical steps to augment human and social connections by trying to alleviate the poverty and hardships of the Bengali peasants through innovative methods of education

---

20. I don't know the source of the poem's translation on the plaque. A slightly different translation appears in Tagore (1960, 89, poem no. 10).

166 EXPEDITION ESCAPE FROM THE CLASSROOM

in the university he established (Visva-Bharati University) and methods of what we call now micro-financing. For he believed that poverty is detrimental to human creativity and the human soul and thus destructive to meaningful human connections and social cohesion. He considered the concept of the nation not necessarily as a political entity but as a way to create the space for people's creativity to flourish and develop their spirituality. "Through many lectures and writings on this issue," writes Sukalpa Bhattacharjee, "Tagore rejects key constitutive machineries and elements of nation-state such as territory, sovereignty and governmental power and builds his thesis of transcendence from the political to the moral realm which could alleviate the Indian masses from suffering and oppression that a modern state intimates in its presence." (Bhattacharjee 2020, 115). In literacy, he saw "a road for travel of the minds of the people to each other's minds for interaction with each other, and thereby find the greater humanity within oneself and oneself within greater humanity" (Tagore, quoted in Rahman 2006, 241).

"Tagore" and Reading Colonialism through Interstellar Lenses

After finding this bust in the Humanities courtyard and after learning something about Tagore and India's struggle against British colonialism, I have begun to take not only the "Mt. Scopus Enclave" students to observe it, but also students from my seminar course "Science Fiction and (International) Politics."

I teach a class on the novel *Childhood's End*, by Arthur C. Clarke, as part of this course. The novel is about the arrival of "Overlords" to earth and their seemingly benevolent rule here. Although they resemble demons (they have hoofs, scales, horns, and long and pointed tails), they speak "perfect English," impose world peace, and relieve earth's states from their "precarious sovereignty." All disease and other material troubles that have haunted humanity since its dawn are also terminated. Humankind is left to engage in art, sports, and philosophy in places such as "New Athens." IR ceases to exist as such: "The old names of the old countries were still used, but they were no more than convenient post divisions" (Clarke 1979, 60).

For many years, I taught *Childhood's End* in the context of Clarke's short discussion of the end of states' "precarious sovereignty." In the 1976 Hebrew translation of the novel, "precarious" was interpreted as something that is in between "questionable" and "dubious" (ריבונותן המפוקפקת)—and the phrase

The Enigma of Portrait Busts **187**

never stops amusing me. Sovereignty can indeed be questionable and dubious.[21] I read the passage to the students with a comic accentuation, and usually we all laugh. But things get less cheerful when I ask, "Would you have liked such benevolent Overlords to arrive here and end our [Israel's and other states'] 'dubious sovereignty'?"

World peace, material abundance, good health—in the more than ten years that I have taught this novel, hardly any of the students have embraced this "offer." Some say that war, along with its sorrows and damages, also has good effects: "uniting the people" and spurring creativity and innovation in many other fields. On one occasion, a student even said, half-jokingly, that he would have committed suicide if war, the ultimate expression of human agency (that's what he said!), were abolished. I experienced his words as a punch in my stomach. I wanted to respond that my cousin Eran committed suicide in the military precisely because of such a mentality, that he was in the grip of a militarist culture of violence that equates manliness and one's value as a human being with combatant service, but something stopped me (Löwenheim 2015). I felt that it would be an insult to Eran's memory if I told his story in response to that student's offhand utterance, that the meaning of Eran's death would be corrupted by the stupor manifested in the student's words.

Other students often refer to their identity being constructed by the Israeli-Palestinian conflict, and more generally, the other conflicts of Israel in the Middle East, as well as their military service, and they cannot see themselves as capable of giving up who they are even if such Overlords arrived here. Fewer claim that it could have been interesting to experience at least the pacifying aspects of such a friendly alien arrival. But almost everybody says, repeatedly and every year, that without any material hardship, human creativity and uniqueness would significantly diminish and humans would deteriorate into an infantile existence (as the novel partially suggests too).

Clarke's novel was published in 1953, several years after the independence of India. In the past few years, along with discussing with the students the hypothetical option of an end to sovereignty, I also talk about an article I found only relatively lately that views *Childhood's End* from a perspective of the termination of British colonial rule in India. According to Matthew Candelaria (2002), Clarke's Overlords maintain similar indirect administration structures to those of the British in India, enforce a single administrative lan-

---

21. And hypocritical too. See Krasner (1999).

guage (English), and treat humans in a paternalistic manner. The novel is "a colonial parable, deftly engineered to make the reader identify with the colonial administrators, the Overlords, and their self-sacrificing mission to better humanity. Throughout the novel, the Overlords are portrayed as British colonial administrators, but they are idealized representations" (Candelaria 2002, 38–39; for a similar argument, see Sun 2018).

Since starting to think about the novel as a colonial parable, I have been taking the class to see the bust of Tagore while teaching it. After we have dealt with the "precarious sovereignty" theme and questioned whether "there is some beneficial side to war," I asked the students to fold their laptops and notebooks into their backpacks and come with me. This year (2021), it was a lovely, warm late morning toward the middle of December. In a docile, colonial manner, the students followed me through the corridors of the campus without asking where we were going. I said, "Just trust me," and they came along. I took them to the Humanities courtyard, and we soon stood around the bust of Tagore.

I invited the students to take a closer look at the bust and read the poem and information on the plaque. They did what I requested for a few moments, with interest and a sense of awe and quiet respect. When I then asked them to describe how they perceived Tagore, they said he looked very sad, old, and *burdened*. I told them that I thought the bust of Tagore was a moving work of art that captures the inner world of the poet and something of what poetry is as well. Then I asked them to read the Wikipedia entry on Tagore. Once they finished, we talked about how *Childhood's End* can be seen as a story that refers to British colonialism in India and its conclusion, along Candelaria's article. In Clarke's novel, humanity eventually transcends its material bodily form and becomes one with the "Overmind," a mysterious energy entity that the Overlords serve. The Overlords lament the transformation of humanity (its childhood's end) and keep human artifacts and other material remnants in their museum of the civilizations they tutored for the union with the Overmind. The spiritual transformation of the humans can be compared to the strategy of nonviolent resistance led by Gandhi and the need for the spiritual and cultural lead of the Indian independence movement that Tagore preached for (and that disappointed him when he felt it was not realized [see: Gupta, 2020: 282–83]).

This year, I had Palestinian students from East Jerusalem (four young women) enrolled for the first time in this seminar. While I was talking about how we can imagine Tagore as a weary colonial subject (his sadness and intro-

The Enigma of Portrait Busts   **169**

version, his recognition that the British subjugation of India will not end soon,[22] his feeling that the British are choking India, and his perception of the spiritual decline of the Indian national struggle) who nonetheless transcended the fate of a submissive colonial subject through his poetry and art, I suddenly noticed that I had become cautious about what I could (or wanted to) say about the colonized person's subjectivity.

How could I talk about this without hurting the feelings of these Palestinian Jerusalemite students? Anything I said might single them out from the rest of the class and highlight the difference between the Israeli students and them, who have no Israeli citizenship, or any other citizenship (they are only permanent residents of Jerusalem, and this so-called permanency is also not always inalienable[23]) and thus are subject to a different set of rights and duties. Moreover, I then realized I was in a trap: these Palestinian students likely perceived me as belonging to the colonizing/occupying side—for example, the course is held in Hebrew. Whatever I said about the colonized/occupied person's experience and subjectivity could be seen as reflecting ignorance, condescendence, or an Orientalist approach. What did I really know about the lived daily experience of the occupation? On the other hand, I did know a little about the history of the British Raj, and I learned something about Tagore's subjectivity and experience with this system.[24] And I wanted

---

22. "The wheels of fate will someday compel the English to give up their Indian Empire. But what kind of India will they leave behind, what stark misery? When the stream of their centuries' administration runs dry at last, what a waste of mud and filth they will leave behind them?" Tagore (1941a, 10–11).

23. In principle, East Jerusalemite permanent residents can apply for Israeli citizenship. But the process is long and full of designed hurdles, resulting in a few hundred approvals per year. In addition, the great majority of Jerusalem Palestinians don't apply from the outset, as they deem the process as cooperation with the Israeli occupation. See Hasson (2017); see also Isa (2023).

24. Tagore can be seen as a man who had an external and internal world. In the external world, he was a colonial subject. His "outer life" was historically determined. But in his inner life, he had freedom, and he was not just a British subject in the domain of general history. "On the debate about historical determination he wrote that his answer 'comes from within where I am nothing but a poet, there I am the creator, there I am by myself, I am free.' He concedes that history brings into being the constituent elements which the creative writer works upon, and some of those elements are generated by the social environment, but the creator is not thereby created. The creator uses those elements and thus reveals his creativity. Tagore argues, or rather declares, that the essential act of creation is explicable in terms of 'the opaque history of inner self,' not in terms of external history. Thus, Tagore reconciles Freedom and Necessity, demarcating freedom of the inner life from the historically determined outer life" (Bhattacharya 2011, 53).

Fig. 31. A close-up of the Tagore bust by Ramkinkar Baij. (Photograph by the author.)

to share this knowledge and insights with the class and connect this to the sci-fi novel.

While I was talking and at the same time weighing my thoughts on these questions, I noticed that one of the Palestinian students, who I know comes from one of the poorest and most heavily policed neighborhoods of East Jerusalem, was listening attentively. It was the first time I had seen her so attuned during the course. She nodded and smiled, with a spark in her eyes. It seemed that she had an understanding or insight while listening to me talk about Tagore's inner and outer experiences and worlds as both a colonial subject and a free creator. Was she encouraged by what I told the class about his ability to retain inner hope and creativity despite the harsh British occupation? As our eyes met, I hoped she would say something, but she remained silent. But it was the first time in this course that I had seen an authentic,

The Enigma of Portrait Busts   **171**

emotive response from this student. It is rare, at least for me, to see a genuine spark in a student's eye during class. I took that spark in her eyes to mean she found something in my words.

When the class ended and the students left the courtyard, the student who said he would rather commit suicide in case of total abolition of war by benevolent aliens approached me and said he was very impressed by the bust and its story and thanked me for the excursion. He also said that he would read something about Tagore. I was happy to hear him saying this.

After he left too, I stayed and observed the bust for a few more moments. I moved around the sculpture and examined it from various angles and positions. Even after the dozens of times I have come to examine it, something in it remains enchanting.[25] I then sat on the low rock at the foot of the bust and checked my phone for new emails. I was happy to see that I had just received a reply from Prof. R. Siva Kumar of the art history department from Visva-Bharati University, to whom I had written the day before.

In 2012, Kumar authored a comprehensive monograph and catalog that accompanied the retrospective exhibition of Ramkinkar Baij at the National Gallery of Modern Art in New Delhi. I asked him a few questions about Baij and the bust of Tagore. Siva Kumar said that he thinks this sculpture is one of the finest and most insightful portraits of the poet. He then added, "The initial portrait Ramkinkar made from life was more conventional. After it was completed, it was destroyed by him and the present one was done by him without the model in his studio. While doing this he also changed Tagore's bodily appearance a bit. By this time, Tagore was relatively frail, but Ramkinkar shows him as broad-shouldered as he was until a few years earlier, giving him a body befitting his brooding head."[26]

I looked at the bust again and saw that he was right: the shoulders indeed were broad, somewhat disproportionally to the stooped head. I wondered whether the original bust would have created in me a similar emotional attachment to this one. I'll never know, of course, but I felt that this "sad" version taught me so much more about despair and hope, colonialism and emancipation, than a more conventional one could have.

---

25. "While resisting the more potent connotations of the word magic, enchanted objects appeal to those who are capable of acts of attention. . . . Enchanted objects restore a sense of wonder to a world that has bowed down for much of the twentieth century to abstraction and theory" (Hepburn 2010, 15).

26. Email correspondence with Prof. Siva Kumar Raman, December 15, 2021.

CHAPTER 5

Layers of Memory and Identity

EXPLORING THE SPACES AND STORIES OF THE HARRY S. TRUMAN RESEARCH INSTITUTE FOR THE ADVANCEMENT OF PEACE

Introduction to the Chapter

This chapter opens on the roof of the Harry S. Truman Research Institute for the Advancement of Peace at the Hebrew University, descends into the foyer, and concludes in the institute's bomb shelter. At each location, I offer detailed descriptions of personal experiences and encounters, all intricately connected to the three overarching goals of this book. In this way, the chapter also demonstrates how a place—here, the Truman Institute—becomes, through an autoethnographic narrative, a canvas for the imprint of broader sociopolitical narratives and the relentless passage of time.

On the roof of the institute, I reflect on a deeply personal conversation with my ex-wife prior to our separation, touching on our shared and conflicting emotions related to our homeland's culture of violence. I also reminisce about my father's doctoral awarding ceremony in 1991. Together, these memories symbolize my profound connection to the Hebrew University and explain my decision to stay in Israel rather than emigrate to Canada. Hence, these personal narratives offer valuable insights into the nexus of emotions, places, politics, and familial bonds. This rooftop experience aligns with the second goal of the book: to forge a meaningful connection with readers through evocative IR autoethnography.

As I descend to the foyer, my attention shifts to the unmistakably "American" ambience and aesthetic design that is revealed upon my entrance to the Truman Institute with the students for a tour, a few days after my divorce. I describe this foreign enclave within the Hebrew University and relay a discussion with the students over the naming of this peace institute after the American president who authorized the bombing of Japan with nuclear weapons, thus aligning with goal 3 of the book: critically IR-izing spaces within the campus.

We then descend into the institute's bomb shelter, embarking on a journey that traverses British Mandate Palestine, the United States, Israel, and the Dominican Republic. Guided by the compelling presence of four intriguing busts and the story of their creator, Maurice Hexter, we navigate through these transitions. These sculptures, originally donated to the Truman Institute by Hexter, were later "exiled" to the shelter due to political considerations, subsequently transforming into potent symbols that encapsulate political history and ongoing national tensions. A substantial portion of my attention is devoted to delving into my interactions with these sculptures and their creator. Maurice Hexter's sculptures act as a conduit to intricate themes such as colonization, historical memory, and the Zionist movement. Their unexpected placement within the bomb shelter evokes contemplation on subjects including establishment art, security, leadership, and the human condition. These critical themes also align with the third goal of the book: to foster critical thinking in international relations and to reimagine objects and spaces within this field.

The chapter also deals with themes of misunderstanding and mistaken identity, culminating in my incorrect identification of another bust as portraying Two-Gun Cohen, a Jewish-Canadian gangster and adventurer. This misidentification leads me to explore personal themes such as boredom, desolation, and facets of my midlife crisis, providing a lens into my teaching anxiety (goal 1 of the book).

Watching a Landscape of Violence from the Roof of the Truman Institute

April 16, 2018, around 2:45 p.m.
I'm with a group of about twenty students from the "Mt. Scopus Enclave" course. After a walk of about fifteen minutes from the secretariat of the IR department (the designated meeting point for our course excursions), we are now entering the building of the Harry S. Truman Research Institute for the Advancement of Peace, at the furthest southeastern end of campus. I took the class here through the longest route possible, via the botanical garden. I needed the walk in the open green garden, appreciating the delay it caused in our arriving here. Now, I am holding open the heavy, metal entry doors of the

174   EXPEDITION ESCAPE FROM THE CLASSROOM

building for the last of the students who come in. I am six days divorced now. I try not to let my emotions show on my face, but on the inside I am shattered. After almost nineteen years of marriage, I experience the divorce as the rupture and collapse of my life. I am disoriented and in deep grief. In many ways, I feel estranged from myself. But I could not have stayed at home with these emotions; I thought it was better to keep the class as scheduled and be with people. Yet now that the tour of today's class is about to start, after my detour through the botanical garden, I think, "How will I endure this ordeal?"

Coming to the Truman Institute is especially hard for me today. I recall that three months ago, I stood here with my now ex-wife on the viewing balcony on the roof of the building. We were looking toward the east. It was one of those crisp, cold winter days in Jerusalem. The Dead Sea and the Judean Desert rested beneath us. The sky was cloudless, and the Moab Mountains in the Hashemite Kingdom of Jordan stretched away on the other side of the Great Rift Valley. I thought the view was magnificent, full of timeless splendor, like the desert depicted in Leopold Pilichowski's *The Opening of the Hebrew University of Jerusalem*.[1] This large oil painting, hung at the entrance of the university's administration building entrance, shows the main dedication ceremony of the institution on April 1, 1925. On the stage of the open Scopus theater, Lord Balfour and many other local and international dignitaries spoke in front of about 20,000 people in the excited audience. It was a day of exuberance for the Zionist Yishuv, the opening of the Hebrew University. About one quarter of all Jews in Palestine attended the ceremony. Behind the stage was the expanse of the white Judean Desert, the blue Dead Sea, and the Moab Mountains.

The Dead Sea is dying nowadays, shrinking and evaporating due to industrial overmining of its minerals and the damming of its tributaries in Israel and Jordan. Its water level descends by more than one meter every year. The wild and open desert of the painting is now much more populated, with Israeli settlements and Palestinian neighborhoods and towns scattered across it. The separation wall scars the landscape and parallels Highway 1 to the Dead Sea. Smoke from the constant burning of waste billows up from the Palestinian town of az-Za'ayyem, at the eastern foot of Mt. Scopus. The Israeli settlement town of Ma'ale Adumim occupies the next ridge. A police base— not a mere "station," for it is more of a fortress and military base than a "blue" civilian police point—also rests not far below Mt. Scopus. This is a landscape of violence, occupation, and environmental degradation.

---

1. See the painting at https://commons.wikimedia.org/wiki/File:Grand_opening_of_the_Hebrew_University_-_Leopold_Philichovsky_painting,_1925.jpg

But when we stood there on the roof, I still saw some of the inspiring views of the desert and the Dead Sea as in Pilichowski's painting. And turning my gaze to the university's open theater just below the Truman Institute's building, I "saw" the 1925 inauguration ceremony. I also recalled the PhD awarding ceremony of the summer of 1991 in that same place: when my father, Avigdor, received his doctorate in Jewish history. Stepping down from the theater stage after the Dean of the Humanities handed him his diploma, he held the scroll with reverence. It was, for him, the fulfillment of a dream of generations of Diaspora Jews (he was born in Budapest in 1941 and emigrated to Israel in 1957): to be a doctor of the Hebrew University, the university of the Jewish people. That this institution even exists was a miracle in his eyes (although, as the representative of the librarians in the administrative staff union, he saw the daily realities and machinations of the institution, which are a bit less ideal and sublime). He hoped to get an academic position then, but it was already too late for him. Fifty-year-old librarians would only rarely be seriously considered for an academic tenure-track position; and, indeed, he was not. I think it broke his heart. When I received my PhD in 2001, at the age of thirty-one, and when I was hired for a tenure-track position here at the department of IR in 2003, my father was already sinking into dementia. I think that at some level, he knew I had entered an academic career and was happy and proud of me. I didn't do it to satisfy him. But even today, I still feel that I "represent" him here, that my presence here somehow amends the condescending treatment he received. When I was given tenure in 2010, he had already passed away.

So, when I stood with my ex-wife, three months ago, on the roof of the Truman Institute and looked out over the Judean Desert and the Hebrew University's open theater, I saw the same view she did but it had completely different meaning for me. She saw only the landscape of violence and conflict. She wanted our family to emigrate to Canada, where we had lived for several years during my postdoc and sabbatical. We had applied and already received permanent residency papers and were set to leave in summer 2018. But leaving for Canada meant that I would have to give up my position at the Hebrew University, and as much as I loved Canada and enjoyed living there, I could not bring myself to do that. I could not leave because of the memory of my late father. Even mustering all the reflexivity, cynicism, and rational thinking I could, I still felt this would be a betrayal of him. Also, I doubted whether I would be able to secure (yes, to secure, in the sense of security) a tenured position in a Canadian university. I am now mid-career and have attained some status here, and I could not see myself starting the torment of a tenure track all over again. Whenever giving a talk at a Canadian university,

EXPEDITION ESCAPE FROM THE CLASSROOM

I always felt like a stranger, even though many others there also had a foreign accent. And while people were interested in my work, I sensed that they don't—they can't—comprehend the intricacies of the place I'm coming from. Knowing how my father was, in a deep sense, unable to put behind the place he left, how rootless he often felt here, and how he struggled with Hebrew (even though he had excellent Hebrew), I was afraid this would happen to me too. I am a Hebrew speaker. As proficient as I am in English, it is not my first language. I didn't want to be an immigrant.

I could understand what my ex-wife meant when all she saw in the landscape below us was conflict, degradation, occupation, and violence. In fact, I believe it was me who sharpened many of the realities of the conflict in this land to her. I, too, saw blood, injustice, violence, and pain when we stood on the roof. But that was not *only* what I saw.

Many other reasons discouraged me from leaving for Canada, bringing about our divorce. I cannot write about them here. All I can say is that since our return from a sabbatical on Vancouver Island in 2013, the issue (the threat, from my perspective) of immigration had deepened the gap between us, making us estranged from each other beyond hope. But as we stood on the roof together, watching the Great Rift Valley, I suddenly understood that not only had a chasm opened between us, but I had become estranged from myself. For the better part of recent years, I had distanced myself from who I am: a Hebrew University professor, a Hebrew-speaking teacher, and a native of this land, rooted in its landscape and history.[2] I had moved away from myself to keep the marriage and the family intact. But this was no solution: a marriage with widening rifts between and within the partners cannot remain "intact." The marriage eventually fell apart. When we finally divorced, along with feeling some relief, I could not help but remember the words of poet Yehuda Amichai: "Whoever leaves the one he loves, the miracles will happen to him in reverse. All wine will turn into blood, and all bread into stone. And the Red Sea will not open wide into a new life but will stay whole like the memory that cannot be traversed, and there he will drown." I knew this would be my life task from now on: to open wide the Red Sea, not to drown in it.

---

2. I adopt here the notion of nativity employed by Meron Benvenisti (2002, 2007): I see myself rooted here and belonging in this land, and, more generally, see both Jews and Palestinians as having legitimate ties to the territory, making both groups indigenous. Like Benvenisti, I consider history as made of layers. Every layer has its own historical and cultural significance, and no layer can be regarded as more "authentic" than another. This perspective challenges attempts by either side to negate or diminish the other's historical connection to the land as well as current rights and needs.

Down from the Roof to the Foyer—American Exterritoriality and Truman's Local Legacy

As the students and I enter (the Truman building, on April 16, 2018), it is quiet and looks almost deserted. Two stories—for researchers' offices and for the institute's administration—encompass a square foyer, and light pours in from the roof windows. The interior has a sense of luxury and elegance (e.g., tubular chandeliers hanging low from the high ceiling; granite floor tiles), but also of outworn design. Cracks in the paint on the walls, cobwebs in the corners, murky windows that haven't been cleaned for years—all hint at neglect and decay in this forty-five-year-old building.

The building of the Truman Institute looks not only derelict but also of a previous era: on the first floor's parapet that faces the foyer hang large and fading photographs from the ceremony of the signing of the peace treaty between Jordan and Israel in the Arava Valley in 1994. Bill and Hillary Clinton look so young. Yitzhak Rabin and King Hussein share an intimate moment as the king lights the cigarette of the prime minister, who was assassinated a year later. On the walls of the third floor, historical pictures from the Camp David 1978 negotiations between Israel and Egypt, with Menachem Begin, Anwar Sadat, Jimmy Carter, and their men (only one woman, First Lady Rosalynn Carter, appears in the pictures). Yet nowhere in the building are photos from the signing ceremony of the 1993 Oslo Accords with the Palestinians on the White House lawn, even though "urban legends" among some of the staff here insist that the Truman Institute played an essential supporting role in the early pre-negotiation between key Israeli and Palestinian participants.[3] This is the peace that failed, that no one wants to remember, apparently.

On the northern side of the foyer hangs a row of posters with the faces of the Truman Peace Prize winners—people such as Dennis Ross, Colin Powell,

---

3. Throughout the years, I have heard various stories about secret pre-negotiation meetings between Israelis and Palestinians on the Truman Institute's premises, but I found no written reference to this. The only indication of the institute's involvement in the inception of the Oslo peace process comes from Ron Pundak, a key initiator of the negotiations on the Israeli side, along with Yair Hirschfeld. Pundak wrote, "As strange as it may sound, had [Yair Hirschfeld] not been invited to Europe exactly on the same week [in December 1992] to participate in a seminar on water in the Middle East, an invitation that let him fly to London, it is most likely that the meeting with Abu Alah would not have materialized on that occasion and the Oslo Process perhaps would not have been launched. *The flight ticket he received from the Truman Institute at the Hebrew University*, which organized the seminar in Switzerland [on water], enabled him to leave for Europe and stop for a swift visit to London" (Pundak 2013, 41; emphasis added). I thank my colleague Dr. Lior Lehrs for the reference. So, this seems to be a very modest contribution, even accidental, but crucial nonetheless.

178   EXPEDITION ESCAPE FROM THE CLASSROOM

Madeleine Albright, and George Mitchell. The last time the peace prize was awarded was in 2013, to George Shultz, former US secretary of state. Most Truman Peace Prize laureates are American officials and politicians. This, together with the portrait of President Truman that welcomes the incoming visitors, the painting of Nathaniel L. Goldstein, former attorney general of the state of New York and first chairman of the Truman Institute's board, and the long list of American benefactors of the institute that is embossed on the wall next to the entrance door to the foyer, always creates a sense of ex-territoriality here. The Truman Institute stands as an enclave where the ideals of peace, diplomacy, and international cooperation are celebrated, seemingly detached from the tumultuous realities beyond its walls. The supposed American official decorum of the place creates an air of authority, presence, and influence, but it also underscores foreignness and the cultural and geographical distance between the United States and the conflicts of the region.

Most of the students have not previously visited this building before I guide them on this tour, and they are struck by the prevailing foreign/American ambiance that permeates the surroundings. They need to get beyond their first impression to see the signs of decay. The students cast inquisitive glances around. Without seeking my permission, a few begin to wander through the foyer, reading the informative signs detailing the institute's history and the contributions of the Truman Peace Prize laureates to peace negotiations. I let them explore.

A few minutes pass, and as I stand in the foyer, waiting for the class to regroup, a student approaches me. She delves right into a thought-provoking question, addressing the apparent contradiction between the Truman Institute's mission of advancing peace in the Middle East and its namesake, who authorized the use of the atomic bombs on Japan.

We're surrounded by the portraits of Truman and the recipients of the Truman Peace Award, a visual paradox that prompts reflection. Other students draw near. I explain that while Truman's decision to drop the atomic bombs is indeed a pivotal aspect of his legacy, one that even led some to consider him a war criminal,[4] the reasons for naming this institute after him relate to other issues. It was Truman's support for the establishment of a Jewish state in Palestine at the November 1947 UN partition vote and the United States'

---

4. Philosopher Elizabeth Anscombe was the single person who openly objected the awarding of an honorary degree to Truman in Oxford in 1956. She considered the atomic bombings as mass murder: "Choosing to kill the innocent as a means to your ends is always murder" (Anscombe 1958).

Fig. 32. In the foyer of the Truman Research Institute for the Advancement of Peace at the Hebrew University. (Photographs by the author.)

180   EXPEDITION ESCAPE FROM THE CLASSROOM

recognition of Israel's independence in May 1948 that brought him accolades from the American Jewry, members of which donated the endowment for the establishment of this institute. For many among the American Friends of the Hebrew University, this turn of events transformed Truman into a symbol of peace and support, especially within the context of Jewish history and aspirations.

The student, and the rest of the group, seem satisfied with my answer. For them, the paradox of Truman being honored by naming a peace institute after him, is settled now that his part in the establishment of our state has been clarified. But then another student comments that naming the institute after Truman raises in him, as a Palestinian from East Jerusalem, a sense of skepticism and frustration. "It is an irony," he says, "that Truman's support for the establishment of Israel and subsequent recognition is seen as a symbol of peace by some, while from my perspective, it marks the beginning of a continuous displacement and dispossession for my own people."

A noticeable tension starts to simmer among the group (all the other students are Israeli Jews), with exchanged glances conveying dismissiveness and irritation. Sensing the rising emotions, I intervene before we plunge into a contentious debate over the historical events that led to the 1948 War and its aftermath. As almost all teachers know, such impromptu arguments often escalate rapidly, with participants failing to genuinely listen to each other's perspectives. Ostensibly rational historical and legal arguments, aimed at demonstrating mastery of facts and historical truths,[5] often mask emotional wounds and traumas. Being emotionally wounded myself today, without the energy for further "battles," I offer the following: "Whether we embrace or reject the naming decision itself, it has the potential to encapsulate a broader essence. As students of IR, this discussion reminds us that understanding history and its impacts requires examining not only the causes and intentions behind decisions but also the outcomes that ripple through generations. It's crucial for us to recognize that different perspectives emerge from different historical experiences. The discipline of IR isn't merely about comprehending policies and choices in a detached, seemingly rational and factual manner. It also means grasping the intricate emotions and acknowledging the pain experienced by those affected by historical events. If the issue of naming this peace institute after Truman can remind us of this complexity, then perhaps

---

5. "They wanted facts. Facts! They demanded facts from him, as if facts could explain anything!" (Conrad 2002, 21).

it's in these conversations that we acknowledge that some questions don't have easy answers, yet we must find a way to live and engage with them, and to foster empathy and understanding in a world filled with contradictions."

I see that the students are thinking about my words. I then suggest that an intriguing approach to addressing such questions from a different perspective is situated just beneath us—in the bomb shelter of the institute, where we will look at four unique marble portrait busts. "In fact, what's down there is the main reason for our visit here today," I say. "This shelter actually turned into a memory vault, a bunker of history and symbolism. As we descend, we'll delve into layers of legacy that history has left behind. But in a deeper way, the story I will tell you there is about complex emotions and personal connections one might form with symbols and historical figures, a testament to the intimate ties one might have to the past. I believe that such emotional connections have influenced your varying viewpoints about naming the institute after Truman. Therefore, from a thematic perspective, I invite you to view the upcoming story as an exercise in observing how emotional engagement with history and its agents of memory can evolve, and then you might critically assess your own emotional connections to history."

We then start moving toward the far end of the foyer, where the stairs leading to the bomb shelter are situated. My aim is to sustain the momentum of my discussion on empathy, emotional connection to history, and the recognition of contradictions in our world, while also shifting the students' attention toward a different facet of the tour. The students follow me, perhaps out of curiosity to see the mentioned busts and maybe due to their reluctance to linger alone in this strange hallway.

An "Archaeological" Discovery at the Bomb Shelter

I lead the group down to the bomb shelter, and a sense of anticipation silences their conversations. The stairway seems to stretch, intensifying the feeling of descending into the building's concealed depths. As I open the shelter's heavy blast door, fluorescent lights hum to life, casting an eerie glow against the concrete walls and revealing before us a row of four gray marble busts.

Upon seeing the busts, some of students exclaim with alarm and surprise, others burst into laughter, and a few step forward to examine the busts more closely. The students don't believe me when I say I didn't set up the scene beforehand. After a few minutes, as their first reactions subside and curiosity

Fig. 33. In the bomb shelter of the Harry S. Truman Research Institute for the Advancement of Peace at the Hebrew University (*from left to right*): busts of Zalman Shazar, third president of the State of Israel; Dr. Eliyahu Elath, Hebrew University president and Israeli diplomat (the inscription on the pedestal mistakenly states this is Professor Ephraim Katzir, fourth president of the State of Israel); David Ben-Gurion, first prime minister of Israel; and Golda Meir, fourth prime minister of Israel. (Busts sculpted by Maurice B. Hexter. Photographs by the author.)

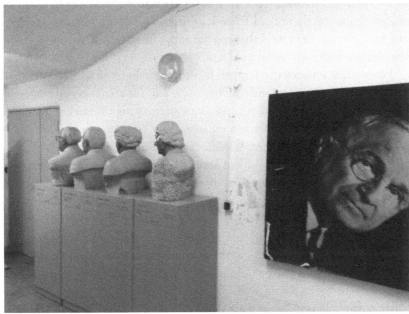

184   EXPEDITION ESCAPE FROM THE CLASSROOM

grows, I suggest, "Find a spot to sit or stand, and listen to the story of how I came across these statues and what happened afterward." The students scatter, some finding seats on the floor, others leaning against the walls. With their attention captured, I begin my narration.

• • •

I first learned about the existence of these four busts, "heads of the nation," from a graduate student in the IR department who knew I was interested in bust sculptures. She happened to be at the Truman Institute during the Home Front Command national emergency exercise in June 2017, when the sirens sounded on campus urging all administrative workers and students to hurry to the closest bomb shelters and other protected spaces (such as underground parking lots) throughout the campus. The academic staff was not included in the drill—perhaps the university's human resources and security departments knew that many professors work from home or perhaps they thought we were more expendable. But no, I'm just being cynical. At any rate, once in the bomb shelter at the Truman Institute, the IR graduate student immediately noticed these four unique busts, photographed them, and sent the images to me. I thanked her excitedly and soon went to examine the pieces myself.

When I first entered the Truman Institute's shelter, the fluorescents took a few seconds to stabilize, and the busts flickered. The scene was a bit unnerving, with a grave and macabre atmosphere permeating the shelter. Imagine: I was here all by myself, not accompanied by a group as we are today. But when the light stabilized, my excitement at finding the sculptures took over the uncanny sensation. I felt I had entered a vault and found a hidden treasure. At the same time, I experienced intense feelings of irony and cynicism. The sculptures were overly impressive, too well made, incredibly realistic, and sculpted in highly polished marble. And even though they represented different sitters, they all looked the same, reminding me immediately of the mass-reproduced "Napoleons" in the Sherlock Holmes story. As I gazed longer at these busts, I realized there was something very naive about them. Alternatively, they seemed as if "printed" by a 3D printer from some computer program in which they were sketched as impeccable objects from a single series. They also had another unique feature: they were sculpted in gray marble instead of white. I had never seen this type of marble before, which I later discovered is called Bardiglio Imperiale and is abundant in the Dominican Republic (a fact that will prove significant in the unfolding of this story).

Of course, I recognized the busts of Golda Meir and Ben-Gurion at first glance, without needing to read the inscriptions on the pedestals. President Shazar was also very familiar from the red 200 New Israeli Shekel banknote.[6] But I did not recognize President Katzir and had to read the inscription on his pedestal to identify him. It took me several months to realize that this was not, in fact, Katzir, but Dr. Eliyahu Elath, president of the Hebrew University between 1962 and 1968. He was also Israel's first ambassador to the United States and among those who conceived the idea to establish the Truman Institute at our university. I recognized him after another IR student, who worked at the photo archive of the university, found a picture of Elath for me, standing next to his bust during the sculptures' dedication ceremony in 1976. The man commemorated in the bust simply does not look like Katzir, and I have no idea why someone thought this was him.[7]

Despite my cynical feelings about the overly impressive sculptures on first seeing them, I also had the sensation of having made an archeological discovery, reminiscent of a scene from one of the Indiana Jones movies or the discovery of a hidden crypt, like that of Tutankhamun. Our campus has an abundance of cemeteries, inside and surrounding it, and I felt that I had found another burial site on Mt. Scopus. The faces of the busts I saw in the shelter seemed frozen in time (they all shared the same small smile). As I looked directly into their hollow eyes, I had the uncanny feeling they looked back.

Standing close to these representations of power and authority, ridiculous and weird as they were, made me curious. I wanted to move the busts, turn them around, touch them. After all, the situation is usually the opposite: we, the citizens, are subject to the whims of politicians and rulers who manipu-

---

6. This banknote has been out of circulation since mid-2017, and when I mentioned to various people that Shazar was the figure on the 200 NIS banknote, this usually did not help to identify him, even though this is the most common banknote in Israel. While many academic articles have been written about banknote recognition technologies for the visually impaired and machines that count cash or detect counterfeit currency, little research has been done on how and whether ordinary daily users of banknotes recognize or know who the persons on the bills are. See, for example, Sørensen (2016); Hymans and Tse-min Fu (2017).

7. Over the years, I repeatedly urged university authorities to correct the inscription on the pedestal—wrongly identifying the bust as Ephraim Katzir instead of Eliyahu Elath—to no avail. Eventually, I recognized the misidentification's value as a conversation starter. It became a means to engage students, visitors, and colleagues in discussions about the university's history, artifacts, and the question of accurate historical representation. As of August 2023, the inscription on the pedestal remained uncorrected.

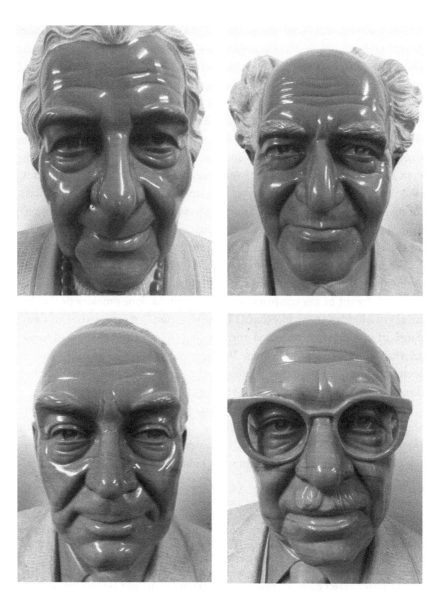

Fig. 34. Close-ups of the Truman Institute busts. Notice the similar smile and the way they stare at you. See also how polished and shiny the marble is. (Photographs by the author.)

Layers of Memory and Identity   **187**

late us (think, again, about Louis XIV's bust from chapter 4). I was tempted to take at least one of them with me to the IR department. But quickly I had a change of heart. I could not take a bust without permission. For all that—my institutional voice took over—this is university property, and I am not a thief. Furthermore, the busts were too heavy for me to even consider moving, let alone carry—each of these marble pieces weighed tens of kilograms, if not more.

But what would have happened if I had really taken these sculptures? Would anyone have noticed that they disappeared from the shelter? (I thought of the theft of Poe's bust.) Given the layer of dust on the statues, it seemed they had been stored in the shelter for years. If I had taken them, I would have placed them at the entrance to our department or in our seminar room. Would they have been noticed *there*? And if indeed they were noticed, what effect would they have had on our seminar participants? To what extent would the department members find these busts suitable or unsuitable in the room? Would they be bothered by the eerie presence of these past leaders (and Elath, the ambassador and administrator) and symbols of government? Or by the constant unnerving gaze of the busts during department meetings and seminars? Would the figures instill more gravity into already serious discussions? When, if at all, would indifference and habituation develop toward the weird sculptures? Or would a cynical and sarcastic attitude emerge toward them?

In any event, I did not steal the busts from the Truman Institute's bomb shelter, nor did I move them anywhere. But I decided to find out how they got there and who created them. I was curious about the contradiction between the presence of the sculptures in the shelter—neglected, almost lonely as they were—and the gravity and formality emanating from them. Somebody invested much effort in creating them, and they obviously were meant to be proudly displayed in public. Why were they stored down here in the "underworld" of this building?

I approached the busts and examined them for any signature or marks indicating who had made them. Yes! The engravings HEXTER and MBH appeared on the back of the busts. The name Hexter sounded very familiar to me. After a few moments, I recalled that we have an endowed chair in the department named after Maurice B. Hexter. I went out of the shelter and connected to the internet (as there is no cellular reception in the underworld[8]) and found that

---

8. Interesting in this regard is the description of Nixon and Brezhnev's meeting in Hell. See Lebow (2003, chap. 1). This is a fictional story that Lebow wrote as a preface to his otherwise scholarly book.

188 EXPEDITION ESCAPE FROM THE CLASSROOM

Maurice B. Hexter, after whom the chair in our department is named, was a sculptor. I read his obituary in the *New York Times*. He died in 1990, at the age of ninety-nine (Fowler 1990). When he was fifty-nine, after a long career as a Jewish social and communal worker and philanthropy administrator in the United States and British Mandate Palestine, he discovered his true calling as a sculptor.

Laconic Formality: Tracing Hexter's Persona through Art and Archive

In the weeks that followed, I developed a slight obsession with Hexter and his sculptures in the Truman Institute's bomb shelter. I visited the fortified basement repeatedly, and after one of my visits I went to speak with someone from the institute's administration to ask for permission to take the busts to display them in the IR department: for what was their use if they were just "buried" in the bomb shelter of the Truman Institute? I was refused. I was told that the sculptures were given to the institute directly by Maurice Hexter. They were initially displayed in the foyer of the Truman Institute. But at some point a member of the institute's board of trustees was offended that they all represented "lefty, socialist" Mapai party (מפא"י) figures, and so in the name of current political correctness they were transferred to the shelter for storage. I was very surprised to learn that somebody considered Ben-Gurion or Meir "lefties," but the person at the administration office insisted that the busts were taken down to the shelter precisely because of that board member's dissatisfaction. I tried not to laugh and mentioned that in Budapest, there is a place called Memento Park—a "cemetery" for sculptures from the Communist era. It displays Soviet and Communist sculptures that were imposed on the Hungarian public space during the Communist period (Fustos and Kovacs 2008). Perhaps, I offered to my interlocutor from the Truman Institute, we should have a Memento Park of our own.

Even though my request to transfer the busts to the IR department was not granted by the powers that be (in IR, I was the department chair then, so I did not have to ask for anyone's approval), I kept coming to the Truman Institute's shelter almost daily to stare at the busts. I brought some of my colleagues and graduate students, who were convinced I was "completely off base" but were polite or surprised enough not to say so explicitly. I was fascinated by the ability to reverse the power relationship between me and the personas commemorated in the busts. *I* was the one who brought people to

Layers of Memory and Identity **189**

observe *them*; *I* could look straight into their hollow eyes; *I* could put my hand on their heads. And I wasn't alone in this fascination: my political theorist friend joked that he felt like grabbing their noses (and he did!),[9] and almost all the other colleagues I brought there also wanted to grab their noses or ears or rest their hand on the top of figures' heads. Some even made "silly faces" while staring directly into the busts' eyes. But even the nose- or ear-grabbers often looked at me first, as if asking for permission, and then performed their trick (I interpreted this as evidence of the power of the representation, à la Alfred Gell). The strong mimetic presence of the busts made everybody cautious when they first approached them—somewhat hesitant, curious, and careful not to damage these supposedly expensive, important, even sanctified artifacts. No one tried to move them.

The sculptures are very realistic, looking almost alive. The technical precision and mimetic element create a strong sense of encounter. But it is precisely these characteristics—along with the grayness of the marble—that greatly reduces the busts' artistic value and raises the desire to joke about them. There is an ambiguity in them, something not entirely understood or settled, but this is not a mystery related to some unpackable inner feature of the sitters themselves, or some complexity of their humanity that the observer struggles to interpret. The mystery I found in the Truman shelter busts was their over-realism, naiveté, and one-dimensionality.[10] I kept trying to seek something about them that didn't meet the eye, but I could not find it.

During this period, I also spent a great deal of time reading about Hexter and reviewing his letters and other documents kept in his personal archive at the National Library on the Giv'at Ram campus. Through my research, I

---

9. About busts' noses and the desire to grab them, see Nathaniel Hawthorne: "And it ought to make us shiver, the idea of leaving our features to be a dusty-white ghost among strangers of another generation, who will take our nose between their thumb and fingers (as we have seen men do by Caesar's), and infallibly break it off if they can do so without detection!" (Hawthorne 2009, 93).

10. Hexter, the sculptor, writes about this case in his autobiography: "A doctor I knew admired some of my work, . . . and asked if I would do a head of his wife. I said yes and we agreed on a fee. When I finished it his wife and daughter admired it greatly, but when the physician joined them, he looked it over for a minute or two and shook his head. Looking straight at his wife he said, 'Dear, you're not that good looking.' He didn't want it. (I'd love to have tapes of the pillow talk at their apartment after *that* showdown.)" (Hexter 1990, 171). Hexter did not go to court over this, and he kept the bust at his New York studio. I think I understand what that physician meant: Hexter's busts look too good, somewhat nonhuman, even in the accepted standards of the bust genre.

190   EXPEDITION ESCAPE FROM THE CLASSROOM

learned that he was the personal representative of the Jewish-American banker Felix Warburg in the management of the Jewish Agency in Palestine during the 1930s (the Jewish Agency was the unofficial "government" of the Jewish Yishuv during the Mandate). Warburg sent him to Palestine in 1929 to administer the Palestine Emergency Fund, following the 1929 Palestine Riots, as well as to guard against misapplication and corruption in the use of the money sent by the American Jewry. He then became an executive member and head of the colonization department of the Jewish Agency and served as the emissary of the non-Zionists in American Jewry to the British authorities during the discussions of the Peel Commission (1937)—the first official committee to discuss the partition of Palestine between Jews and Arabs. Hexter was also a member of the Hebrew University's board of trustees. He played an instrumental role during the Weizmann-Einstein-Magnes friction in the 1930s, when the famous scientist threatened to withdraw his support from the Hebrew University due to disagreements with its chancellor, Judah L. Magnes, about curriculum and faculty recruitment.

While in his position in the 1930s as the de facto treasurer of the Jewish Agency, Hexter got to know the heads of the Yishuv and even gained their trust. But Warburg did not trust *them* completely: he knew the Zionists were reading his cables to Hexter. Thus, when they had sensitive information to exchange, Hexter would have to take the train to Cairo and telephone Warburg from there (Hexter 1990, 87). I wondered about his mood on those trips and whether the long journeys were indeed worth the while. What secrets did he relay to Warburg? He did not share this in his autobiography. What he did relate in that book was, among other things, his acquaintance with figures such as Ben-Gurion, Weizmann, Meir, and Dayan, and his involvement in the Zionist settlement enterprises and colonization projects, such as the development of the Hula Valley near the Sea of Galilee or the settlement method of Tower and Stockade (Homa U-Migdal, ‎חומה ומגדל‎).

Reading Hexter's book and other sources about him revealed to me the difference between non-Zionists and anti-Zionists in those days. The non-Zionists among American Jews did not disapprove of Zionism and its efforts to obtain refuge for Jews in Palestine (unlike anti-Zionists). Still, they believed that a Jewish state should be avoided for the time being. Alternatively, they supported territorial solutions for Jews elsewhere, not just in Palestine (e.g., Australia, Canada, Dominican Republic). This objection to Jewish statehood was mainly due to their fear that the civic status of Jews in the Western world would be undermined if a Jewish state was established in Palestine (Parzen 1967, 222).

Layers of Memory and Identity   **191**

I cannot say precisely what drew me so powerfully to Hexter, the person. Indeed, through him I learned much about the history of the Yishuv in the 1930s. Also, he was an efficient and devoted "public servant," a trusted emissary, and something of a "Forrest Gump"—he seemed to have been everywhere and to have known everyone (Zionists and non-Zionists in Palestine, American philanthropists and bankers, British officials and politicians, Palestinian Arab leaders, and even German bureaucrats and a Caribbean tyrant). In terms of his personality, as revealed from his autobiography as well as his letters and other documents in his archive, he seems to have been a laconic, formal, introverted, and sometimes reserved person.[11] He was not revealed to me to be a brilliant humorist.[12] I even found an element of tedium in his letters to his Israeli friends in the 1970s and 1980s, such as Eliyahu Elath or Walter Eytan (former director general of the Israeli foreign office). They often included a clipped recent op-ed from the *New York Times* criticizing Israel and a comment (by Hexter) that things could not get worse in Israel or "Palestine," as he continued to call the country (although he was always surprised that things *did* get worse). Hexter, the man, was revealed to me as similar to the busts he created: official and formal in his style, somewhat stiff, gray, and predictable, very polished, and with only a small sense of self-irony.

Chasing Fiction: Hexter's Misidentified Bust and Imaginative Desires

Thus, when I found another bust of Hexter's in the storage room of the university's curator (in the bomb shelter of the Central Library), made of red-brown porphyry marble, I hoped it would be "Two-Gun" Cohen: Morris A. Cohen, a Jewish Polish-British-Canadian gangster and adventurer whose career peaked when he served as chief of security for Chinese president Sun Yat-sen in the 1920s. I felt that connecting Hexter to a colorful character like

---

11. In a letter of April 6, 1989, to Walter Eytan, the retired director general of the Israeli foreign office and Hexter's friend, Hexter writes, "A friend of mine, who is quite well to do, insists on wasting his money and has employed a ghostwriter to prepare my 'autobiography'" (Hexter 1989). Indeed, there is a discernable difference in style between the letters and the autobiography, which was written with the "editorial cooperation" of Murray Teigh Bloom.

12. About the 1936 Arab Revolt, "Hexter privately joked that the growing Arab casualty toll was due to the fact that 'for every Arab killed by the [British] military, seven Arabs die laughing at the ineptitude of the British,' but he still regarded Jewish inflexibility, not British laxity, as the primary cause of the troubles" (Medoff 2001, 73).

192   EXPEDITION ESCAPE FROM THE CLASSROOM

Two-Gun Cohen would "redeem" him from his grayness and rigidity. A metal label at the foot of the bust stated, "Maurice M. Cohen" (indeed, "Maurice" is not "Morris" and "M" is not "A," but I ignored that). Moreover, I saw a resemblance between the bust and the rogue Jewish adventurer, who always carried two guns on his person. The curator had no record or registry of the sitter or who sculpted the bust (although it was obviously a Hexter), so I hoped my wish would come true. What fascinated me especially about this was that apart from his actual adventures, Two-Gun Cohen is renowned for inventing stories about his supposed exploits and inspiring anyone who wrote about him to follow suit (Levy 2002). But why would Hexter sculpt him? Perhaps because Cohen was instrumental in convincing the Chinese government to at least stay neutral during the United Nations' 1947 Palestine partition vote. Cohen also knew Eliyahu Elath, Hexter's good friend, whose bust is now misidentified as Ephraim Katzir. Why not Cohen too? I thought.[13] Or maybe Hexter sculpted him because Hexter himself always carried two guns during his trips in Palestine.[14]

Eventually, however, I discovered the sitter was not Two-Gun Cohen—the label I found had obviously been intended for some other sculpture or portrait, likely lost over the decades. The director of the university's archive informed me that Maurice M. Cohen was a distinguished donor who received an honorary doctorate from the Hebrew University in 1990. And Hexter's

---

13. Cohen helped the Zionists already at the 1945 UN San Francisco Conference, when it was decided that Palestine would remain a mandated territory. "Lobbying efforts, orchestrated by the charismatic Morris Cohen, were critical to overcoming Arab opposition and winning over the Chinese." Interestingly Morris Cohen knew Eliyahu Elath, a Zionist diplomat then, and introduced him to key Chinese officials. In November 1947, when China's UN delegate Liu "announced that he intended to vote against the partition proposal . . . Cohen showed Liu a letter Sun Yat-Sen had sent him many years earlier thanking him for his services and saying that China would never do anything to harm the Jewish people. On the strength of the letter and after some discussion, Liu reversed his position on the partition proposal. While it is clear that he said he would not vote against partition, there is contradictory evidence as to whether he said he would vote for partition or merely abstain" (Goldstein 2004, 229, 231).

14. This is mentioned by Walter Eytan in a letter of November 1, 1988, that he sent to Hexter in response to a piece Hexter sent him about his days in Palestine: "Another thing I liked was your carrying a revolver, even two: I take it your gun toting days are now behind you" (Eytan 1988). In his autobiography Hexter says that he had two revolvers, one with British permit, as a member of the executive of the Jewish Agency, and another one unregistered, just in case the British repealed his gun permit. In addition, he had a boxer guard dog whom he named Thanatos (death) (Hexter 1990, 84–86).

Fig. 35. Eliyahu Elath with his bust, sculpted by Maurice B. Hexter. At the foyer of the Truman Institute (1976). Later, the bust was misidentified as Ephraim Katzir. (Photograph by Werner Braun. Courtesy of the Hebrew University Photo Archives.)

porphyry bust was of a Jewish-American industrialist named Robert I. Wishnick, a chemical products manufacturer from Connecticut who donated to many Jewish-American organizations as well as to the Hebrew University of Jerusalem. The bust appears in a 1973 catalog of Hexter's works, on the last page (Hexter 1973).

So ended the uncertainty about the sitter's identity, my foray into "fictional IR," and my attempt to instill some color into Hexter's historical personality.

A Technician or an Artist?

Hexter turned out to be a very competent communal administrator and, according to his own admission, a better technician than an artist.[15] Almost

---

15. "How good is my stuff? Some of it, I think, is very good, and some is pretty bad.

Fig. 36. "A Bust of an Oriental Jew," by Maurice B. Hexter (currently in the storage room). (Photograph by the author.)

all the people he sculpted were officials, politicians, community leaders, philanthropists, and also "generic" types such as the "Oriental Jew" (figs. 37 and 38), another bust of his that I found in the curator's storage. He never sculpted anyone as rogue as Two-Gun Cohen (unless you consider his lost/stolen/broken "Moshe Dayan" [see chapter 4], which was an attempt in that direction). But I so wished the porphyry bust to be Two-Gun Cohen, so I could breathe life into Hexter's legacy, adding a dynamic figure to his otherwise formal repertoire. By associating Hexter with a swashbuckling persona like Two-Gun Cohen, I wanted to introduce shades of intrigue and complexity, elevat-

---

When I was eighty, in 1971, Leonard Block gave me a marvelous birthday party, which started with an exhibit of many of my works at the Whitney Museum, then on to the Carlyle Hotel for dinner. John Bower, director of the museum and a great authority on American art, in a warming little talk—*I* was warmed—called me a 'gifted amateur whose works breathe the humanity of man himself.' I was 'not a great artist in the international sense,' he said, but I had impressive technical skills. A fair estimate, I think" (Hexter 1990, 171).

Fig 37. "A Bust of an Oriental Jew," with sculptor Maurice B. Hexter and Eliyahu Elath, during the dedication ceremony, March 6, 1968. (Photograph by Werner Braun. Courtesy of the Hebrew University Photo Archives.)

ing Hexter's work from mere formality to a tapestry of vibrant narratives. Of course, I also wanted to add such dimensions to my own research, but eventually my narrative became one of a failed attempt. Despite my hopes, the truth of the bust's identity remained distinct from my aspirations, leaving my quest to breathe life into Hexter's legacy an unfulfilled venture and reminding me of the fact that reality is sometimes nothing more than what we see.

Nonetheless, Passion and Emotion in Grayness

Perhaps what kept fascinating me was Hexter's deep and unrelenting *passion* for sculpting (even if formal and gray busts) and the question of why he spent so much time sculpting the Truman Institute's now forsaken marble figures (he probably had not imagined that this would happen to them). Each bust required an investment of many work hours—months, if not years. The minute detail and high level of technical artisanship in the figures indicate that Hexter tried to make them look as dignified and beautiful as possible and hoped that the sculptures would commemorate the sitters long after their deaths. He was proud of these busts (Hexter 1976). I felt sorry for him that his dear work was so treated.

Hexter did not *have* to sculpt these Zionist leaders; he chose to do so. Sculpting usually did not bring him any material benefit—like many other

196 EXPEDITION ESCAPE FROM THE CLASSROOM

of his works that he donated to various institutions in the United States and Israel, he gave these busts to the Truman Institute (plus the lost/stolen statue of Moshe Dayan).[16] The Truman Institute's busts were donated after three of the five sitters had finished serving in their official positions (Ben-Gurion died in 1973), so that, to a large extent, they no longer had political clout (Hexter 1990, viii). To me, the busts represented an emotional connection the sculptor felt to those represented and to the history they symbolized. "Looking back," he writes, "I can see that the years in Palestine were the happiest in my life. In spite of the great problems and constant dangers, I have never felt so alive" (1990, 116–17). Reading this, the busts are revealed as a personal mea culpa from Hexter to Zionism and its historical leaders,[17] and perhaps also as a lamentation for a lost period and opportunity, a representation of a path not taken. They are also a sculptural expression of his feelings of appreciation and friendship.

One can clearly sense his misgivings and undecisive approach to Israel throughout his letters and autobiography. During a visit to Israel in 1949, Ben-Gurion offered to appoint him minister of welfare in his government (he had a PhD in social work). Hexter was flattered by the offer and saw it as a golden opportunity to employ his experience and education as a social

---

16. He tells in his autobiography that some of his sculptures were sold for tens of thousands of dollars (Hexter 1990, 170). In 1979, his bust of Egyptian president Anwar Sadat won the gold medal of the American National Sculpture Society. The bust was sold to the Aspen Institute, but its whereabouts are unknown today (email correspondence with the Aspen Institute). Hexter tells in a letter to Lady Rosemary d'Avigdor-Goldsmid (May 9, 1979) that the Egyptian ambassador to the United States inquired "what it would cost to have 1,000 miniatures made in bronze [of that bust] so that President Sadat can distribute them to friends." It does not seem that the initiative materialized. Hexter decided to sculpt Sadat "the day he announced his intention to visit Israel to begin the peace discussion" (Hexter 1987, 3). However, he probably never made a bust of Menachem Begin, Sadat's partner in the peace process, because he considered him "the greatest danger to our people ever, surpassing even Hitler. . . . He is a mad man and has led us down into a morass from which I fear there is no escape unless there is a sharp change in the thinking of the vast mass of oriental immigrants . . . [whose anti-Muslim memories] Begin was shrewd enough to corral and exploit" (Hexter 1982).

17. In 1937, "an American non-Zionist and a member of the Jewish Agency's executive, Maurice Hexter supplied the anti-Zionist American consul in Jerusalem, George Wadsworth, with antinational propaganda. Hexter informed Wadsworth of the trepidation with which western Jewry regarded the establishment of a Jewish state under the leadership of 'persecuted and less culturally advanced East European Jewry.' Wadsworth absolutely concurred and relayed the substance of his informant's remarks to Secretary of State Cordell Hull" (Knee 1977, 218).

worker. But Hexter's considerations against taking the offer prevailed over the considerations in favor. In fact, the counter-considerations were a "persistent dark cloud." For, as his wife argued, "[The Israelis] had just been through one war and others were likely." Had he been single, he told Ben-Gurion, nothing would have stopped him from accepting the offer (Hexter 1990, 133). At a time when I had to decide whether to stay in Israel or leave for Canada and for similar reasons to the "persistent dark cloud" of violence over this country, I empathized with Hexter. Finally, I managed to see something more than meets the eye in his busts.

The Element of Historical Coincidence

What further increased my interest in Hexter was the story of how he learned to sculpt. This story points to the element of coincidence in history. Historical chance is a familiar phenomenon, almost taken for granted, and we are all aware of countless episodes of coincidences, some more important and some less (consider the unintended contribution of the Truman Institute to the Oslo accords, discussed in note 3 of this chapter). But Hexter's story contains a fascinating accidental element in how he was exposed to the world of professional sculpting. It illustrates how great historical changes might affect the life of a person who seems far from them (in this case, Hexter), and continue to resonate even decades later, in another place and context, to touch another person's life (in this case, mine).

The story of how Hexter turned from being a communal administrator, manager of philanthropic enterprises and funds, and social worker into a sculptor begins with the Évian Conference, convened in 1938 to discuss the problem of Jewish refugees from Germany. Most of the countries that participated in the conference were unwilling to increase the quota of refugees they claimed to be able to receive. The Dominican Republic stood out in this context, declaring it was ready to accept 100,000 Jewish refugees. A year earlier, the ruler of the Dominican Republic, General Rafael Trujillo, had massacred a large number of Haitians (Haiti shares with the Dominican Republic the territory of the Caribbean island of Hispaniola). His forces murdered between 17,000 and 35,000 Haitians due to racist motives and a desire to preserve the whiteness and Christianity of the Dominican Republic. (Trujillo disliked the voodoo rites of the Haitians who "infiltrated" his country. One of the more expressive busts Hexter sculpted is called "Voodoo Priest," made of

198   EXPEDITION ESCAPE FROM THE CLASSROOM

Dominican black granite. See the image in Hexter 1987, 61.) The United States occupied the Dominican Republic between 1916 and 1924, and the US administration kept its eye open to what was happening there even after its forces were evacuated. In an attempt to clear himself of the image of a bloodthirsty tyrant and influence, Trujillo declared his readiness to absorb the German Jewish refugees.

About 5,000 Jewish refugees were eventually granted visas by the Dominican Republic, but only about 700 settled there in a rural locality called Sosúa. Maurice Hexter, who had already returned to the United States from Palestine and now (1939) worked for the Joint Distribution Committee (JDC; a Jewish organization established during World War I to help Jewish war refugees), was appointed by the organization as its liaison to this Jewish colony in the Dominican Republic. The JDC trained the Jewish colonists in Sosúa in farming and agriculture, among other things, by bringing Jewish instructors from the kibbutzim in Palestine. Hexter was very helpful in this regard thanks to his earlier heading of the colonization department of the Jewish Agency. In the Dominican Republic, Hexter also forged a relationship of trust and friendship with General Trujillo (Wells 2009; Hexter 1990, 2 and 124–26). An incident during one of Hexter's visits to the Dominican Republic in 1948 eventually led to his sculpting (and to my finding his busts in the bomb shelter, almost seventy years later):

> While I was wandering around the island during one visit, I came across an Italian sculptor working in stone. He was there because Trujillo felt that the marble deposits of his country should become better known. Since he always believed in direct action—good and bad—he imported three Italian experts to exploit the deposits. One of them was the sculptor.
>
> He was generous with his time. He showed me the various tools—hammers, points, chisels, rifflers—used in working with stone, even permitted me to work in one of the studios. My early works weren't very good, but I fell in love with the process. I felt a marvelous inner peace carving stone. . . .
>
> Stone sculpture *endures*, my Italian friend pointed out, which can't be said of bronze, for example. Bronze was frequently melted down for weapons in times of war. As my work improved, he suggested that . . . I ought to visit his native city, Pietrasanta, where there was a remarkable school. (Hexter 1990, 149–50)

Indeed, Hexter retired from Jewish communal work toward the end of the 1950s and later began sculpting. He rented a studio in Pietrasanta, where he sculpted the busts of the Zionist leaders that I found in the Truman Institute's shelter.

The Unintended Art Installation in the Bomb Shelter and the Night Train to Cairo

The visit to the bomb shelter in April 2018 with my students runs well, despite my initial fears that my sorrow would take over me. My enthusiasm and passion are unmistakable, and the students can also perceive my emotional attachment to the historical figures and events. It's clear they are listening with empathy, attempting to process their thoughts on these individuals, artifacts, and historical occurrences: Hexter, his busts, General Trujilo and the Jews of Sosúa, Two-Gun Cohen and my misidentification of the bust of Wishnick, and the misrepresentation of Eliyahu Elath. When I finish my narration, one student says she thinks this is actually a perfect place for the busts: in the eerie environment of the shelter, the row of four gray sculptures under the supervision of President Truman's watchful gaze is an unintentional art installation. She tells us about a video installation she recently saw in the Tel Aviv museum in which people in an apartment building in Tel Aviv go endlessly down the stairwell—hurrying, stampeding, and shoving—into the shelter of the building as a siren howls in the background. The tenants never reached the shelter, though, and were cursed to continue "going down" endlessly. As opposed to those civilians who cannot reach the shelter, the student says, these "heads of the nation" are permanently safe in the concrete underworld of the Truman Institute. Perhaps, she adds, if our *living* leaders were housed in similar conditions, they would be more critical about going to wars and undertaking military "operations" every few years. I see that most of the other students do not like what she said. The common perception in Israel is that such events are enforced on us, and this is not a matter of choice. Several other students are distressed that such "national symbols" are treated so disrespectfully, being forsaken in such a grim place. After hearing my stories about the busts and their creator, a few say they will write to the university's management asking that the busts be taken out of the shelter and presented in a more appropriate place.

• • •

I don't think they ever wrote these letters, as the busts remained in the shelter for more than a year after that visit. Surprisingly, they are now (2023)

EXPEDITION ESCAPE FROM THE CLASSROOM

again in the institute's foyer, but that was because the administration of the institute wanted to make *me* happy when I became the acting director of the Truman Institute in 2019. In fact, I wasn't entirely pleased with this move—the story of the busts and their creator is much better told in the bomb shelter. While I felt sorry that Hexter's work was stored in the underworld of the institute, I tended to agree with the student who said that the whole shelter scene was unintentionally artful, and with some political lessons to it too. It was much more effective than the busts' current "respectable" presentation in the entry to the institute, and even effective than displaying the busts in the IR seminar room would have been. But the transfer of the busts to the foyer, which was intended as a surprise for me, the new director, cost the institute quite a bit of money, and I did not want it to spend this sum again to return them to the shelter. While I am no longer the acting director (I just filled in for the 2018–19 academic year), the busts remained at the entrance to the institute's lobby.

In any event, a large part of the resonance of their presence in the shelter was related to the fact that they were *banished* there due to an impulse of a self-important person (to whose will others ascribed importance) and not because anyone disliked them simply on aesthetic grounds.[18] Thus, the whole affair contained an excellent lesson on the concept and practice of importance.

Busts, Age, and Wisdom

During the tour in April 2018, as I am telling the students how Hexter first arrived in Palestine in 1929, his colonization initiatives and financial responsibilities here, and his (indecisive) non-Zionism, one student suddenly interjects and asks why I think Hexter sculpted these people as they looked when they were older adults. After all, in the 1930s, when Hexter served in the

---

18. Once, during a visit to the shelter with a colleague from overseas, my visitor exclaimed, "They are hideous!" She found the busts to be excessively pompous and believed they misrepresented the subjects, whom she recalled as more humble and intelligent leaders. Her exclamation reminded me of a similar response, by Dr. Zaius, the ape Minister of Science and Chief Defender of the Faith, in the 1970 film *Beneath the Planet of the Apes* (director Ted Post): "They are obscene!" he exclaims, as the invading army of the apes rushes through the Hall of [human] Leaders in subterranean New York City. They smash the busts of the human leaders one by one (at 1:28:32 in the film).

Jewish Agency, the sitters were much younger. "Interesting," I say. "In fact, they did not 'sit' for Hexter—he made the busts using photographs of the notables; they did not come to his studio. So why didn't he indeed use photographs of them when younger?" I admit that I had never thought about this before. "What do you think?" I return the question to the student. "Well," he says, "perhaps he made them as old people because old age symbolizes wisdom and authority. But if I were to become a bust one day," he adds, "I rather want to be represented as a young and muscular man. Also, I think that most of people's brightest reflections and ideas arrive before age thirty." (He was twenty-six.)

A week or so after this, when I went to check on Tagore's bust in the Humanities courtyard, I thought about what that student had said about old age and wisdom. Tagore, whom Ramkinkar Baij purposefully sculpted as "sad" and weary, is seen as wise and, in certain respects, even authoritative (although he also looks despairing and burdened). This is precisely because Baij made him so human and distinctive. But while Hexter sculpted his busts as relatively older people, they do not look weary or sad. They seem like a part of a series of "grays" and they all have a similar smile, in this way seeming more like clones than unique and individual sculptures. Despite this, their faces show very little sign of the difficulties they must have encountered in their years of political and public service and responsibility. Notably, I see no sign of burden, regret, or doubt in their faces. Of course, marble does not change with age (unlike bronze), and so their faces remain frozen in time. Whereas the Tagore bust, outside in the courtyard, is exposed to the elements, Hexter's busts were protected in the building and its shelter, and thus remained intact. But even considering all this, his busts never convinced me as representations of wisdom and authority.

Solving Mysteries after the Tour

Following the April 2018 class trip to the Truman Institute busts, the student who asked about the "age" of the busts sent me an email:

> When you told us that Hexter sometimes took the train to Cairo to report to Warburg, I was startled, because even today, almost a century later, our farthest-reaching trains are to Beer Sheva and Sderot. Cairo is out of the question. Moreover, trains are a subject which I think you could have de-

202   EXPEDITION ESCAPE FROM THE CLASSROOM

> veloped further in the context of consolidation of territorial control and economic development [and free travel and international connections, I thought]. Lastly, during the tour, I had the impression that I was the only one in the group who did not know that Palestine was connected by train to Egypt.

He was right. No one in the class raised an eyebrow or asked anything about the train line to Cairo that I casually mentioned (for example, no one wondered how the passengers crossed the Suez Canal). I must admit that I, too, when reading Hexter's book, did not check the practicalities of the train ride in detail.[19] I just assumed there was a train (and I didn't give a single thought to the—important, in hindsight—question of the Suez crossing).

This student, stauncher than the rest of us, went to the National Library in Giv'at Ram and asked to borrow Paul Cotterell's book *The Railways of Palestine and Israel* (1984), which is mentioned in the Hebrew Wikipedia entry on the British Mandate Palestine Rail Company as a "major [information] source" for the entry. The library indeed had the book, but the student said the librarians had him "left high and dry" for an hour or so until they brought the book from the closed stacks. After he skimmed through the book (which is not for loan), he corroborated the Wikipedia entry and even sent me a photo of the timetable of the Mandate-era train. He also solved the mystery about the canal crossing: initially, there was a shuttle service at El-Qantara, and passengers had to board another train on the western bank of the canal. It was only in the 1940s, after the rebuilding of the El Ferdan Bridge, that direct railway trips between Palestine and Egypt became available.[20] Unrelatedly (or, on second thought, perhaps indeed relatedly), he also discovered that the Egyptian town of El-Qantara has a British War Cemetery too—"Kantara Indian Cemetery Memorial, dedicated to the 283 Indian casualties originally buried or commemorated in Kantara Indian Cemetery, which in 1961 *was declared unmaintainable.*"[21]

I was happy he checked all this: first, it signified that he carefully listened to what I said during the visit to the shelter—not a thing to be taken lightly. I was happy that he had this passion for the truth and fact-checking. Second, it seemed to prove that he, too, was emotionally moved by the visit to the

---

19. Email correspondence with Amit Leibson.
20. Email correspondence with Amit Leibson.
21. See https://www.cwgc.org/visit-us/find-cemeteries-memorials/cemetery-details/54500/kantara-war-memorial-cemetery/ (italics added).

shelter busts. Otherwise, why would he go through all the trouble of going to the National Library, far from Mt. Scopus, to check whether indeed there was a train to Cairo?

• • •

When I sat to write this chapter a few years after the depicted events, I realized how I valued that trip with the students to the Truman Institute, how their attentive listening, comments, thoughts, associations, and interest in the story of Hexter, the busts, and their banishment to the bomb shelter helped me pass another day during the painful period right after my divorce. But beyond that, this and other visits to the bomb shelter—and even trips to the foyer of the Truman Institute after the busts were restored to the "world of the living"—all reminded me of the pain I have carried for years now stemming from my realization that my ex-wife had been right in many ways.

The conflict in this land is terrible and is ingrained in people's identity, emotions, basic thinking, and understanding of the world. Israel's is a deep-seated culture of violence. But this was not enough to have me leave for Canada—a country with its own various forms of colonial violence and injustice. And while I am connected—perhaps too connected—to this campus, it, too, will never be my genuine "home." It is an institution, not an ideal—and an institution that exists under an ever-stronger regime of neoliberal managerialism and student-customer satisfaction. There are clear political limits to what I can discuss with my students, and those limits will probably increase over the years until I retire. And my colleagues at times seem as "fossilized" as the busts—I cannot count on most of them to be meaningful interlocutors. The Truman Institute busts highlighted my solitude in this place and my ambivalence toward it. But they also sometimes provided me with a much-needed laugh and an opportunity for human connection. And despite my ironic response to Hexter, I also discovered shared experiences and dilemmas in his story. And this, too, was something that was worthwhile.

Conclusions

ANALYTICAL AXES, WRITING DRAWBACKS, AND THE AUTHOR-BOOK SEPARATION

This book has been an exploration of certain places and spaces within Hebrew University's Mt. Scopus campus in Jerusalem. It is also an introspective reflection on my interactions with students and my dealings with department colleagues, university management, and the discipline of International Relations. The campus outings grew out of a teaching anxiety I experienced in my mid-forties, and even though they did not completely cure my anxiety, they did ameliorate my uneasiness through the act of "escaping" the regimented environment of the classroom (yes, even to the bomb shelter . . .) and adding a more dynamic and lively dimension to some of my courses. Gradually, the sporadic outings turned into a planned—but still relatively flexible[1]—course ("The Mt. Scopus Enclave") and resulted in this book, which is the first research text I had written in eight years, having distanced myself from writing. Through my record of these journeys, I seek to bring to light my teaching anxiety and its causes, to establish meaningful connections with readers and create empathy in our discipline, and to inculcate critical observation skills and spatial curiosity through the practice of IR-izing places and objects in the campus.

In this concluding chapter, I expand on the conceptual logic of the four outings presented here. Then, I will consider the process of writing this book in terms of the experience of regaining some self-confidence as an author.

---

1. Flexibility was maintained by nurturing an element of improvision and surprise in the course. For example, each year I sent reading materials before and after the tours, depending on the various developments and conversations during the outings themselves. In essence, I asked the students to read backward: first come to the class/tour and read after it and compare the experience of the outing to the readings. On other occasions, I asked the students to write tour reports after each outing and to find relevant reading materials for these reports. Thus, we effectively created the syllabus of the course together.

Conclusions **205**

Finally, I will turn to the issue of how to create some separation between author and text in autoethnographic, narrative, and personal writing. Such separation is important for writers to maintain forward momentum and not remain "locked" within a certain book—or, to use a term from chapter 1 of this book, to avoid becoming "bolted" to your text.

Conceptual Axes for the Four Outings

Dr. Orit Gazit, my friend and colleague in the Department of International Relations here at Jerusalem, sharply observed that the outing chapters revolve around three main conceptual axes: (1) space / history-politics-security; (2) space / mind-and-knowledge-production; and (3) space/profession. By this, she meant that the spaces of the campus are environments that several other factors and themes interact with and this interaction creates a motion that propels the outings. These axes embody the three goals of the book in different formulations, and they provide a basis for a positivist-analytical conceptualization of the book's logic. In the following four subsections, I consider the tours of each chapter and how the axes manifest in them and propel them.

British Jerusalem War Cemetery Tour

The tour to the British Jerusalem War Cemetery in chapter 2 revolves mainly around the space / history-politics-security axis.

Themes of Space

HETEROTOPY: The cemetery is first and foremost a heterotopic space. It is a "space of otherness." Located adjacent to the university campus, it blends elements of Jerusalem's landscape with the physical characteristics of English and Australian environments (namely, gardening, architecture, monuments). It is both local and foreign, symbolizing a connection between different cultures, geographies, and nations. Moreover, the fact that very similar cemeteries exist also in the Gaza Strip creates interesting and thought-provoking parallels and comparisons between "our" cemetery at Mt. Scopus and these sites in "enemy" territory.

INVISIBILITY OF SPACE: Despite its proximity and accessibility, the cemetery remains largely unnoticed by the students. This "invisibility" highlights how certain spaces can be disregarded or suppressed in daily life, perhaps due to their association with death, war, or foreignness.

Themes of History

MILITARY BURIAL HISTORY: The cemetery serves as a testament to the British conquest of Palestine from the Ottomans during World War I, and more generally to the human cost of war. By visiting the site, students confront the layers of history embedded in their environment, spanning different nationalities and eras. They are exposed to the history of military burial and learn about the relative modernity of this practice, through which we also engage with various other issues, such as the clock and war, war as a series of events and fronts, and the commemoration of the war dead.

IMPERIAL HISTORY: The cemetery's existence here speaks to the geopolitical power dynamics and imperial legacies that shaped the Middle East. Its maintenance by the Commonwealth War Graves Commission symbolizes an ongoing connection to imperial history.

THE BOTANICAL GARDEN'S LOCATION: The historical story on how the controversy between the Hebrew University and the Australian government in the 1930s eventually led to the planting of the botanical garden in its current location, within the campus, and not on the original plot, beneath the cemetery's Australian monument, resonates with political and security issues that were dealt with in chapter 3.

MY PERSONAL CONNECTION: My private visits and personal connection with the cemetery add another historical layer, blending personal experience with the broader historical context, as well as with the history of the outings to the cemetery within the university course. Therefore, the stories and experiences I share with the students add to an everyday history of this site (think, the incident with the dog).

Themes of Politics

BLURRED BOUNDARIES: The burial of both imperial and enemy soldiers within the same grounds prompts reflection on the often fluid nature of political allegiances and enmities, illustrating how war can blur lines between friend and foe.

LEGAL STATUS OF THE PLACE: The lack of orderly land registration of this site (see note 12 of chapter 2) attests to the possible continuation of con-

Conclusions **207**

flict between Britain and Israel over landownership rights, stemming from the location of the cemetery in the Mt. Scopus enclave and Britain's reluctance to acknowledge Israeli sovereignty in this space. This disagreement led to frictions between the two states during the 1950s and 1960s over British access to the cemetery, and today it is exemplified by the fact that the annual Memorial Day ceremony here takes place on the Saturday before November 11, probably to discourage the participation of official Israeli representatives, due to the Jewish Sabbath. Notably, Israeli officials do participate in the ceremonies in other British cemeteries throughout the country.

THE "USE" OF THE CEMETERY: Youths from Issawiya use the cemetery for drinking and smoking at night. This crowded neighborhood lacks open spaces and suffers from an intentional neglect on the part of Israeli authorities. Consequently, the cemetery provides an accessible open space for the nocturnal gathering of these youths.

ABUSE OF THE WAR DEAD FOR POLITICAL PURPOSES: The fasces symbol on the Italian soldiers' tombs attests to the abuse of the war dead by imposing an anachronistic political meaning over history. The burial of Bar-Kosevah's soldiers in an official Israeli military service serve a similar purpose.

Themes of Security

SIGNIFICANCE OF THE SOLDIER'S BODY: Exploring the value and symbolism of the fallen soldier's body, as well as the efforts states are willing to exert in order to retrieve and identify lost soldier bodies, raises questions about national security, sacrifice, and the embodiment of military values.

WAR'S AFTERMATH: The mixed burial of foes and friends also serves as a reminder of the shared human costs of conflict and the necessity for reconciliation and healing after the chaos of war (recall the alleged words of Ataturk about the "Johnnies" and the "Mehmets" and their healing impact on Australia and New Zealand).

IR-IZATION PROCESS: The effort to IR-ize the location emphasizes how international relations concepts are not merely theoretical but are embedded in concrete physical sites, reinforcing the importance of spatial and material awareness.

Summary of the Cemetery Tour

Thus, revolving around the space / history-politics-security axis, the tour of the British Jerusalem War Cemetery acts as a multidimensional case study,

208 EXPEDITION ESCAPE FROM THE CLASSROOM

offering unique insights into how space, history, politics, and security interact. It's not merely an academic exercise but a practical exploration of complex themes that are intended to resonate with both students and readers. By making visible the often-invisible threads connecting these elements, it fosters a critical understanding of political dynamics and personal connection to broader world events. The site thus bridges historical memories with contemporary realities, and personal reflections with collective national and international narratives.

Tour of the Botanical Garden

In the third chapter, the tour of the botanical garden on campus turns mainly on the space/profession axis.

Themes of Space

VIRTUAL VERSUS PHYSICAL SPACE: The transition from physical to virtual teaching during the COVID-19 pandemic alters the spatial experience of the botanical garden. Virtual platforms like Google Street View and Google Earth both enable and limit the experience, filtering the sensory richness of the space yet becoming necessary tools in the face of challenges such as lockdowns and extreme weather conditions that evolve here due to climate change.

SPATIAL POLITICS: The limited resolution and outdated imagery of Israel on international web platforms bring up questions about digital obscuring and its impact on spatial transparency. This political aspect of space emphasizes how control and representation of space can be wielded as a form of power.

SPACE AND IDENTITY: The COVID-19 pandemic's impact on relationships with physical spaces, such as the Mt. Scopus campus, has led to some volatility in my perceptions of place and personal identity. The traditional connections I had with physical spaces are challenged, leading to reflections on the essence and complexities of space.

INTERCONNECTED SPACES: The botanical garden's juxtaposition with the Palestinian neighborhood of Issawiya illustrates the inseparability of spaces that might appear distinct. Their interwoven nature highlights contrasts and tensions, such as certitude versus illusion and security versus danger, showing how space can reflect broader social and political realities. Seen as inter-

Conclusions **209**

connected with Issawiya, the garden is a geography of danger and a space for viewing oppression outside it. Moreover, the recurring violent incidents within Issawiya and from it turn the garden into a frontier where boundaries blur between the supposedly peaceful and orderly, on the one hand, and the violence-ridden areas, on the other hand.

KNOWABLE SCIENTIFIC SPACE: The garden is mapped and ordered according to various phytosociological areas, and every plant in it is scientifically known. In this way, the garden served in the 1930s and 1940s as an epistemic space that anchored Zionist landownership claims in scientific knowledge. Today, deserted by science, its meticulous and orderly organization exemplifies a botanical "mini-Israel" to the visitor and gives meaning to the otherwise imagined notion of "country."

Themes of Profession

THE ROLE OF EDUCATOR: The chapter reflects my conscious efforts to bring the complexities of the garden to the students' attention, aiming to reveal the political and disciplinary questions that it embodies. The educator's profession here involves not merely conveying information but fostering critical thinking and empathy with the residents of Issawiya due to their systemic discrimination and oppression. Yet, their often-violent resistance to this oppression complicates my own ability to empathize with them (recall, the harm to the garden due to Molotov cocktails), let alone the ability of many of the students to empathize. While I belong to the powerful side, my job is nonetheless to open my mind to the plight of the residents and share my experiences and thoughts with the class, a move that is received by some of my students with animosity.

MORAL AND ETHICAL CHALLENGES: Contemplation of rootedness, empathy, resistance to violence, and the acknowledgment of systemic discrimination and oppression presents a complex professional challenge. Educating within such a conflicted context requires a careful balance between academic insight and moral responsibility.

IR-IZATION OF SPACE: The chapter emphasizes the process of integrating IR perspectives into the study of the botanical garden. IR-izing the garden brings political theories into the study of the physical environment, bridging academia with real-world situations. By exposing the students to the colonial and imperial histories of botanical gardens in general, I try to capture the distinct nature of the garden, which nonetheless served colonial purposes

210   EXPEDITION ESCAPE FROM THE CLASSROOM

but not in the prevalent imperial manner of acclimatizing beneficial plants or showcasing the splendor of the empire at the metropolitan center. The colonial purpose of our garden rested mainly in its being a research center for understanding the causes of deforestation in Palestine and examining the means necessary to return the "authentic" floral landscape of the land.

BOTANICAL LEGACY AND TEACHING ANXIETY: The comparison between the bond among the early Hebrew University botanists and their students and my current relationship with IR students represents my longing for deeper professional connections. This reflects the anxiety of teaching political subjects, where the quest for meaningful connection with students is a persistent challenge.

Summary of the Botanical Garden Tour

The virtual tour of the Mt. Scopus Botanical Garden acts as a multifaceted exploration of space and the profession of academic education. By interweaving spatial analysis with the intricacies of teaching international relations, the chapter invites readers to reflect on the complexity of seemingly simple spaces. The garden becomes not only a site of botanical interest but also a miniature of broader social, political, and ethical dilemmas. The space/profession axis uncovers the deeply interconnected nature of location and the task of education, emphasizing the educator's vital role in joining the physical with the theoretical and moral realms. The botanical garden thus transcends its immediate function, symbolizing the interconnected challenges and responsibilities faced by educators and students alike within the Mt. Scopus enclave campus, which, supposedly uninvolved, overlooks the occupation and oppression of the Palestinians in Issawiya.

Bust Tour

The chapter on the enigma of busts and the campus bust hunt revolves mainly along the space / mind-and-knowledge-production axis, but it also explores themes around the space / history-security-politics axis. I explore both below.

Space / Mind-and-Knowledge-Production Axis

Themes of Space

THE PLACEMENT OF BUSTS: The placement of busts, such as the one of Rabindranath Tagore, within the campus represents the merger of tangible space with intellectual or mental space. The bust symbolizes cerebral power and authority, ideas, histories, and politics, thereby creating an environment where physical space becomes a medium for intellectual exploration and cultural exchange.

THE SEARCH FOR MISSING BUSTS: Looking for the missing or stolen busts of Moshe Dayan and Elisabeth, Queen of the Belgians, takes us to various hidden corners and areas of the campus (e.g., the Institute of Archaeology) and adds a layer of intrigue and mystery to the campus, reflecting underlying social or political peculiarities.

Themes of Mind and Knowledge Production

THE IDEA OF STUDYING "BUSTOLOGY": This idea as a subject of contemplation informs the mind and knowledge aspect within the axis of this chapter. The presence of busts in an academic environment like the Mt. Scopus campus connects the physical and mental spaces, where objects of art/commemoration become a gateway to intellectual curiosity and philosophical inquiry. By engaging with bustology and introducing it to my students, I expand the boundaries of traditional disciplinary thinking, interweaving subjects like art, commemoration, power, history, politics, and philosophy. This de Certeau-ian "poaching" from different fields emphasizes a cross-disciplinary approach that feeds into innovative knowledge production and knowledge transmission. In venturing beyond IR to invent and undertake "bustology," I highlight the dynamic nature of knowledge production (but also treat this process with some humor).

INFLUENCE ON TEACHING AND STUDENT ENGAGEMENT: Taking students out of the conventional classroom setting to seek and observe these head sculptures throughout the campus creates a new type of learning environment, which includes walking from one bust to another (with all the beneficial aspects of walking as a learning method). This conceptual space transcends the limitations of structured learning, fostering curiosity, critical thinking, tactile knowledge, and a personalized connection to the subject matter and the expanses of the campus.

Space / History-Security-Politics Axis

Themes of Space

SPACES OUTSIDE THE CAMPUS: The development of bustology or the "introduction to busts" also takes us to Versailles, where Bernini's famous bust of Louis XIV is displayed; to Richmond, Virginia, to the Poe Museum

212   EXPEDITION ESCAPE FROM THE CLASSROOM

and the Raven Inn to recall the story of the theft of Edgar Allan Poe's bust and the literary ransom; and to nineteenth-century London, to help Sherlock Holmes solve the mystery of the "Six Napoleons" or, more currently, the "Six Thatchers." Student smartphones and more accurate imagery of these places on Google Earth and Google Street View help us to compare our virtual Mt. Scopus campus to locations outside of Israel.

Themes of History

HISTORICAL FIGURES: Busts serve as durable monuments to historical figures, encapsulating the ideologies, struggles, and societal roles they played. The Louis XIV bust stands as a representation of sovereign power and the enigma of legitimacy, weaving historical monarchy with contemporary governance. On our campus, the bust of Theodor Herzl at the entrance to the Faculty of Law building exemplifies the role of Orientalism in nineteenth-century Zionism with the Assyrian beard "Herzl" wears.

Themes of Politics

Busts like that of Tagore or Herzl acquire political meaning when they are used to explore the colonial history of India with the students, some of whom are colonial subjects themselves (e.g., East Jerusalemites). This requires extra sensitivity and contemplation. The Tagore bust also becomes a political tool, as seen in India's international "bust diplomacy" campaign. Busts can thus symbolize alliances, cultural connections, and geopolitical intentions. Studying Herzl's bust can lead to a discussion of *Altneuland*, a novel about a Zionist utopia; most students are vaguely aware of the novel but do not realize how different current Israel is from the country depicted in the novel.

Themes of Security and Power

The exploration of power and violence, as seen through the busts, links to broader security concerns within the political landscape. The sovereign power symbolized by Louis XIV's bust connects to the foundational violence that underpins political authority, raising questions about security, control, and the paradoxes of power. The Arthur Conan Doyle story "The Adventure of the Six Napoleons" exemplifies Foucault's notion of politics as a continuation of war by other means. The bust of Moshe Dayan, missing or stolen from

Conclusions   **213**

our campus, resonates with his obituary for Roee Rothberg, which I quote in chapter 3. Dayan's words—that we, Israelis, are a generation of settlers who conquered the land from the Palestinians and therefore shouldn't be surprised at Palestinian hatred of us—express a truth that almost cannot be uttered here today. Thus, Dayan's words have disappeared in much the same way his bust has.

Summary of the Bust Tour

Hence, the chapter's engagement with busts extends into an examination of the spatial connections between the mind and the environment, the multidimensional exploration of knowledge, and the intricate weaving of space with history, security, and politics. I try to show how curiosity and innovative thinking can transform static physical objects into dynamic symbols, inviting readers and students to journey beyond traditional academic boundaries.

The Truman Institute Outing

The last outing, to the Truman Institute, discussed in chapter 5, mainly deals with the space / profession and space / mind-and-knowledge-production axes.

Themes of Space

INFLUENCE ON PERSONAL REFLECTION: The rooftop of the Truman Institute conjures reminders of key life decisions and occurrences—the conversation with my ex-wife on the view from the rooftop and the recollection of my father's PhD awarding ceremony. This physical location becomes imbued with emotional significance, shaping my connection to and understanding of the campus where I work and write.

PERSONAL AND POLITICAL RESONANCE: The story of Hexter's decision not to immigrate to Israel parallels my own non-immigration to Canada, which culminated in divorce. This personal history intertwines with broader historical and political contexts, creating a layered narrative that resonates deeply with the space of the Truman Institute.

Themes of Mind–Knowledge Production

MARBLE BUSTS AS EMOTIONAL CATALYSTS: The gray marble busts of Zionist leaders sculpted by Maurice B. Hexter serve as complex emotional

214　EXPEDITION ESCAPE FROM THE CLASSROOM

triggers. Their "hyperrealistic" and "Soviet" appearance generates in me an uncanny feeling, connecting to personal and political narratives.

HEXTER'S COMPLEX RELATIONSHIP WITH ZIONISM: Hexter's multifaceted connections to Zionism and Israel reflects his roles as both an active participant and a reluctant contributor. His story resonates with my own conflicting feelings about Israel and the Hebrew University, illustrating the personal dimensions of historical and political narratives.

CREATIVITY, IMAGINATION, AND THE EXPLORATION OF IDENTITY: The imaginative story I tell about a supposed bust of the gangster and adventurer Two-Gun Cohen reflects a creative engagement with historical artifacts. This playful narrative not only speaks to my personal fears and aspirations but also illustrates academic freedom's potential to foster innovative thinking.

LEARNING THROUGH "IDLENESS" AND REFLECTION: The reflective engagement with these busts and the creative process of story- and myth-making demonstrate a unique approach to learning. Far from idleness, this contemplative approach emphasizes a deep and personal connection to the subject matter and to the place where I "discovered" the busts of the four Zionist leaders: the bomb shelter under the Truman Institute.

A JOURNEY OF SELF-REFLECTION AND PROFESSIONAL GROWTH: The gray, introverted character of Hexter triggers personal introspection—specifically my fear of becoming a similarly "gray" person. The space of the university, combined with historical artifacts, allows me to explore identity, commitment, and rejection within the professional context.

Summary of the Truman Institute Tour

The Truman Institute tour dealt with the complex interplay between space, profession, and intellectual development. Personal narratives and historical context intertwine on the institute's rooftop, linking individual choices with Israel's history. The brief tour of the institute's foyer, coupled with the debate surrounding the naming of the institute after President Truman, sheds light on the intricate emotions that individuals can develop around symbols and historical figures. Then, in the bomb shelter, the hyperrealistic busts by Maurice B. Hexter evoke emotions and mirror conflicted feelings about Zionism, illustrating the fusion of personal and political dimensions. The bomb shelter, somewhat reminiscent of Hexter's introverted persona, prompts introspection on identity and commitment in professional development. This outing shows how personal experiences, history, and academic exploration converge in a physical space, underlining the nuanced nature of my embeddedness within the Mt. Scopus campus.

Writing Drawbacks

The writing of this book took about five years. Soon after I sent the book to be reviewed (in September 2022), an untenured colleague asked me how I was progressing in writing and whether he could learn from me about his own book. I told him I didn't recommend learning from this project on how to write a book.

But I was half joking when I told him that. In a previous conversation with the same person, about six months earlier, when we talked about my evident boredom during many of our departmental seminars, I told him that perhaps I would have been less disengaged if speakers had talked more about the difficulties and even failures during their research, or shown us the absurd and amusing elements in their work, instead of marshaling proof after proof of the seriousness, importance, and rigor of their research. So many seminars and the papers presented in them digress into argumentation contests, as authors, rather than saying something interesting about the world, aim mainly to prevent others from refuting their arguments.[2] My colleague agreed that seminars could be improved if they were conducted along the more open lines I suggested (and also if they were less rigid and ritualistic in structure). But he also said that he would not dare to discuss the vulnerabilities of his work and his own academic identity in departmental seminars for fear of being tagged as "crazy." He said "crazy" with a little smile, and I smiled back. I didn't want to embarrass him or press further on the meaning of academic craziness—he is on his tenure track, and I didn't want to instill any further fears, doubts, or "dangerous" ideas in him during this stressful period.

But later, at home, I felt another crack open in my heart.[3] I suddenly experienced a gestalt moment: perhaps this is how many colleagues and students perceived me. I had sensed this attitude over the years, and it had surely slowed me down and contributed to my teaching and writing anxieties. My students often resisted or objected to my personal disclosures of doubt, regret, and "weakness" in the classroom. In the introduction to this book, I proposed that this response was related to their desire to connect through me, the professor, to officialdom and state power and other structures of political authority. In the same way, I sensed that many of my colleagues

---

2. This is "fortress writing"—"a form of writing that portrays the researcher and the research as invulnerable, inoculating the inquiry against anticipated challenges and preempting critique" (Ravecca and Dauphinee 2018, 127). See also Badley (2015).

3. "Of course, all life is a process of breaking down, but the blows that do the dramatic side of the work . . . don't show their effect all at once" (Fitzgerald 1995, 520).

218   EXPEDITION ESCAPE FROM THE CLASSROOM

too were put off by my rejection of the IR "proper" and by my parallel move to IR-ize the campus. My intention in IR-izing spaces such as the botanical garden or artifacts such as the campus busts was to question the ontological firmness of International Relations as a distinct and real-world concept or phenomenon. Indeed, my cynicism and sometimes manifested boredom during meetings and seminars were not beneficial in this regard. People don't like to feel they are being mocked or condescended to.[4] I genuinely ask for my colleagues' forgiveness if I offended anyone. But beyond that, my open questioning of the managerial line of intensified "excellence" and quantified knowledge production (through perceived "antics" or "idleness") surely added to my image as "crazy"—or, at least, strange. For this logic of intensification is deeply rooted and internalized now in the academic world in general and in my university too.[5]

Following the university rector's email in June 2019 announcing that department chairs would have to publish quarterly lists of the new publications of their faculty members (which I described more fully this book's introduction), I wrote to him that I wanted—I *needed*—time. He was kind in his response, and no one *openly* pressured me to write even a single article more. But I emotionally internalized the climate of coerced excellence and was embarrassed by not being able to publish. During my family's "Canadian crisis" and after my divorce, I had to collect the pieces of my broken life. I also had to recuperate after more than four years in demanding administrative positions. Throughout this period, I struggled to find a way to face my growing teaching anxiety. The modest "performance" and reception of my previous book, *The Politics of the Trail*, further paralyzed me. But to return to "mainstream" and strategic writing and teaching was something I could not do. I felt that I could no longer serve as a conduit of state and international power for the students and could not reify the authority of the state and state's system by writing about it from the vantage point of an omniscient and disengaged social scientist. I had to make my personal voice heard and maintain my human and professional dignity by doing so.

---

4. "In January 2014, a professor of English and Comparative Literature at the University of Warwick was suspended by members of its senior administration. Amongst the charges laid against him justifying the suspension were allegations of 'inappropriate sighing,' 'making ironic comments,' and 'projecting negative body language'— behaviors which were said to undermine the authority of, who was then, the professor's head of department" (Prasad and Segarra 2017, 727).

5. One of the seminal works on the adoption of "excellence" as the raison d'être of the current neoliberal university is Readings (1996).

Of course, autoethnography and personal writing are not the only ways to achieve what I sought. But this is where I want to contribute further. If academics indeed exhibit a recurring theme in their writing throughout their entire career (Dauphinee 2013), then mine is the need to (a) seek professional companionship with students and colleagues, and (b) maintain and develop my individuality and sovereignty within my profession and resist, as much as I can, co-option into institutionalized power structures.[6] It took me several years to realize that the two aims might oppose each other.

Some will argue that empathy or companionship should not be a major aim for a professor in the academic profession of IR. Along with those who are put off by my playing with the "proper" boundaries of IR, others might see my narratives as whitewashing Israel's occupation of the Palestinians, or even the supposed apartheid regime that Israel maintains. I don't think there is apartheid here (at least not yet, but we might be close to it given the systemic and deep-rooted oppression of the Palestinians by Israel), and I also don't see myself engaging in Israeli *hasbara* (public diplomacy), as a reviewer once suggested when responding to a paper of mine in the 2010s. This reviewer thought that by revealing my humanity and doubts about the complexities of the situation in Israel, I was glossing over the systemic violence Israel employs toward Palestinians. The opponents to approaches such as mine often demand that Israeli scholars unequivocally denounce Israeli violence and oppression and disregard occasions when Palestinian violence is motivated by hatred and fanaticism because such violence is always, according to them, a legitimate resistance to the occupation. I concur that Israel employs systemic oppression and that on many occasions Palestinian violence is indeed resistance. This, however, does not make the overall situation less complex, nor does it annul my right, as a member of the power-wielding and oppressing community, to lament the situation and reveal its intricacies.

Having said this, I am well aware that, as a product of the culture of violence in Israel, I might have many blind spots about its workings and effects. Even if a person wants to resist and challenge their own culture, there are limits to what they can achieve, mainly because they are part of the culture and unable to see it as an outsider. Related to this is the argument that colonial violence constitutes the subjectivity not only of its sufferers but also of

---

6. From a Foucauldian perspective, my very essence and position as a tenured university professor could stand in sharp contradiction to that supposed resistance. But this is less the case from a de Certeau-ian position, which stresses the notion of "making do" and "ripping off" from within systems.

218 EXPEDITION ESCAPE FROM THE CLASSROOM

its inflictors. This violence becomes part of a person's identity and self, and a strong emotional and ideational connection between violence and members of the occupying society evolves even if they don't wield the violence personally (Kotef 2020). (This is reminiscent of Simone Weil's concept of rootedness and uprootedness.)

I struggled for many years with such arguments and reservations, which fed upon my teaching anxiety and solidified my writer's block. Eventually, and much thanks to the love and acceptance of my partner, Dr. Daphna Sharef-Davidovich (a material-culture historian), I realized that even if from a "broader" IR point of view my narratives are seen as marginal and unimportant or personally self-absorbed (or even saturated with colonial-inflictor violence), they still have value as long as others can learn something about themselves or about the everyday political spaces *they* inhabit from the stories of my pursuit of individuality. I also drew much encouragement from Claud Lévi-Strauss's powerful words at the end of his *Tristes Tropiques*:

> Other societies are perhaps no better than our own; even if we are inclined to believe they are, we have no method at our disposal for proving it. However, by getting to know them better, we are enabled to detach ourselves from our own society. Not that our society is peculiarly or absolutely bad. But it is the only one from which we have a duty to free ourselves. . . . The society we belong to is the only society we are in a position to transform without any risk of destroying it, since the changes, being introduced by us, are coming from within the society itself. (Lévi-Strauss 1973, 392)

Beyond the innate importance of Lévi-Strauss's ethnographic insights here, a person can switch "society" with "self" and see whether the result speaks to them.

My narratives have value for my students too: Hagar Kotef argues that many Israelis are *not* blind to the violence that they inflict or that is inflicted in their name, but rather think this violence is morally just and necessary. They become emotionally and ideologically attached to it and detached from the pain the Palestinians suffer. Therefore, she argues, potential "solutions" to the conflict here, or to other conflicts in colonial and postcolonial settings (such as in the United States), do not necessarily begin with a need to open the eyes of members of the dominating society to the violence they exact because they know about this violence and it makes them into who they are (Kotef 2020). While I see logic in her argument, both theoretically and empirically (although hers is a political theory piece, not empirical research), my experience on the campus tours showed me that this is not always or even often the case. My students regularly refuse to see the violence around us (recall their responses to the words of Yitzhak Rabin in 1967 upon his receiving an honorary doctorate in Scopus) and, more importantly, to acknowledge it *within* us.

The "expeditions" take us out to the various spaces and embodiments of conflict, oppression, and violence on the campus and in its close vicinity. The traces of violence are more present in some sites than in others. But the outings *do*, sometimes inadvertently, open the eyes of students—Israelis and Palestinians—to different forms of violence and its naturalization (and I'm sure there are many more forms I have not yet identified) in our immediate and daily environment *and* within ourselves. Moreover, as more East Jerusalemites enroll in the IR department and in my course, Israeli students sometimes get to hear directly from their Palestinian fellow students what it is like to live in a neighborhood like Issawiya (I had two students from the neighborhood during the last two runs of the course) or what it feels like to have to clear campus security every day as a Palestinian woman wearing a hijab, for instance. I am not naive enough to believe this will bring peace, not even within the class or between me and some students, but I do see how people start looking around more critically and empathetically following these excursions. Documenting these experiences in a published IR book— reflecting on the outings' planning and conduct, innate difficulties, and encountered conflicts—formalizes them and has a distancing effect, allowing us to see our own society and ourselves from the outside.[7] This may enable some students to understand Lévi Strauss's words about transforming our own society when learning about other societies.

The Author-Book Separation

Now the question remains of how to avoid repeating the experience of "sinking into the pond of professional oblivion" I refer to in the introduction to this book. The answer is to lower expectations and be more realistic. Perhaps

---

7. The fact the book is written in English can also contribute to the distancing effect: "Research on bilingualism and emotions has shown stronger emotional responses in the native language (L1) compared to a foreign language. . . . [There is] greater emotional distance when making decisions in the second language as compared to the native tongue" (Dylman and Bjärtå 2019, 1284). See similar findings also in Schroeder and Chen (2021).

220   EXPEDITION ESCAPE FROM THE CLASSROOM

in partial contradiction to what I just wrote above, I must remind myself that this is, in the end, only a book. Because I am its author, it contains a part of my identity and subjectivity—but, importantly, not *all* of my identity and subjectivity. The book and I are not identical. Furthermore, I know that for it to have any impact in the world, people first have to read it, preferably from cover to cover. Yet this is very unlikely—it is not professionally efficient or strategic these days to read a book from cover to cover. Reading is time-consuming. And a book like the present one also cannot be easily summarized into a few sentences or a thesis that would allow it to be used as a reference in a literature review, for example. Still, I would be happy if people read the book in the fashion observed by Michel de Certeau when he discusses the difference between writing and reading: "Writing accumulates, stocks up, resists time through the establishment of a place and multiplies its production by the expansionism of reproduction. Reading takes no measures against the erosion of time (one forgets oneself *and* also forgets), it does not keep what it acquires, or it does so poorly, and each of the places through which it passes is the repetition of the lost paradise" (de Certeau 1984, 174). As this is a book about many stories and processes of teaching and learning IR, and as it is not always a coherent or continuous narrative, I hope that readers can draw multiple lessons from it about their own experiences and circumstances in a political culture or in academia. And if the book, like previous ones, eventually falls into a pond of oblivion, perhaps one day someone will stumble upon it. Patience is advised, I tell myself.

Final Thoughts, Summer 2023

Upon finishing revisions and edits of this book in preparation for publication, in summer 2023, I read the following paragraph, which was supposed to be the last passage of this concluding chapter (written in 2022):

> Hence, I hope that people will read (parts of) this book, and I hope they will draw beneficial and empowering lessons from it. But even if they don't, I know that the *process* of writing the book did strengthen me, and its publication will help me to develop methods of teaching that will (a) reduce friction between me and the students or allow me to make more fruitful political and academic use of it, and (b) cause more students to learn something. With this book completed, I know I have found some

closure and am ready to meet the students with an easier heart. For me, this is not something to be taken lightly.

But in light of the of the current crisis in Israel, which started with Netanyahu's government judicial overhaul in January 2023 and the escalation of ensuing protests against it, I deleted that paragraph. I am not sure whether I will be able to open the next academic year (October 2023) with less friction with the students or whether they will come to campus with a mindset to learn anything. It has been said that, whereas Netanyahu once used hatred and fear to gain rule, since the establishment of his sixth, religious-ultranationalist, almost openly fascist government in January 2023, he rules to spread hatred and fear. Various parts of Israeli society are pitted against one another, and communal violence, civil unrest, and oppressive authoritarian government (along the Hungarian or even Turkish "models") never seemed so close.

This situation opened the eyes of many Israelis, especially those in the so-called Center and Center-Left, to the corrupting influences of the occupation on Israel itself, especially with regard to how messianic settlers have overtaken main institutions and mechanisms of the state with their open and explicit intention to implement anti-democratic norms in the Occupied Territories within Israel "proper." However, resistance to the occupation has not (yet?) become a major theme of the anti-government protest movement. A significant outcome of the protest movement was the changing attitude toward the "sanctity" of the military, exemplified mainly in the decision of air force pilots and intelligence offensive cyber-capabilities operators to cease their volunteering to reserve service (with a substantial impact on the operational war-readiness of the IDF in general). But the very fact that these reservists were the most powerful "weapon" that the resistance and protest movement relied upon reveals the protest's strong militaristic elements. Those who supported the acts of the reservists and those who objected to them often framed the debate in security-militaristic terms, and less in civil notions.

In recent months, not a day passes without my recalling the conversation with my ex-wife on the roof of the Truman Institute. I ask myself every day, Was it worth staying here? Moreover, as each new day brings with it a new governmental threat to civil rights and also to academic freedom, I fear not simply for my ability to teach freely next year and in the years to come, but also for my academic position. I keep being reminded of those who signed the "academics for peace" petition in Turkey in 2016 and who were shortly fired from their university positions (Baser, Akgönül, and Öztürk 2020). On YouTube, one finds videos of some of them teaching in public squares and gardens in Istanbul. Such an exile from the university, from the classroom, is not what I thought of when developing the "Mt. Scopus Enclave" course.

But the government has not closed our university yet. And perhaps this government will eventually fall from power. I don't know what classes will look like next academic year, or how my course will be conducted. Uncertainty weighs heavily on me. The recent events have cast a long shadow over everything I have worked for, and I find myself grappling with questions that have no easy answers. The societal unrest, the threat to democracy, to the rule of law, and to academic freedom, and the divisiveness that permeates our daily lives are realities that smother criticism and creativity, generating even a sense of existential threat. As I conclude this book, I do so with a sense of foreboding, recognizing that the challenges we face as a society are complex and deeply entrenched. I often fear that this is the last book I will publish as a free scholar. This book is not just a reflection of my thoughts but a chronicle of a time and place that will, I hope, serve as a warning and a call to action for those who read it elsewhere.

Epilogue

On October 7, 2023, everything changed. The brutal and murderous surprise attack launched by the terrorist organization Hamas against the Israeli kibbutzim and towns near the border of the Gaza Strip and the terrible war that broke out following the unimaginable atrocities committed against the Israeli civilian population deeply tore the heart of every Israeli. The murder of women, babies, and children; the slaughter of entire families; the butchering of participants in a music festival; the massacre of the elderly and the disabled within their own homes; the rape of women and the marching of them in the streets of Gaza as war trophies; and the abduction of young children and old Holocaust survivors into Gaza (more than 230 were kidnapped)—these were just some of the atrocities that were intentionally captured on video by the terrorists' GoPro and body cameras and were uploaded to the internet (they were deleted a few days later when the leadership of Hamas realized the self-inflicted damage these videos caused them). Many years will pass before this trauma is healed, and I do not know what Israeli society will look like in the foreseeable future. It is not impossible that Israeli society will become more militaristic, more nationalistic, more religious, and more entrenched in the position of the victim (and this time, rightfully so!). The memory of the Holocaust will come again to the fore of Israeli policies and public discourse, as many Israelis and their supporters in the international community perceived the pogroms carried out by the terrorists of Hamas and the hateful Gazan mob that crossed the Gaza Strip fence following the armed and organized terrorist squads not only as an ISIS-like evil, but also as Nazi-inspired. I am skeptical whether Israelis will be capable of showing empathy and understanding for Palestinian suffering, in the Gaza Strip and elsewhere, following these events, and it is also difficult for me to see how I myself can muster such feelings. As someone who has studied and written about the phenomenon of revenge in war (Löwenheim and Heimann 2008) and knows how dangerous and destructive revenge can be, I am now concentrating on trying to prevent feelings of hatred and vengeance from overwhelming me

224   EXPEDITION ESCAPE FROM THE CLASSROOM

and trying to think about the future—the future of myself and my family, and of society here in general.

What kind of people will we be when we rise up from the ashes of the war, asked writer David Grossman, in a *Haaretz* newspaper column he published a few days after the massacre in the kibbutzim. I cannot say what kind of person I myself will be. If I've learned anything from the last two weeks, it's that we really don't have the ability to predict or control what will happen. "Oded, please don't let this war change you," one of the Palestinian students from East Jerusalem wrote to me a few days after the war broke out. "This world is cruel, and you and I decided at some point in life not to be a part of this cruelty. . . . The easiest and most natural thing in this place is to feel like the others around us. . . . The supreme goal of my life, and I think yours too, is to think about other directions for both sides."

It took great courage and a big soul to write what that student, who defines himself as a devout Muslim, wrote to me. He continued to write me similar messages in the following days, despite the unprecedented bombings, killings, and destruction that the Israeli military inflicted on the Gaza Strip (and in view of the expected continuation of violence in the near future). I admit that I was not able to show the same magnanimity as him. Admittedly, I was not happy about the bombings, the death of the innocents, and vast destruction in Gaza, but I felt there was no other option now, and this is what I also told him. For the first time in three decades of studying and working in the academic field of International Relations, I was unable to see any other way to deal with the terrible crisis other than the massive use of military force. Hamas deceived Israel for years by pretending that it was possible to reach rational settlements with it, meanwhile brainwashing the residents of Gaza with deeply antisemitic hatred. It used the time and resources at its disposal (including donations from the international community) for military buildup backed by Iran, and planned and carried out an act of genocide in the name of a distorted and fanatical interpretation of Islam. The siege imposed by Israel on the Gaza Strip for years (which itself resulted from Hamas's violent takeover of the Strip from the Palestinian Authority in 2007), the ongoing Israeli occupation of the Palestinians in the West Bank and East Jerusalem, the continuing provocations of far-right Israeli politicians on Temple Mount/ Haram al-Sharif in Jerusalem, the acts of dispossession, violence, and control that the Israeli military and the settlers employ against the Palestinian civilian population in the West Bank and East Jerusalem, and even the previous "rounds" of fighting between Israel and Hamas—none of these can be used

Epilogue   **225**

as a justification or "context" for heinous acts of genocide, such as those committed on October 7.

The first semester of the 2023–24 academic year at the Hebrew University was supposed to open on October 15, but due to the outbreak of the war, the opening of the semester was postponed several times. The scheduled date now is December 3. Various estimates in our Faculty say that between 30 and 40 percent of our students are drafted for reserve service in the military. No one knows how many of the East Jerusalem students will show up for classes—most of them are probably very scared to come to campus at such a time, and others are surely full of anger and hatred for Israel and decided to cancel their university registration. Our classrooms will be half-empty for weeks, and the atmosphere will be charged and tense. There is hardly anyone in Israel in these days who doesn't know someone who was killed or injured or even kidnapped on October 7. Who will have the emotional and mental energies needed to study? What will I be able to teach in such a situation? How will I ever overcome my own sense of fear, distrust, deadlock, and despair? Sometimes we'll probably have to interrupt classes and run to a protected space or a bomb shelter. I am doubtful whether I'll be allowed to take the students out of the classroom for our "expeditions" under such conditions. I have written in the past with some irony about the bomb shelters on campus, but now, unfortunately, they might become very necessary. My campus tours will have to return to virtual platforms and rely on tools such as Google Earth and Google Street View, much like during the pandemic period. And to where shall I "take" the class in these tours? Certainly not to the British War Cemetery—this will be highly insensitive and unwise in a period when our own military cemeteries are holding funerals one after the other.

• • •

Yesterday, on October 19, I came to campus for the first time since the outbreak of the war. I was sitting in my office at the Harry S. Truman Research Institute for the Advancement of Peace (I now have an office there . . .). I was the only faculty member attending the institute that day, and among the few people on the entire Mt. Scopus campus (there were no more than ten cars in the parking lot). The campus was desolate and deserted, even more so than during the worst period of the COVID-19 pandemic. I sat down at my desk in the office and tried to read a seminar paper. But I could not concentrate. I decided to leave the office to wander around the campus a bit, and my feet led me to the botanical garden. I was the sole visitor in the garden. Signs of

226   EXPEDITION ESCAPE FROM THE CLASSROOM

neglect were evident: garbage cans rummaged through by cats and porcu-
pines in search of food scraps; bags of garden prunings left untouched for
weeks; and paths obscured by dirt from recent rains and winds. I thought
about the time of the Mt. Scopus enclave, when the garden was a buffer zone
between the Israeli region and the territory controlled by the Kingdom of
Jordan (1948–67), and how desolation and disorder took over Eig's garden,
which nonetheless survived the enclave years. I sat down on a bench under
a group of large, old pine trees, looked out over the houses of the Issawiya
neighborhood below Mt. Scopus, and thought about whether it is safe for me
to sit here now—someone from the neighborhood might shoot at the garden
or throw a Molotov cocktail. The images of the storming Gazan mob through
the broken fence of the Strip also came to my mind. Being a "peacenik" won't
guarantee safety—Hamas kidnapped elderly women from kibbutzim along
the Gaza border, even though they were peace activists and humanitarians.

I moved from the bench into the oak grove, where I was less visible from
Issawiya. The last time I was in Issawiya was in November 2019, in a "police
watch" patrol (see chapter 3). Today, I don't know if I would have gone down
to the neighborhood for another patrol like this, even if I had been invited
by its residents. I fear for my safety. I am also mentally exhausted and feel
very lonely. So many events have transpired here since that visit to Issawiya.
The COVID-19 pandemic; the repeated election campaigns that have eroded
the Israeli public's trust in democracy; the riots in the mixed Arab-Jewish
cities in Israel during the previous round of warfare between Hamas and
Israel in May 2021; the consequent legitimacy that the far-right parties in
Israel gained and their entry into the government; the Netanyahu coalition's
attempt to carry out a judicial coup d'état in 2023 (a plan which is still on
the table!); and now, this war. Besides the terrible fear the war raised in me,
I also feel betrayed. I was amazed by the refusal of some of the heads of the
most prestigious universities in the United States (e.g., Harvard, Columbia)
to unequivocally condemn Hamas in light of their fear of the reactions of
the pro-Palestinian student associations or as a result of the infiltration of
distinctly antisemitic ideas under the guise of progressive agendas into the
mainstream of the American Left. Also, I was appalled by the fact that not a
few so-called liberal and progressive professors saw Hamas's crimes against
humanity in the "context" of Israeli colonialism, refusing to acknowledge that
Israelis, too, are natives of this country and that they have the right to self-
defense. I was astounded that, apart from two colleagues, none of my *numerous* acquaintances and purported friends at universities in the United States,

Epilogue **227**

the United Kingdom, Canada, Australia, and other countries reached out to me. Some of these individuals benefited from my help in advancing their careers—whether through letters of recommendation, reviewing their students' doctoral theses, or assessing papers and books for journals and presses where they served as editors. Yet, after the war broke out, they didn't even email to check on my well-being or that of my family. I'm uncertain about presenting the chapter from this book on the botanical garden at the upcoming International Studies Association conference in April 2024 in San Francisco. Although my proposal to present this chapter as an ISA paper was accepted, I'm hesitant. The registration deadline is approaching, and I'm apprehensive about potentially facing an atmosphere hostile to Israelis at the conference (or worse: to tackle hypocrisy). It's both surprising and disheartening that the ISA managing board hasn't voiced any support for Israel during these trying times.

• • •

Amid all this, I keep reminding myself that violence almost always breeds more violence. Hatred leads to more hatred, and cruelty to more cruelty. The vicious circle of war is a self-fulfilling prophecy, and it is very difficult to break it. Long-term security for Israel in the Middle East can't be built on escalating levels of Muslim and Arab animosity—hatred will always find its way to circumvent or trick "deterrence" mechanisms, either through new and/or surprising technologies, unexpected alliances, or by other unknown unknowns. While many, if not most, Israelis are guided now by terrible righteous anger and vengeance, we must find ways to prevent hatred from spreading and seeping into more places and other hearts and minds. The vanquishing of Hamas must involve the use of military means. But for the long run, and once the war ends, such means will not suffice. I am reminded of the tragic results of previous employment of military power, in our conflicts here in the Middle East (e.g., the growth of Hezbollah following the 1982 Lebanon War and the eighteen years of Israeli occupation of southern Lebanon; see Sobelman 2016), and in other "wars on terror" (for example, the American invasion of Afghanistan in 2002 and the resilience of the Taliban). I still believe that only justice and democracy for all, in a setup that will guarantee the rights and security of all in the territory of Mandatory Palestine, will ensure peace in this country. I still believe in the duty not to seek revenge and in preserving empathy toward Palestinians who reject Hamas's atrocities. Yet I'm skeptical about the possibility of witnessing justice, security, and democracy for all in

228 EXPEDITION ESCAPE FROM THE CLASSROOM

my lifetime. The hazards of ending the occupation are evident from events like the Hamas seizure of Gaza in 2007 and the 2023 War. Conversely, the perils of persisting with the occupation are just as apparent.

I'm not a political leader or a luminary visionary, I'm just a university teacher. And I don't always have clear answers to or helpful suggestions for such dilemmas. But I still see my role as Max Weber thought about the job of the professor: to clearly present uncomfortable facts to the students. Many of these facts involve grappling with dilemmas like the ones outlined here. In the foreseeable future, I'm committed to highlighting the intricacies of righteous anger, vengeance, mistrust, fear, and hatred to my students. I'll emphasize the significance of maintaining human connections—both among Israelis and with Palestinians—within and beyond our campus. Some window, even a crack, of hope must be kept open. And beyond my classes, my hope is that people who will read this book might find inspiration or direction in it. Perhaps someone smarter or braver than me will know how to act more effectively in light of the stories I've shared. I hope such a person reads this. Therefore, despite the war and the judicial coup d'état, despite my own anger, fear, mistrust, and doubt, I'll step into the classroom for the forthcoming term. I will once again confront the pain and anxiety of teaching international politics. And when the war ends, I will take my classes on campus outings once more.

Bibliography

Abeliovich, Ruthie, and Edwin Seroussi, eds. 2019. *Borderlines: Essays on Mapping and the Logic of Place*. Warsaw: De Gruyter.

Abu Hatoum, Nayrouz. 2021. "For 'A No-State Yet to Come': Palestinians Urban Place-Making in Kufr Aqab, Jerusalem." *Environment and Planning E: Nature and Space* 4, no. 1 (March): 85–108.

Agha, Zena. 2020. "Israel Can't Hide Evidence of Its Occupation Anymore." *Foreign Policy*, August 3. https://foreignpolicy.com/2020/08/03/israel-cant-hide-evidence -of-its-occupation-anymore/

Agnon, Shmuel Yosef. 1989. *Shira*. A novel. New York: Schocken.

Ambo, Theresa, and Theresa Rocha Beardall. 2023. "Performance or Progress? The Physical and Rhetorical Removal of Indigenous Peoples in Settler Land Acknowledgments at Land-Grab Universities." *American Educational Research Journal* 60, no. 1: 103–40.

Anderson, Leon. 2006. "Analytic Autoethnography." *Journal of Contemporary Ethnography* 35, no. 4 (August): 373–95.

Anscombe, G. E. M. 1958. "Mr. Truman's Degree." Pamphlet published by the author. https://www.theahi.org/wp-content/uploads/2013/10/Anscombe-Mr.-Trumans -Degree-1958.pdf

Arendt, Hannah. 2006. *Eichmann in Jerusalem: A Report on the Banality of Evil*. New York: Penguin. First published 1963.

Arnon-Ohana, Yuval. 2008. *Guarding Mt. Scopus*. [In Hebrew.] Jerusalem: Ariel.

Auchter, Jessica. 2016. "Paying Attention to Dead Bodies: The Future of Security Studies?" *Journal of Global Security Studies* 1, no. 1 (February): 36–50.

Azaryahu, Maoz. 1995. *State Rituals: The Celebrations of Independence and the Commemoration of the Fallen, 1948–1956*. [In Hebrew.] Beer Sheba: Ben Gurion University Press.

Badley, Graham Francis. 2014. "Titles Я Us!" *Qualitative Inquiry* 20, no. 5: 635–40.

Badley, Graham Francis. 2015. "Playful and Serious Adventures in Academic Writing." *Qualitative Inquiry* 21, no. 8: 711–19.

Baer, Madeline, and Heidi Nichols Haddad. 2023. "Localizing the International Relations Classroom: Evaluation of Academic Partnerships with City Government." *International Studies Perspectives* 24, no. 3: 231–47. https://doi.org/10.1093/isp/ek ac008

Baghdadchi, Amir. 2005. "On Academic Boredom." *Arts and Humanities in Higher Education* 4, no. 3: 319–24.

Bainbridge, Simon. 2015. "Battling Napoleon after Waterloo: Re-enactment, Representation, and the 'Napoleon Bust Business.'" In *Tracing War in British Enlightenment and Romantic Culture*, edited by Neil Ramsey and Gillian Russell, 132–50. Houndmills: Palgrave Macmillan.

230 Bibliography

Balivis, Geula, and Mordechai Peleg. 1981. "The Effect of Air Pollution on Lebanon Cedars." [In Hebrew.] Jerusalem Municipality Department of Improving the City's Appearance and the Hebrew University's Department of Human Environment, March. Botanical Garden Library.

Barak, Oren. 2007. "'Don't Mention the War?': The Politics of Remembrance and Forgetfulness in Postwar Lebanon." *Middle East Journal* 61, no. 1: 49–70.

Barthes, Roland. 1982. *Empire of Signs*. New York: Farrar, Straus and Giroux.

Bar-Yosef, Eitan. 2017. "Bonding with the British: Colonial Nostalgia and the Idealization of Mandatory Palestine in Israeli Literature and Culture after 1967." *Jewish Social Studies* 22, no. 3: 1–37.

Baser, Bahar, Samim Akgönül, and Ahmet Erdi Öztürk. 2020. "'Academics for Peace' in Turkey: A Case of Criminalising Dissent and Critical Thought via Counterterrorism Policy." In *Critical Terrorism Studies at Ten*, edited by Richard Jackson, Harmonie Toros, Lee Jarvis, and Charlotte Heath-Carry, 78–100. London: Routledge.

Basu, Anjan. 2021. "Remembering India's First Modern Sculptor, Ramkinkar Baij." *The Wire*, May 25. https://thewire.in/the-arts/remembering-indias-first-modern-sculptor-ramkinkar-baij

Beattie, Amanda Russell. 2019. "The Reflexive Potential of Silence: Emotions, the 'Everyday' and Ethical International Relations." *Journal of International Political Theory* 15, no. 2 (June): 229–45.

Beattie, Jennifer. 2006. "Ontological Security in World Politics: State Identity and the Security Dilemma." *European Journal of International Relations* 12, no. 3: 341–70.

Belting, Hans. 2011. *An Anthropology of Images: Picture, Medium, Body*. Princeton: Princeton University Press.

Ben Menachem, H. Report to Hebrew University's management, November 11, 1938, Hebrew University Central Archive, Botanical Garden file no. 2350.

Bennion, Elizabeth A. 2015. "Experiential Education in Political Science and International Relations." In *Handbook on Teaching and Learning in Political Science and International Relations*, edited by John Ishiyama, William J. Miller, and Eszter Simon, 351–68. Cheltenham: Edward Elgar.

Benvenisti, Meron. 1990. *Jerusalem's City of the Dead*. Jerusalem: Keter Publishers.

Benvenisti, Meron. 2002. *Sacred Landscape: The Buried History of the Holy Land Since 1948*. Berkeley: University of California Press.

Benvenisti, Meron. 2007. *The Son of the Cypresses: Memories, Reflections, and Regrets from a Political Life*. Berkeley: University of California Press.

Berger Ziauddin, Silvia. 2017. "(De)territorializing the Home: The Nuclear Bomb Shelter as a Malleable Site of Passage." *Environment and Planning D: Society and Space* 35, no. 4: 674–93.

Berlin, Isaiah. 2013. *The Hedgehog and the Fox: An Essay on Tolstoy's View of History*. Princeton: Princeton University Press.

Bernhardt, Peter. 2008. *Gods and Goddesses in the Garden: Greco-Roman Mythology and the Scientific Names of Plants*. New Brunswick, NJ: Rutgers University Press.

Besky, Sarah, and Jonathan Padwe. 2016. "Placing Plants in Territory." *Environment and Society*, no. 7: 9–28.

Bhattacharjee, Sukalpa. 2020. "Tagore's Ideas on Nationalism: A Contemporary Perspective." In *The Idea of Surplus*, edited by Mrinal Miri, 115–34. New Delhi: Routledge India.

Bhattacharya, Sabyasachi. 2011. *Rabindranath Tagore: An Interpretation*. New Delhi: Penguin Books India.

Bibliography

Black, Jeremy. 2007. "What Is War? Some Reflections on a Contested Concept." *RUSI Journal* 152, no. 6 (December): 42–45.

Bleiker, Roland. 2019. "Visual Autoethnography and International Security: Insights from the Korean DMZ." *European Journal of International Security* 4, no. 3: 274–99.

Bolotin, M. 1965. "A Cedars Survey in the Jerusalem Area." [In Hebrew.] *LaYa'aran: The Journal of the Israel Forestry Association* 15, no. 1 (March): 16.

Boneh, Omri, Nir Har, and Roee Harel. 2014. "An Overview of the Geographical Distribution and Condition of the Cedar Species in the Countries of the Mediterranean Basin and the Factors Influencing the Development of Cedar Trees Planted in Forests in Israel." [In Hebrew.] *Ya'ar* [Forest] 13 (September): 4–17.

Bowdridge, Michael, and Sean Blenkinsop. 2011. "Michel Foucault Goes Outside: Discipline and Control in the Practice of Outdoor Education." *Journal of Experiential Education* 34, no. 2: 149–63.

Bradberry, Leigh A., and Jennifer De Maio. 2019. "Learning by Doing: The Long-Term Impact of Experiential Learning Programs on Student Success." *Journal of Political Science Education* 15, no. 1: 94–111.

Brannick, Teresa, and David Coghlan. 2007. "In Defense of Being 'Native': The Case for Insider Academic Research." *Organizational Research Methods* 10, no. 1 (January): 59–74.

Braverman, Irus. 2009. *Planted Flags: Trees, Land, and Law in Israel/Palestine*. Cambridge: Cambridge University Press.

Brilliant, Richard. 2007. "Faces Demanding Attention." *Gesta* 46, no. 2: 91–99.

Brock, Kathy L., and Beverly J. Cameron. 1999. "Enlivening Political Science Courses with Kolb's Learning Preference Model." *PS: Political Science and Politics* 32, no. 2 (June): 251–56.

Brown, Marshall. 1992. "Introduction: Contemplating the Theory of Literary History." *PMLA* 107, no. 1 (January): 13–25.

Budreau, Lisa M. 2010. *Bodies of War: World War I and the Politics of Commemoration in America, 1919–1933*. New York: New York University Press.

Callahan, William A. 2017. "Cultivating Power: Gardens in the Global Politics of Diplomacy, War, and Peace." *International Political Sociology* 11, no. 4 (December): 360–79.

Campbell, Joseph. 2008. *The Hero with a Thousand Faces*. Novato, CA: New World Library.

Candelaria, Matthew. 2002. "The Overlord's Burden: The Source of Sorrow in Childhood's End." *ARIEL: A Review of International English Literature* 33, no. 1 (January): 37–58.

Carroll, Khadija von Zinnenburg. 2018. "NonWest by North: Marianne North and William Colenso's Responses to Plant Life and the Classification of Economic Botany." *Third Text* 32, nos. 2–3: 290–310.

Chabon, Michael. 2008. *The Yiddish Policemen's Union*. New York: HarperCollins.

Chaudhuri, Shantanu Ray. 2021. "The Art of Ramkinkar Baij," *Daily Eye*, September 10. https://thedailyeye.info/post.php?id=a0eef496f28be5f9&title=The-Art-of-Ra mkinkar-Baij

Chazkel, Amy. 2020. "Toward a History of Rights in the City at Night: Making and Breaking the Nightly Curfew in Nineteenth-Century Rio de Janeiro." *Comparative Studies in Society and History* 62, no. 1 (January): 106–34.

Clarke, Arthur C. [1953] 1979. *Childhood's End*. London: Pan Books.

Cohen, Hillel. 2007. *The Rise and Fall of Arab Jerusalem: Palestinian Politics and the City since 1967*. London: Routledge.

232 Bibliography

Cohen, Uri, and Adi Sapir. 2016. "Models of Academic Governance during a Period of Nation-Building: The Hebrew University in the 1920s–1960s." *History of Education* 45, no. 5: 602–20.

Cohn, Carol. 1987. "Sex and Death in the Rational World of Defense Intellectuals." *Signs: Journal of Women in Culture and Society* 12, no. 4 (July): 687–718.

Conrad, Joseph. 2002. *Lord Jim*. Edited with an introduction and notes by Jacques Berthoud. Oxford: Oxford University Press.

Cotter, Holland. 2021. "With Splendor and Saints, Hispanic Society Shows Its Treasures." *New York Times*, October 21.

Cottman, Paul. 2008. *A Politics of the Scene*. Stanford: Stanford University Press.

Cox, David William. 2014. *Battlefield Tourism: Pilgrimage and the Commemoration of the Great War in Britain, Australia, and Canada, 1919–1939*. London: Bloomsbury.

Cox, Margaret, and Peter Jones. 2014. "Ethical Considerations in the Use of DNA as a Contribution toward the Determination of Identification in Historic Cases: Considerations from the Western Front." *New Genetics and Society* 33, no. 3: 295–312.

Cristiano, Fabio, and Emilio Distretti. 2017. "Along the Lines of the Occupation: Playing at Diminished Reality in East Jerusalem." *Conflict and Society* 3, no. 1 (June): 130–43.

Curtis, John O. 1979. *Moving Historic Buildings*. Washington, DC: US Department of the Interior.

Cusumano, Eugenio. 2021. "Private Military and Security Companies' Logos: Between Camouflaging and Corporate Socialization." *Security Dialogue* 52, no. 2 (April): 135–55.

Dahamshe, Amer. 2017. *Local Habitation and a Name: A Literary and Cultural Reading of the Arabic Geographical Names of the Land*. [In Hebrew.] Tel Aviv: Dvir.

Dahamshe, Amer. 2020. "Palestinian Arabic versus Israeli Hebrew Place-Names: Comparative Cultural Reading of Landscape Nomenclature and Israeli Renaming Strategies." *Journal of Holy Land and Palestine Studies* 20, no. 1: 62–82.

Dai, Lili. n.d. "Mount Scopus." [In Hebrew.] Israeli Society for Science Fiction and Fantasy. https://www.sf-f.org.il/archives/2776

Daley, Paul. 2015. "Ataturk's 'Johnnies and Mehmets' Words about the Anzacs are Shrouded in Doubt." *The Guardian* April 20. https://www.theguardian.com/news/2015/apr/20/ataturks-johnnies-and-mehmets-words-about-the-anzacs-are-shrouded-in-doubt

Dar, Yechezkel, and Shaul Kimhi. 2001. "Military Service and Self-Perceived Maturation Among Israeli Youth." *Journal of Youth and Adolescence* 30, no. 4 (April): 427–48.

Datta Gupta, Sobhanlal. 2020. "Tagore's View of Politics and the Contemporary World." In *The Cambridge Companion to Rabindranath Tagore*, edited by Sukanta Chaudhuri, 279–93. Cambridge: Cambridge University Press.

Dauphinee, Elizabeth. 2013. "Writing as Hope: Reflections on the Politics of Exile." *Security Dialogue* 44, no. 4 (August): 347–61.

Davidovitch, Nadav, and Rakefet Zalashik. 2010. "Pasteur in Palestine: The Politics of the Laboratory." *Science in Context* 23, no. 4: 401–425.

de Certeau, Michel. 1980. "On the Oppositional Practices of Everyday Life." *Social Text* 1, no. 3 (Autumn): 3–43.

de Certeau, Michel. 1984. *The Practice of Everyday Life*. Translated by Steven Rendall. Berkeley: University of California Press.

Dening, Greg. 1980. *Islands and Beaches: Discourse on a Silent Land, Marquesas, 1774–1880*. Honolulu: University Press of Hawaii.

Dening, Greg. 2002. "Performing on the Beaches of the Mind: An Essay." *History and Theory* 41, no. 1 (February): 1–24.

Derrida, Jacques. 1992. "The Mystical Foundation of Authority." In *Deconstruction and the Possibility of Justice*, edited by Drucilla Cornell, Michel Rosenfeld, and David Gray Carlson, 3–67. New York: Routledge.

Dolev, Diana. 2006. "An Ivory Tower in the National Precinct: The Architectural Plan for the University Campus in Givat Ram." [In Hebrew.] *Zmanim: A Historical Quarterly*, no. 96 (Autumn): 86–93.

Dolev, Diana. 2016. *The Planning and Building of the Hebrew University, 1919–1948: Facing the Temple Mount*. Lanham, MD: Lexington Books.

Dolev, Diana. 2017. "Academia and Spatial Control: The Case of the Hebrew University Campus on Mount Scopus, Jerusalem." In *Constructing a Sense of Place*, edited by Haim Yacobi, 227–45. London: Routledge.

Dudai, Nativ, and Zohar Amar. 2017. "Tree Wormwood (Artemisia Arborescens) at Montfort Castle: The Possible Introduction of a Medicinal Plant from Western Europe to the Latin East in the Crusader Period." In *Montfort: History, Early Research and Recent Studies of the Principal Fortress of the Teutonic Order*, edited by Adrian Boas and Rabei G. Khamisy. Leiden: Brill.

Dutta, Krishna, and Andrew Robinson. 1995. *Rabindranath Tagore: The Myriad-Minded Man*. London: Bloomsbury.

Dylman, Alexandra S., and Anna Bjärtå. 2019. "When Your Heart Is in Your Mouth: The Effect of Second Language Use on Negative Emotions." *Cognition and Emotion* 33, no. 6: 1284–90.

Ehrenschwendtner, Marie-Luise. 2009. "Virtual Pilgrimages? Enclosure and the Practice of Piety at St. Katherine's Convent, Augsburg." *Journal of Ecclesiastical History* 60, no. 1 (January): 45–73.

Eig, Alexander. 1929a. Letter to Judah L. Magnes, July 28. Hebrew University Central Archive. file no. 3490/21424.

Eig, Alexander. 1929b. "The Botanical Garden and the Garden of the Prophets." Hebrew University Central Archive, file no. 3490/21424.

Eig, Alexander. 1931. "The Trip to Syria and South Harkor, August 6, 1931–September 6, 1931." Hebrew University Central Archive, file no. 3490/21424.

Eig, Alexander. 1937. Letter to the management of the Hebrew University, July 16. Hebrew University Central Archive, Botanical Garden file no. 2350/14580.

Eig, Alexander. 1938. "The Montague Lamport Memorial Botanical Garden of the Hebrew University." *Palestine Journal of Botany* 1, no. 1: 106–8.

Eldar, Shlomi. 2011. "Star of David in the Heart of the Gaza Strip: Tombstones of Jewish Soldiers in a British Cemetery in Gaza." [In Hebrew.] *News 13*, December 21. https://13news.co.il/item/news/domestic/ntr-854595/

Enloe, Cynthia. 2014. *Bananas, Beaches, and Bases: Making Feminist Sense of International Politics*. Berkeley: University of California Press.

Ettinger, Aaron. 2020. "Scattered and Unsystematic: The Taught Discipline in the Intellectual Life of International Relations." *International Studies Perspectives* 21, no. 3 (August): 338–61.

Evald, Björn Christian. 2008. "The Tomb as Heterotopia (Foucault's 'Hétérotopies'): Heroization, Ritual and Funerary Art in Roman Asia Minor." *Journal of Roman Archaeology*, no. 21: 624–34.

Eytan, Walter. 1988. Letter to Maurice B. Hexter. November 1. Hexter's personal archive, National Library, Jerusalem. The documents are not cataloged or numbered. ARC. 4 o 1729[L].

Ferguson, R. Brian. 2018. "War Is Not Part of Human Nature." *Scientific American*, September 1. https://www.scientificamerican.com/article/war-is-not-part-of-human-nature/

Festus, Moses Onipede. 2019. "Patterns of Meaning in Selected Nigerian Military and Paramilitary Logos: A Systemic Functional Multimodal Discourse Approach." *International Journal of Systemic Functional Linguistics* 2, no. 2 (December): 61–70.

Fitzgerald, Scott. 1995. "The Crack-Up." In *The Art of the Personal Essay: An Anthology from the Classical Era to the Present*, edited by Philip Lopate, 520–32. New York: Anchor Books.

Flynn, Brian W., James E. McCarroll, and Quinn M. Biggs. 2015. "Stress and Resilience in Military Mortuary Workers: Care of the Dead from Battlefield to Home." *Death Studies* 39, no. 2: 92–98.

Foucault, Michel. 2002. *The Order of Things: An Archaeology of Human Sciences*. London: Routledge. First published 1966.

Fowler, Glenn. 1990. "Maurice B. Hexter, 99, a Leader in Jewish Social Causes, Is Dead." *New York Times*, October 29. https://www.nytimes.com/1990/10/29/obituaries/maurice-b-hexter-99-a-leader-in-jewish-social-causes-is-dead.html

France, Anatole. 1948. *Penguin Island*. West Drayton: Penguin Books. First published 1908.

Frank, Arthur W. 2013. *The Wounded Storyteller: Body, Illness, and Ethics*. Chicago: University of Chicago Press.

Frumin, Suembikya, Mitia Frumin, and Ehud Weiss. 2019. "When Alexander Eig Met Nikolai Ivanovich Vavilov—An Influential Meeting for Israeli Botany." *Israel Journal of Plant Sciences* 66, nos. 1–2 (March): 7–18.

Fuchs, Ron. 1996. "The Planning of the British War Cemeteries in Mandatory Palestine." [In Hebrew.] *Cathedra: For the History of Eretz Israel and Its Yishuv*, no. 79 (March): 114–39.

Fustos, Erika J., and Helen Kovacs. 2008. *In the Shadow of Stalin's Boots: Visitors' Guide to Memento Park*. Budapest: Premier Press.

Gell, Alfred. 1999. "The Technology of Enchantment and the Enchantment of Technology." In Alfred Gell, *The Art of Anthropology: Essays and Diagrams*, 159–86. Edited by Eric Hirsch. Oxford: Berg.

Genette, Gérard. 1997. *Paratexts: Thresholds of interpretation*. Cambridge: Cambridge University Press.

Ghatak, Ritwik, dir. 1975. *Ramkinkar Baij: A Personality Study*. 30:47 min. Available at: https://www.youtube.com/watch?v=GCBWrdN1eRY

Ghose, Partha. 2020. "Rabindranath and Science." In *The Cambridge Companion to Rabindranath Tagore*, edited by Sukanta Chaudhuri, 337–51. Cambridge: Cambridge University Press.

Gilat, Moti. 1969. *Mt. Scopus*. [In Hebrew.] Ramat Gan: Masada.

Gilbert, Martin. 2007. *Churchill and the Jews: A Lifelong Friendship*. New York: Henry Holt.

Gilpin, Robert. 1996. "No One Loves a Political Realist." *Security Studies* 5, no. 3 (September): 3–26.

Goldstein, Jonathan. 2004. "The Republic of China and Israel, 1911–2003." *Israel Affairs* 10, no. 1–2: 223–53.

Goyal, Yogita. 2019. "On Transnational Analogy: Thinking Race and Caste with W. E. B. Du Bois and Rabindranath Tagore." *Atlantic Studies* 16, no. 1 (January): 54–71.

Grainger, John D. 2007. *The Battle for Palestine, 1917*. Woodbridge: Boydell Press.

Gray Hill, John. 1891. *With the Bedouins: A Narrative of Journeys and Adventures in Unfrequented Parts of Syria*. London: Unwin.

Gross, Neil, and Ethan Fosse. 2012. "Why Are Professors Liberal?" *Theory and Society* 41, no. 2 (March): 127–68.

Guignon, Charles, and David R. Hiley. 2003. "Introduction: Richard Rorty and Contemporary Philosophy." In *Richard Rorty*, edited by Charles Guignon and David R. Hiley, 1–40. Cambridge: Cambridge University Press.

Guillaume, Xavier, and Jef Huysmans. 2018. "The Concept of the 'Everyday': Ephemeral Politics and the Abundance of Life." *Cooperation and Conflict* 54, no. 2: 278–96.

Guillaume, Xavier, Rune S. Andersen, and Juha A. Vuori. 2016. "Paint It Black: Colours and the Social Meaning of the Battlefield." *European Journal of International Relations* 22, no. 1 (March): 49–71.

Hagmann, Jonas, and Thomas J. Biersteker. 2014. "Beyond the Published Discipline: Toward a Critical Pedagogy of International Studies." *European Journal of International Relations* 20, no. 2 (June): 291–315.

Hamann, Julian, and Wolfgang Kaltenbrunner. 2022. "Biographical Representation, from Narrative to List: The Evolution of Curricula Vitae in the Humanities, 1950 to 2010." *Research Evaluation* 31, no. 4 (October): 438–51. https://doi.org/10.1093/reseval/rvab040

Hansen, Magnus Paulsen, and Peter Triantafillou. 2022. "Methodological Reflections on Foucauldian Analyses: Adopting the Pointers of Curiosity, Nominalism, Conceptual Grounding and Exemplarity." *European Journal of Social Theory* 24, no. 4: 559–77.

Harel-Shalev, Ayelet, and Shir Daphna-Tekoah. 2019. *Breaking the Binaries in Security Studies: A Gendered Analysis of Women in Combat*. New York: Oxford University Press.

Hartnett, Liane. 2022. "Love Is Worldmaking: Reading Rabindranath Tagore's Gora as International Theory." *International Studies Quarterly* 66, no. 3 (2022): sqac037. https://doi.org/10.1093/isq/sqac037

Hasson, Nir. 2017. *Urshalim: Israelis and Palestinians in Jerusalem, 1967–2017*. [In Hebrew.] Tel Aviv: Sifrey Aliyat Hagag.

Hasson, Nir. 2019. "Policemen in Issawiya Were Recorded Complaining about Their Activity in the Neighborhood: 'This Is Really Just to Provoke Them.'" *Haaretz*, October 13.

Hasson, Nir. 2023. "The Head of the Shin Bet Pleaded with Smotrich Not to Cancel the Budget for Promoting Higher Education in East Jerusalem." *Haaretz*, July 13.

Hawthorne, Nathaniel. 2009. *The Marble Faun*. Oxford: Oxford University Press. First published 1859.

Head, Naomi. 2016. "A Politics of Empathy: Encounters with Empathy in Israel and Palestine." *Review of International Studies* 42, no. 1 (January): 95–113.

Hepburn, Allan. 2010. *Enchanted Objects: Visual Art in Contemporary Fiction*. Toronto: University of Toronto Press.

Hexter, Maurice B. 1973. *My Stone Age*. New York: Usdan Center for the Creative Arts.

Hexter, Maurice B. 1976. Letter to Eliyahu Elath, January 15. Hexter's personal archive, National Library, Jerusalem. The documents are not cataloged or numbered. ARC. 4 0 1729[L].

Hexter, Maurice B. 1979. Letter to Lady Rosemary d'Avigdor-Goldsmid, May 9. Hexter's personal archive, National Library, Jerusalem. The documents are not cataloged and numbered. ARC. 4 o 1729[L].

Hexter, Maurice B. 1982. Letter to Lady Rosemary d'Avigdor-Goldsmid, October 4. Hexter's personal archive, National Library, Jerusalem. The documents are not cataloged or numbered. ARC. 4 o 1729[L].

Hexter, Maurice B. 1987. *My Thirty-Year Love Affair 1956–1986: A Retrospective of the Sculpture of Maurice B. Hexter*. Tokyo: Dai Nippon Printing.

Hexter, Maurice B. 1989. Letter to Walter Eytan, April 6. Hexter's personal archive, National Library, Jerusalem. The documents are not cataloged and numbered. ARC. 4 o 1729[L].

Hexter, Maurice B. 1990. *Life Size: An Autobiography*. West Kennebunk: Phoenix Publishing.

Hill, Arthur W. 1915. "The History and Functions of Botanic Gardens." *Annals of the Missouri Botanical Garden* 2, nos. 1–2 (January–April): 185–240.

Huizinga, Johan. 2002. *Homo Ludens: A Study of the Play Element in Culture*. Abingdon, Oxon: Routledge.

Hülsse, Rainer. 2010. "I, the Double Soldier: An Autobiographic Case-Study on the Pitfalls of Dual Citizenship." In *Autobiographical International Relations*, edited by Naeem Inayatullah, 70–78. London: Routledge.

Hymans, Jacques, and Ronan Tse-min Fu. 2017. "The Diffusion of International Norms of Banknote Iconography: A Case Study of the New Taiwan Dollar." *Political Geography* 57 (March): 49–59.

Inayatullah, Naeem. 2020. "Teaching Is Impossible: A Polemic." In *Pedagogical Journeys through World Politics*, edited by Jamie Frueh, 17–26. Cham: Palgrave Macmillan.

Inayatullah, Naeem. 2022. *Pedagogy as Encounter: Beyond the Teaching Imperative*. London: Rowman & Littlefield.

Isa, R. 2023. "Precarious Living in Jerusalem: Return, Fear, and Sumud." *Journal of Palestine Studies* 52, no. 1: 87–91.

Isser, Yaara. 2016. *Palestinian Neighborhoods in East Jerusalem. Research and Evaluation: Issawiya*. [In Hebrew.] Jerusalem: Jerusalem Institute for Israel Research.

Jackson, Patrick Thaddeus. 2020. "Time for Class." In *Pedagogical Journeys through World Politics*, edited by Jamie Frueh, 41–53. Cham: Palgrave Macmillan.

Jansen, Jonathan D. 2009. *Knowledge in the Blood: Confronting Race and the Apartheid Past*. Stanford: Stanford University Press.

Jones, James F. 1991. *Rousseau's Dialogues: An Interpretive Essay*. Geneva: Droz.

Kamczycki, Artur. 2013. "Orientalism: Herzl and His Beard." *Journal of Modern Jewish Studies* 12, no. 1: 90–116.

Kaplan, Rachel, and Stephen Kaplan. 1989. *The Experience of Nature: A Psychological Perspective*. Cambridge: Cambridge University Press.

Kaplan, Stephen. 1995. "The Restorative Benefits of Nature: Toward an Integrative Framework." *Journal of Environmental Psychology* 15, no. 3 (September): 169–82.

Kay, Jilly Boyce. 2020. "'Stay the Fuck at Home!': Feminism, Family, and the Private Home in a Time of Coronavirus." *Feminist Media Studies* 20, no. 6 (May): 883–88.

Kerzhner, Tamara, Sigal Kaplan, and Emily Silverman. 2018. "Physical Walls, Invisible Barriers: Palestinian Women's Mobility in Jerusalem." *Regional Science Policy and Practice* 10, no. 4 (November): 299–314.

Khosravi, Shahram. 2010. *"Illegal" Traveller: An Auto-ethnography of Borders*. New York: Palgrave Macmillan.

Kim, Jung-Hwa, and Kyung-Jin Zoh. 2017. "Inventing Modern Taste at the Changgyeongwon Botanical Garden." *Landscape Research* 42, no. 5: 574–91.

Kinsella, Helen M. 2021. "Of Colonialism and Corpses: Simone Weil on Force." In *Women's International Thought: A New History*, edited by Patricia Owens and Katherina Rietzler, 72–92. Cambridge: Cambridge University Press.

Kliot, Nurit. 2004. "Afforestation for Security Purposes: Spatial Geographical Aspects." [In Hebrew.] In *Studies in Eretz Yisrael: Aviel Ron Book*, edited by Y. Gal, Nurit Kliot, and A. Peled, 205–17. Haifa: Department of Geography, University of Haifa.

Knee, Stuart E. 1977. "Jewish Non-Zionism in America and Palestine Commitment 1917–1941." *Jewish Social Studies* 39, no. 3: 209–26.

Kohl, Jeanette. 2013. "Casting Renaissance Florence: The Bust of Giovanni de' Medici and Indexical Portraiture." In *Carvings, Casts & Collectors: The Art of Renaissance Sculpture, Conference Papers*, edited by P. Motture, E. Jones, and D. Zikos, 58–71. London: Victoria and Albert Museum.

Korica, Maja. 2022. "A Hopeful Manifesto for a More Humane Academia." *Organization Studies* 43, no. 9 (2022): 1523–26. https://doi.org/10.1177/01708406221106316

Kotef, Hagar. 2020. "Violent Attachments." *Political Theory* 48, no. 1 (February): 4–29.

Krasner, Stephen. 1999. *Sovereignty: Organized Hypocrisy*. Princeton: Princeton University Press.

Kristeva, Julia. 1982. *Powers of Horror: An Essay on Abjection*. New York: Columbia University Press.

Kumar, Nita. 2015. "The Educational Efforts of Rabindranath Tagore." In *Rabindranath Tagore in the 21st Century*, edited by Debashish Banerji, 131–44. New Delhi: Springer.

Kumar, R. Siva. 1999. "Modern Indian Art: A Brief Overview." *Art Journal* 58, no. 3 (Fall): 14–21.

Kurowska, Xymena. 2020. "The Secondary Gains of Neoliberal Pain: The Limits of Consolation as a Response to Academic Anguish." *Political Anthropological Research on International Social Sciences (PARISS)* 1, no. 1: 117–36.

Kushnir, Tuvia. 1949. *Nature Research and Letters*. Tel Aviv: Am Oved.

Lebow, Richard Ned. 2003. *The Tragic Vision of Politics: Ethics, Interests and Orders*. Cambridge: Cambridge University Press.

Leimkugel, Frank. 2005. *Botanischer Zionismus: Otto Warburg (1859–1938) und die Anfänge institutionalisierter Naturwissenschaften in "Erez Israel."* Berlin: Botanischer Garten und Botanisches Museum.

Lévi-Strauss, Claude. 1973. *Tristes Tropiques*. Translated by John and Doreen Weightman. New York: Atheneum.

Levin, Ayala. 2011. "The Mountain and the Fortress: The Location of the Hebrew University Campus on Mount Scopus in the Israeli Imaginary of National Space." [In Hebrew.] *Theory and Criticism* 38–39 (Winter): 11–34.

Levy, Daniel S. 2002. *Two-Gun Cohen*. New York: Macmillan.

Levy, Eyvone. 2011. "Repeat Performances: Bernini, the Portrait and Its Copy." *Sculpture Journal* 20, no. 2 (December): 239–49.

Levy, Yagil. 2012. *Israel's Death Hierarchy: Casualty Aversion in a Militarized Democracy*. New York: New York University Press.

Bibliography

Linklater, Andrew. 2007. "Towards a Sociology of Global Morals with an 'Emancipatory Intent.'" In "Critical International Relations Theory after 25 Years," special issue, *Review of International Studies*, no. 33 (April): 135–50.

Liphschitz, Nili. 2007. *Timber in Ancient Israel: Dendroarchaeology and Dendrochronology*. Tel Aviv: Emery and Claire Yass Publication in Archaeology.

Lloyd, David William. 2014. *Battlefield Tourism: Pilgrimage and the Commemoration of the Great War in Britain, Australia, and Canada, 1919–1939*. London: Bloomsbury.

Loveday, Vik. 2018. "The Neurotic Academic: Anxiety, Casualization, and Governance in the Neoliberalising University." *Journal of Cultural Economy* 11, no. 2: 154–66.

Löw, Shimon. 2015. "'Clear Are the Paths of India'": The Cultural and Political Encounter Between Indians and Jews in the Context of the Growth of their Respective National Movements." PhD diss., Hebrew University of Jerusalem. [In Hebrew.]

Lowenhaupt Tsing, Anna. 2005. *Friction: An Ethnography of Global Connection*. Princeton: Princeton University Press.

Lowenhaupt Tsing, Anna. 2015. *The Mushroom at the End of the World*. Princeton: Princeton University Press.

Löwenheim, Oded. 2007. *Predators and Parasites: Persistent Agents of Transnational Harm and Great Power Authority*. Ann Arbor: University of Michigan Press.

Löwenheim, Oded. 2010. "The 'I' in IR: An Autoethnographic Account." *Review of International Studies* 36, no. 4 (October): 1023–45.

Löwenheim, Oded. 2014. *The Politics of the Trail: Reflexive Mountain Biking along the Frontier of Jerusalem*. Ann Arbor: University of Michigan Press.

Löwenheim, Oded. 2015. "Back to Hebron's Tegart Fort: An Autoethnography of Shame, Love, Loss, and the De-securitization of the Self." *Journal of Narrative Politics* 1, no. 2 (September): 133–49.

Löwenheim, Oded, and Gadi Heimann. 2008. "Revenge in International Politics." *Security Studies* 17, no. 4: 685–724.

Luque-Ayala, Andrés, and Flávia Neves Maia. 2019. "Digital Territories: Google Maps as a Political Technique in the Re-making of Urban Informality." *Environment and Planning D: Society and Space* 37, no. 3 (June): 449–67.

Macalister, R. A. Stuart. 1905. "Further Observations on the Ossuary of Nicanor of Alexandria." *Palestine Exploration Fund Quarterly* 37, no. 3: 253–57.

Mitzen, Jennifer. 2006. "Ontological Security in World Politics: State Identity and the Security Dilemma." *European Journal of International Relations* 12, no. 3 (September): 341–70.

Magolda, Peter M. 2001. "What Our Rituals Tell Us about Community on Campus: A Look at the Campus Tour." *About Campus* 5, no. 6 (January–February): 2–8.

Malpas, Jeff. 2018. *Place and Experience: A Philosophical Topography*. London: Routledge.

Mantz, Felix. 2019. "Decolonizing the IPE syllabus: Eurocentrism and the Coloniality of Knowledge in International Political Economy." *Review of International Political Economy* 26 no. 6: 1361–78.

Marnin-Distelfeld, Shahar, and Edna Gorney. 2019. "Why Draw Flowers? Botanical Art, Nationalism, and Women's Contribution to Israeli Culture." *Anthropology of the Middle East* 14, no. 1: 45–69.

Martin, Susan K. 1995. "Gender, Genera, Genre, and Geography: Colonial Women's Writings and the Uses of Botany." *Journal of the Association for the Study of Australian Literature*: 30–39.

Matthews, Jack. 1994. "The Raven Caper and the Writing Curse." *Antioch Review* 52, no. 1 (Winter): 157–65.

Mattusch, Carol C. 1988. *Greek Bronze Statuary: From the Beginnings through the Fifth Century B.C.* Ithaca: Cornell University Press.

Mattusch, Carol C. 2015. "Broken but Not Forgotten: Fragments of Bronze Statues from the Northern Limes." *Journal of Roman Archaeology* 28, no. 2: 751–60.

Mazza, Roberto. 2007. "Jerusalem During the First World War: Transition from Ottoman to British Rule (1914–1920)." Phd diss., SOAS University of London.

McGinn, Colin. 2015. *Prehension: The Hand and the Emergence of Humanity.* Cambridge, MA: MIT Press.

McOuat, Gordon R. 1996. "Species, Rules and Meaning: The Politics of Language and the End of Definitions in 19th Century Natural History." *Studies in the History of the Philosophy of Science* 27, no. 4 (December): 473–519.

Medoff, Rafael. 2001. *Baksheesh Diplomacy: Secret Negotiations Between American Jewish Leaders and Arab Officials on the Eve of World War II.* Lanham, MD: Lexington Books.

Mercer, Jonathan. 1995. "Anarchy and Identity." *International Organization* 49, no. 2 (Spring): 229–52.

Merivale, Patricia. 1974. "The Raven and the Bust of Pallas: Classical Artifacts and the Gothic Tale." *Proceedings of the Modern Language Association* 89, no. 5 (October): 960–66.

Mishory, Alec. 2019. *Secularizing the Sacred: Aspects of Israeli Visual Culture.* Leiden: Brill.

Molloy, Sean. 2020. "Realism and Reflexivity: Morgenthau, Academic Freedom, and Dissent." *European Journal of International Relations* 26, no. 2 (June): 321–43.

Morin, Ran. 2019. "Three Trees: Environmental Projects on Mount Scopus, Jerusalem (2003–2015)." In *Borderlines: Essays on Mapping and The Logic of Place*, edited by Ruthie Abeliovich and Edwin Seroussi, 174–83. Warsaw: De Gruyter.

Morris, Benny. 2002. "The Red Time." [In Hebrew.] *Yisrael: A Journal for the Study of Zionism and the State of Israel* 1 (Spring): 143–48.

Mosse, George L. 1991. *Fallen Soldiers: Reshaping the Memory of the World Wars.* New York: Oxford University Press.

Mosse, George L. 2000. *Confronting History: A Memoir.* Madison: University of Wisconsin Press.

Murdin, Paul. 2009. *Full Meridian of Glory: Perilous Adventures in the Competition to Measure the Earth.* New York: Springer.

Neves, Katja. 2009. "Urban Botanical Gardens and the Aesthetics of Ecological Learning: A Theoretical Discussion and Preliminary Insights from Montreal's Botanical Garden." *Anthropologica* 51, no. 1 (January): 145–57.

Ochs, Juliana. 2011. *Security and Suspicion: An Ethnography of Everyday Life in Israel.* Philadelphia: University of Pennsylvania Press.

O'Donnell, Katherine, and Suzanne Sharock. 2017. "The Contribution of Botanic Gardens to Ex Situ Conservation through Seed Banking." *Plant Diversity* 39, no. 6 (December): 373–78.

Onol, Isil. 2011. "Haptic Interaction with Visual Information: Tactile Exhibition as Inclusive Interface between Museum Visitors and the Bronze Bust of Sophocles." PhD diss., University of Huddersfield.

Osborne, Michael A. 2000. "Acclimatizing the World: A History of the Paradigmatic Colonial Science." *Osiris*, no. 15 (January): 135–51.

Otto, Rudolf. 1936. *The Idea of the Holy: An Inquiry into the Non-rational Factor in the Idea of the Divine and Its Relation to the Rational*. Translated by J. W. Harvey. London: Oxford University Press.

Padan, Yael. 2019. "Seeing Is Believing: Miniature and Gigantic Architectural Models of the Second Temple." *Journal of Tourism and Cultural Change* 17, no. 1 (January): 69–84.

Page, Edward C. 2015. "Undergraduate Research: An Apprenticeship Approach to Teaching Political Science Methods." *European Political Science* 14, no. 3 (September): 340–54.

Pahre, Robert, and Carie Steele. 2015. "Teaching Politics in the National Parks." *Journal of Political Science Education* 11, no. 3: 301–18.

Paliewicz, Nicholas S., and Marouf Hasian Jr. 2017. "Popular Memory at Ground Zero: A Heterotopology of the National September 11 Memorial and Museum." *Popular Communication* 15, no. 1 (January): 19–36.

Paravalos, Peter. 2006. *Moving a House with Preservation in Mind*. Lanham, MD: Altamira Press.

Park-Kang, Sungju. 2015. "Fictional IR and Imagination: Advancing Narrative Approaches." *Review of International Studies* 41, no. 2: 361–81.

Park Kang, Sungju. 2022. *Tears of Theory: International Relations as Storytelling*. Lanham, MD: Rowman and Littlefield.

Parzen, Herbert. 1967. "A Chapter in Arab-Jewish Relations during the Mandate Era." *Jewish Social Studies* 29, no. 4 (October): 203–33.

Paz, Yair. 1995. "The Botanical Garden and the Garden of the Prophets: On Two Projects for the Setting Up of Teaching Gardens in the Hebrew University." [In Hebrew.] In *History of the Hebrew University of Jerusalem, Consolidation and Growth*, vol. 1, edited by Hagit Lavsky, 443–72. Jerusalem: Hebrew University Magness Press.

Paz, Yair. 1997. "The Hebrew University in Mount Scopus as a 'Temple.'" [In Hebrew.] In *The History of the Hebrew University of Jerusalem: Roots and Beginnings*, vol. 2, edited by Michael Heyd and Shaul Ben Menachem Katz, 281–308. Jerusalem: Magness Books.

Paz, Yair. 2017. "Going Up and Down': The Symbolic-Political Connection to Mt. Scopus and the Hebrew University's Campus during the Enclave Period, 1948–1967." [In Hebrew.] *Cathedra* 163 (April): 69–104.

Penslar, Derek. 1990. "Zionism, Colonialism, and Technocracy: Otto Warburg and the Commission for the Exploration of Palestine, 1903–1907." *Journal of Contemporary History* 25, no. 1 (January): 143–60.

Perks, Tom, Doug Orr, and Elham Al-Omari. 2016. "Classroom Re-Design to Facilitate Student Learning: A Case Study of Changes to a University Classroom." *Journal of the Scholarship of Teaching and Learning* 16, no. 1: 53–68.

Persico, Tomer. 2017. "The End Point of Zionism: Ethnocentrism and the Temple Mount." In "Changing Perspectives on the Temple Mount," special issue, *Israel Studies Review* 32, no. 1, (Summer): 104–22.

Phillips, Margaret, and Lynn Jones. 2018. "Where Are They Now? Winners of a Library Prize for Undergraduate Research: A Survey at the University of California, Berkeley." *SAGE Open* 8, no 2 (April–June): https://journals.sagepub.com/doi/full/10.11 77/2158244018772627

Pinsker, Leon. 2007. "Autoemancipation." Quoted in *Israel in the Middle East: Documents and Readings on Society, Politics, and Foreign Relations, Pre-1948 to the Present*, edited by Itamar Rabinovich and Jehuda Reinharz, 14–15. Waltham, MA: Brandeis University Press.

Pisharoty, Sangeeta Barooah. 2017. "In Talk of Dismantling Ramkinkar Baij's Gandhi Statue in Guwahati, an Unhappy Déjà Vu," *The Wire (India)*, August 9. https://thew ire.in/culture/ramkinkar-baij-guwahati-gandhi

Power, Martin J., Patricia Neville, Eoin Devereux, Amanda Haynes, and Cliona Barnes. 2013. "'Why Bother Seeing the World for Real?': Google Street View and the Representation of a Stigmatised Neighbourhood." *New Media and Society* 15, no. 7 (November): 1022–40.

Prasad, Ajnesh, and Paulina Segarra. 2017. "Academe under Siege and the Atrophy of Today's Universities." *Ephemera: Theory and Politics in Organization* 17, no. 3: 727–32.

Pundak, Ron. 2013. *Secret Channel: Oslo—The Complete Story*. [In Hebrew.] Tel Aviv: Sifrei Aliyat Hagag.

Rahman, Anisur. 2006. "Roots of Action Research and Self-Reliance Thinking in Rabindranath Tagore." *Action Research* 4, no. 2 (December): 231–45.

Randolph, Adrian W. D. 2014. *Touching Objects: Intimate Experiences of Italian Fifteenth-Century Art*. New Haven: Yale University Press.

Rapp, David. 2002. "Meir Dizengoff's Only Child." *Haaretz*, December 20. https://www .haaretz.com/israel-news/culture/1.4993218

Ravecca, Paulo, and Elizabeth Dauphinee. 2018. "Narrative and the Possibilities for Scholarship." *International Political Sociology* 12, no. 2 (June): 125–38.

Readings, Bill. 1996. *The University in Ruins*. Cambridge, MA: Harvard University Press.

Richardson, Margaret Ann. 2019. "Journeying through Inner and Outer Worlds: The Significance of Travel across the Works of Rabindranath Tagore." *Studies in Travel Writing* 23, no. 4 (October): 358–77.

Riemer, Jeffrey W. 1977. "Varieties of Opportunistic Research." *Urban Life* 5, no. 4 (January): 467–77.

Roberts, Nicholas. 2011. "Re-remembering the Mandate: Historiographical Debates and Revisionist History in the Study of British Palestine." *History Compass* 9, no. 3 (March): 215–30.

Rosenberg, Stephen G. 2004. "The Jewish Temple at Elephantine." *Near Eastern Archaeology* 67, no. 1 (March): 4–13.

Rosenberg, Uri, dir. 2016. *The People of the Garden* [אנשי הגן]. https://vimeo.com/189 837700

Roth, Philip. 2004. *The Plot Against America*. London: Vintage.

Rowley, Tom. 2017. "Meet the Palestinian Family Who Have Tended the Graves of Our War Dead for 60 Years." *The Telegraph*, May 13.

Sa'di-Ibraheem, Yara. 2021. "Indigenous Students' Geographies on the Academic Fortress Campus: Palestinian Students' Spatial Experiences at the Hebrew University of Jerusalem." *Journal of Holy Land and Palestine Studies* 20, no. 2 (November): 123–45.

Salter, Mark, ed. 2015. *Making Things International 1: Circuits and Motion*. Minneapolis: University of Minnesota Press.

Salter, Mark, ed. 2016. *Making Things International 2: Catalysts and Reactions*. Minneapolis: University of Minnesota Press.

Salter, Mark B. 2007. "Governmentalities of an Airport: Heterotopia and Confession." *International Political Sociology* 1, no. 1 (March): 49–66.

242 Bibliography

Saunders, Robert A., and Rhys Crilley. 2019. "Pissing on the Past: The Highland Clearances, Effigial Resistance and the Everyday Politics of the Urinal." *Millennium* 47, no. 3 (June): 444–69.

Schlesinger, Max. 1934. Letter to Mrs. Vera Bryce Salomons of Reahvia, Jerusalem, November 27. Hebrew University Central Archive, Botanical Garden file # 2350.

Schrader, Benjamin. 2014. "Auto-archaeology and the Political Affect of War." *Journal of Narrative Politics* 1, no. 1 (March): 4–23.

Schroeder, Scott R., and Peiyao Chen. 2021. "Bilingualism and COVID-19: Using a Second Language during a Health Crisis." *Journal of Communication in Healthcare* 14, no. 1 (January): 20–30.

Scott, Susie. 2018. "A Sociology of Nothing: Understanding the Unmarked." *Sociology* 52, no.1: 3–19.

Selzer, Assaf, and Yair Paz. 2009. "Remained in the Mountain: The Historical Campus Buildings from the Mandate Period in Mt. Scopus." [In Hebrew.] In *The History of the Hebrew University in Jerusalem: Academic Growth during a National Struggle*, vol. 3, edited by Hagit Lavsky, 463–87. Jerusalem: Magness Press.

Sen, Amartya. n.d. "Tagore and His India." The Nobel Prize (website). https://www.nobelprize.org/prizes/literature/1913/tagore/article/ (accessed: February 27, 2024). First published August 28, 2001.

Sengupta, Ratnottama. 2012. "Busts Trace Rabindranath Tagore's Footprint across the Globe." *Times of India*, May 20. https://timesofindia.indiatimes.com/city/kolkata/busts-trace-rabindranath-tagores-footprint-across-the-globe/articleshow/13309634.cms

Shaffer, Aaron. 1983. "Gilgamesh, the Cedar Forest, and Mesopotamian History." *Journal of the American Oriental Society* 103, no. 1 (January–March): 307–13.

Shah, Nisha. 2017. "Death in the Details: Finding Dead Bodies at the Canadian War Museum." *Organization* 24, no. 4: 549–69.

Shalhoub-Kevorkian, Nadera. 2017. "The Occupation of the Senses: The Prosthetic and Aesthetic of State Terror." *British Journal of Criminology* 57, no. 6 (November): 1279–1300.

Sharf, Avi. 2022. "One Pixel Forward, Two Backward: Why Google Is Censoring Again [Israel]." [In Hebrew.] *Haaretz*, September 29.

Sharon, Ossnat. 2016. "'In Your Darkness, Jerusalem': Reading 'Jerusalem of Iron' by Meir Ariel in 1967 and Today." [In Hebrew.] *Hayo Haya* [Once upon a time], no. 11: 84–103.

Sheffi, Na'ama, and Anat First. 2019. "Land of Milk and Honey: Israeli Landscapes and Flora on Banknotes." *National Identities* 21, no. 2: 191–211.

Sheridan, Michael. 2016. "Boundary Plants, the Social Production of Space, and Vegetative Agency in Agrarian Societies." *Environment and Society* 7, no. 1 (September): 29–49.

Sherwood, Harriet. 2013. "Tending the War Graves of Gaza City." *The Guardian*, August 18.

Shim, David. 2016. "Between the International and the Everyday: Geopolitics and Imaginaries of Home." *International Studies Review* 18, no.4 (December): 597–613.

Simmel, Georg. 1971. "The Adventurer." In *On Individuality and Social Forms*, 187–98. Chicago: University of Chicago Press.

Singer, Wendy. 2001. "Introduction. Endless Dawns of Imagination: Portfolio—Einstein and Tagore." *Kenyon Review* 23, no. 2 (Spring): 7–33.

Bibliography

Sledge, Michael. 2005. *Soldier Dead: How We Recover, Identify, Bury, and Honor Our Military Fallen.* New York: Columbia University Press.

Sobelman, Daniel. 2016. "Learning to Deter: Deterrence Failure and Success in the Israel-Hezbollah Conflict, 2006–16." *International Security* 41, no. 3: 151–96.

Sondarjee, Maïka, and Nathan Andrews. 2023. "Decolonizing International Relations and Development Studies: What's in a Buzzword?" *International Journal* 77, no. 4: 551–71. https://doi.org/10.1177/00207020231166588

Sørensen, Anders Ravn. 2016. "'Too Weird for Banknotes': Legitimacy and Identity in the Production of Danish Banknotes 1947–2007." *Journal of Historical Sociology* 29, no. 2 (June): 182–206.

Spary, Emma. 2000. *Utopia's Garden: French Natural History from Old Regime to Revolution.* Chicago: Chicago University Press.

Spruyt, Hendrik. 1996. *The Sovereign State and Its Competitors: An Analysis of Systems Change.* Princeton: Princeton University Press.

Spruyt, Hendrik. 2017. "War and State Formation: Amending the Bellicist Theory of State Making." In *Does War Make States? Investigations of Charles Tilly's Historical Sociology,* edited by Lars Bo Kaspersen and Jeppe Strandsbjerg, 73–97. Cambridge: Cambridge University Press.

Stamatopoulou-Robbins, Sophia. 2019. *Waste Siege: The Life of Infrastructure in Palestine.* Stanford: Stanford University Press.

Starkey, Paul. 2018. "The Cedars of Lebanon in Literature and Art." In *Travelers in Ottoman Lands: The Botanical Legacy,* edited by Ines Aščerić-Todd, Sabina Knees, Janet Starkey, and Paul Starkey, 251–74. Oxford: Astene.

Steele, Brent J. 2010. "Of 'Witch's Brews' and Scholarly Communities: The Dangers and Promise of Academic Parrhesia," *Cambridge Review of International Affairs* 23, no. 1 (March): 49–68.

Steele, Brent J. 2013. *Alternative Accountabilities in Global Politics: The Scars of Violence.* London: Routledge.

Steele, Brent J. 2020. "Journey to the Unknown: Survival, Re-awakening, Renewal, and Reformation." In *Pedagogical Journeys through World Politics,* edited by Jamie Frueh, 279–92. Cham: Palgrave Macmillan.

Sterling-Folker, Jennifer. 2020. "Confessions of a Teaching Malcontent: Learning to Like What You Do." In *Pedagogical Journeys through World Politics,* edited by Jamie Frueh, 77–90. Cham: Palgrave Macmillan.

Sucharov, Mira. 2021. *Borders and Belonging: A Memoir.* Cham: Palgrave Macmillan.

Sun, Mengtian. 2018. "Alien Encounters in Liu Cixin's *The Three-Body Trilogy* and Arthur C. Clarke's *Childhood's End.*" *Frontiers of Literary Studies in China* 12, no. 4 (December): 610–44.

Sylvester, Christine. 2013. *War as Experience: Contributions from International Relations and Feminist Analysis.* London: Routledge.

Sylvester, Christine. 2019. "Who Curates Recent American Wars? Looking in Arlington Cemetery and at the Wall that Heals." *Critical Military Studies* 18, no. 1 (March): 1–15.

Tagore, Rabindranath. 1916. *Nationalism.* New York: Macmillan.

Tagore, Rabindranath. 1939. "The Congress." *Modern Review,* July 1939. In *The Mahatma and the Poet: Letters and Debates between Gandhi and Tagore, 1915–1941,* edited by Sabyasachi Bhattacharya, 174. New Delhi: National Book Trust, India, 1997.

244 Bibliography

Tagore, Rabindranath. 1941a. *Crisis in Civilization: A Message on Completing His Eighty Years*. Birbhum: Santiniketan Press.

Tagore, Rabindranath. 1941b. "Tagore's Last Article." *The Militant*, October 4. Available at https://www.marxists.org/history/etol/newspape/themilitant/1941/v05n40/tagore.html

Tagore, Rabindranath. 1960. *Wings of Death: The Last Poems of Rabindranath Tagore*. Translated from the Bengali by Aurobindo Bose. London: John Murray.

Tagore, Rabindranath. 2006. *The English Writings of Rabindranath Tagore: A Miscellany*. Vol. 2. Edited by Sisir Kumar Das. New Delhi: Sahitya Akademi.

Tal, Alon. 2013. *All the Trees of the Forest: Israel's Woodlands from the Bible to the Present*. New Haven: Yale University Press.

Tallis, Raymond. 2003. *The Hand: A Philosophical Inquiry into Human Being*. Edinburgh: Edinburgh University Press.

Theobald, Andrew. 2006. "Incidents on Mount Scopus: UNTSO Effectiveness and the 1958 Death of Lieutenant Colonel George Flint." *Middle Eastern Studies* 42, no. 5 (September): 803–17.

Thomson, Janice E. 1996. *Mercenaries, Pirates, and Sovereigns: State-building and Extraterritorial Violence in Early Modern Europe*. Princeton: Princeton University Press.

Tichi, Cecelia. 2001. *Embodiment of a Nation: Human Form in American Places*. Cambridge, MA: Harvard University Press, 2001.

Tuan, Yi-Fu. 1979. "Space and Place: Humanistic Perspective." In *Philosophy in Geography*, edited by Stephen Gale and Gunnar Olsson, 387–427. Dordrecht: Springer.

University of Oxford. 2020. "Oxford Archaeologists Win Access to Restricted Satellite Images of Israel and the Palestinian Territories." News and Events Arts Blog, August 11. https://www.ox.ac.uk/news/arts-blog/oxford-archaeologists-win-access-restricted-satellite-images-israel-and-palestinian#

US National Oceanic and Atmospheric Administration. 2020. "Notice of Findings Regarding Commercial Availability of Non-U.S. Satellite Imagery with Respect to Israel." *Federal Register*, July 21. https://www.federalregister.gov/documents/2020/07/21/2020-15770/notice-of-findings-regarding-commercial-availability-of-non-us-satellite-imagery-with-respect-to

Vavilov, Nikolaï. 1997. *Five Continents*. Translated by Doris Löve, edited by Semyon Reznik and Paul Stapleton. Rome: International Plant Genetic Resources Institute. First published in Russian in 1962.

Végső, Roland. 2013. "Stalin's Boots and the March of History (Post-Communist Memories)." *Cultural Critique* 83 (Winter): 31–62.

Vroman, Kerryellen, Rebecca Warner, and Kerry Chamberlain. 2009. "Now Let Me Tell You in My Own Words: Narratives of Acute and Chronic Low Back Pain." *Disability and Rehabilitation* 31, no. 12 (January): 976–87.

Wagner, Sarah E. 2013. "The Making and Unmaking of an Unknown Soldier." *Social Studies of Science* 43, no. 5 (May): 631–56.

Wagner, Sarah E. 2015. "A Curious Trade: The Recovery and Repatriation of U.S. Missing in Action from the Vietnam War." *Comparative Studies in Society and History* 57, no. 1: 161–90.

Wahrman, Jacob. 1997. "From the Gray Hill Estate to the 'Plot of the University' at Mt Scopus." [In Hebrew.] In *The History of the Hebrew University: Roots and Beginnings*, vol. 2, edited by Saul Katz and Michael Heyd, 163–200. Jerusalem: Magness Press.

Walker, R. B. J. 2002. "They Seek It Here, They Seek It There." In *A Political Space: Read-*

ing the Global Through Clayoquot Sound, edited by Warren Magnusson and Karena Shaw, 237–62. Minneapolis: University of Minnesota Press.

Warburg, Otto. 1931. Letter to Hebrew University's chancellor, Judah L. Magnes, April 10. Hebrew University Central Archive, Botanical Garden file #2350.

Wasinski, Christophe. 2008. "'Post-Heroic Warfare' and Ghosts—The Social Control of Dead American Soldiers in Iraq." *International Political Sociology* 2, no. 2: 113–27.

Weber, Max. 1958. "Science as a Vocation." *Daedalus* 87, no. 1 (Winter): 111–34.

Weil, Simone. 1945. "The Iliad, or the Poem of Force." *Politics* (November): 321–31.

Weil, Simone. 2005. *The Need for Roots: Prelude to a Declaration of Duties towards Mankind*. Translated by Arthur Wills. London: Routledge. First published 1949.

Weiss, Haim. 2016. "'Suddenly a Bridge Has Been Established for Over Two Millennia': From Secular Archeology to Religious Archeology—The Case of Bar Kosevah, Yigael Yadin, and Shlomo Goren." [In Hebrew.] *Theory and Criticism* 46 (Summer): 143–67.

Weiss, Yfaat. 2017a. "Performing Sovereignty—The Village of Issawiya in the Mount Scopus Demilitarized Zone, 1948–1967." In *Welcome to Jerusalem*, edited by Margret Kampmeyer and Cilly Kugelmann, 172–83. Cologne: Jewish Museum in Berlin.

Weiss, Yfaat. 2017b. "Resting in Peace in No Man's Land: Human Dignity and Political Sovereignty at the British Commonwealth's Jerusalem War Cemetery, Mount Scopus." *Jerusalem Quarterly* 72 (Winter): 67–85.

Weizman, Eyal. 2012. *Hollow Land: Israel's Architecture of Occupation*. London: Verso Books.

Wells, Allen. 2009. *Tropical Zion: General Trujillo, FDR, and the Jews of Sosúa*. Durham: Duke University Press.

Willis, Emma. 2014. *Theatricality, Dark Tourism, and Ethical Spectatorship: Absent Others*. New York: Palgrave Macmillan.

Yanovsky, Yvgeny. 2015. "Clocks." *In Making Things International 1: Circuits and Motions*, edited by Mark B. Salter, 348–63. Minneapolis: University of Minnesota Press.

Yehoshua, Sagit. 2014. "The Israeli Experience of Terrorist Leaders in Prison: Issues in Radicalisation and De-radicalisation." In *Prisons, Terrorism, and Extremism*, edited by Andrew Silke. London: Routledge.

Yehoshua, A. B. 2012. *Can Two Walk Together: A Play in Two Acts*. [In Hebrew.] Tel Aviv: Hkibutz Hameuhad.

Yilmaz, Ahenk. 2014. "Memorialization on War-Broken Ground: Gallipoli War Cemeteries and Memorials Designed by Sir John James Burnet." *Journal of the Society of Architectural Historians* 73, no. 3 (September): 328–46.

Yuval, Rivka, and Esther Tal. 2012. "In the Paths of the Campus: A Tour of the Edmond J. Safra Campus in Givat Ram." Booklet published by the Public Relations Department, Hebrew University of Jerusalem.

Záhora, Jakub. 2018. "Mundane Self-Legitimizations of Power: Distribution of the Sensible in the Israeli Settlements in the West Bank." PhD diss., Univerzita Karlova (Prague). https://dspace.cuni.cz/handle/20.500.11956/103917

Zambernardi, Lorenzo. 2017. "Excavating Soldier Deaths: A Study of Changing Burial Practices." *International Political Sociology* 11, no. 3 (September): 292–307.

Zembylas, Michalinos. 2012. "Pedagogies of Strategic Empathy: Navigating through the Emotional Complexities of Anti-racism in Higher Education." *Teaching in Higher Education* 17, no. 2 (April): 113–25.

Zerbini, Andrea, and Michael Fradley. 2018. "Higher Resolution Satellite Imagery of

Israel and Palestine: Re-assessing the Kyl-Bingaman Amendment." *Space Policy* nos. 44–45 (August): 14–28.

Zidani, Sulafa. 2021. "Whose Pedagogy Is It Anyway? Decolonizing the Syllabus through a Critical Embrace of Difference." *Media, Culture & Society* 43, no. 5: 970–78.

Zohary, Michael. 1938. "Alexander Eig and His Scientific Project." [In Hebrew.] *Davar* daily, August 29.

Zohary, Michael, and Naomi Feinbrun-Dotan. 1978. *Flora Palaestina*. 4 vols. Jerusalem: Israel Academy of Sciences and Humanities, 1966–1978.

Zweig, Stephen. 1964. *The World of Yesterday: An Autobiography*. Lincoln: University of Nebraska Press.

Index

1929 Palestine Riots, 190

Academic impasse, 17, 21, 142, 144
Adventure (Simmelian concept of), 29n2
The Adventure of the Six Napoleons (a
   Sherlock Holmes story), 139, 154
Albright, Madeleine, 178
al-Husseini, Haj Amin (mufti), 150
Allenby, Edmund (field marshal), 90
Alliance of the Hoodlums, 150
Allure of the Global in IR, 11
Al-Tawjeehi (Palestinian matriculation),
   47
Altneuland (novel), 161, 212
Amichai, Yehuda (poet), 178
Anscombe, Elizabeth (philosopher), 31,
   178
Anti-occupation organizations, 13
ANZAC (Australian and New Zealand
   Army Corps), 64, 94
Arad, Ron (missing in action Israeli
   pilot), 89
Arbutus trees, 110, 121
Arendt, Hannah, 61n4
Arneson, Robert (sculptor), 149n5
Ataturk (Mustafa Kemal), 94
Attention restoration theory (Stephen
   Kaplan's), 29
Augusta Victoria compound, 45
Autoethnography, resistance to 7–9

Baij, Ramkinkar (sculptor), 139, 164–71
Bar-Kosevah, Shimon (Jewish rebel), 91
Basic research, 13
Battle of Hattin (1187), 156
Battle of Megiddo (1918), 75
Begin, Menachem, 92, 177
Ben-Avi, Itamar, 37, 39

Ben-Gurion, David, 52, 141, 182, 185, 196
Benjamin, Walter, 14, 139, 155
Bentwich, Norman (lawyer, professor),
   138, 146
Ben-Yehuda, Eliezer, 37
Bernini, Gian Lorenzo (sculptor), 151–52
Biden, Joe, 45
Blomfield, Reginald (architect), 84
Body count (in war), 61
Bolt neighborhoods (of Jerusalem), 44
Breaking the Silence (human rights
   organization), 13
British Raj, 168–69
Buber, Martin (professor), 142
Burnet, John (architect), 59

Carter, Jimmy, 177
Carter, Rosalynn, 177
Cassini, G. D. (astronomer), 153
Cave of Nicanor, 115, 122–23
Cedars of God Forest, 135
Cedrus libani, 134–37
Chaos narratives, 15
Childhood's End (novel), 166
Churchill, Winston: Avenue, 57, 59, 72,
   81, 95; "Churchill's Palm," 137
Cohen, Morris A., "Two Gun," 191–92
Commonwealth War Graves Commis-
   sion (CWGC), 58, 63n8, 77n25
COVID-19 lockdown in Israel, 100, 104
Cross of Sacrifice, 59, 72, 74, 77, 82, 84

Dayan, Moshe, 120n20, 155
Dead Sea, 35, 50, 80, 99, 174–75
de Certeau, Michel, 34, 52–56, 105, 139,
   161, 211, 217, 220
Defenders of the Mountain Road, 101
Derrida, Jacques, 153

248 Index

Doar HaYom (periodical), 37
Dogs, explosive-sniffing, 112
Dolev, Diana (2016 book cover), 44, 124
Dome of the Rock, 50
Dominican Republic, 184, 197–98

Egyptian Expeditionary Force, 60
Eig, Alexander (botanist), 126–27n33, 129–30, 132–35
Einstein, Albert (images of on campus), 50n20
Elath, Eliyahu (diplomat and university administrator), 185, 187, 191, 192n13
El Ferdan Bridge, 202
Elisabeth, Queen of the Belgians, bust of, 155–56
Empathic listening, 28, 30
Empire of signs, 29
Enkidu (mythical hero), 135
Epic of Gilgamesh, 135
Évian Conference (1938), 197
Excellence, academic, 2, 3, 216

Fasces symbol, 90, 91, 207
Flâneurist (spirit of outings), 109
Flavius Josephus, 35, 36, 122
Foucault, Michel, 155, 160, 212
Founders Wall (Hebrew University), 50
Frank, Arthur, 15
Frank Sinatra Student Center, 2002 bombing of, 45–46
Franz Joseph (emperor of Austria), sideburns of, 160
French Hill (neighborhood), 44, 78

Gallipoli, British cemeteries in, 64n10, 86n30, 94
Gaza, British War Cemetery in, 92–93
Gell, Alfred, 151, 152
Google Earth, 98, 99, 101–5, 208, 212, 225
Google Maps, 46, 101
Google Street View, 98, 101, 102, 116, 119, 208, 212, 225
GoPro (trademark), 223
Goren, Shlomo (military rabbi), 91
Gray Hill, Sir John, 122
Great Powers, 6, 10
Great War (World War I), 60, 70, 76, 87, 88

Green Line, 14, 38, 39
Gush Etzion, 80

Hadassah Mount Scopus University Hospital, 38, 63, 72, 80, 81, 82, 135
Halacha (Jewish religious law), 87
Haram al-Sharif (Arabic name of Temple Mount), 50, 124, 224
Harry S. Truman Research Institute for the Advancement of Peace, 19, 25, 29, 31, 172, 173, 225
Haruba Street, blocking of, 46
Haunted places (concept by de Certeau), 34
Hebron (city), 12, 19
Heraldry, 76
Herzl, Theodor, 134, 159, 160, 212
Heterotopia, 23, 50, 57, 68–70, 205
Hexter, Maurice B., 187–99
Hobbesian Leviathan, 82–83
Huizinga, Johan, 71
Humbaba (mythical beast), 135

IDF (Israel Defense Forces), 13, 16, 39, 40, 41, 42, 46, 64, 76, 92, 93, 103, 121, 221
Important / unimportant topics of study, 50–51, 54
Incoherent narratives, 15, 52
Innovative Pedagogical Methods 1, 165, 211, 213, 214
Introduction to IR, 5, 13
IR-ization, process of, 22, 25, 54, 59, 99, 145, 207, 209
Isaiah, Book of, 135
Israel Plant Gene Bank, 132
Issawiya (Palestinian neighborhood), 24, 43, 45, 46–47, 80, 81, 110, 112, 118–20, 130, 133, 207, 219, 226

Jabotinsky, Vladimir Ze'ev, 140, 141
Jerusalemite Brigade, 42
Jerusalem Municipality, 111
"Jerusalem of Gold" (song by Naomi Shemer), 40, 41
"Jerusalem of Iron" (song by Meir Ariel), 40, 41
Jewish Agency, 190, 192, 196, 198, 201

Joint Distribution Committee (JDC), 198

Jordanian Arab Legion, 45

Judean Desert, 35, 41, 91, 99, 109, 110, 174, 175

Judicial reform/coup of 2023, 42n6, 221, 226, 228

Kafka, Franz, 98

Katzir, Ephraim, 182, 185, 192, 193

Kohen tradition, 74n3

Krav Maga, 81

Kristeva, Julia, and concept of the abject, 79, 115

Kubrick, Stanley, 71

Kyl-Bingaman Amendment, 102

Lamport, Montague, 128

Lamport, Solomon, 128

Lebanon War of 1982, 92

Lebanon War of 2006, 71

Le Guin, Ursula, vii, 11

Lévi-Strauss, Claude, 34, 218

Lindbergh, Charles, 51

Lord Jim (novel), 180n5

Louis XIV, 152–53

Magav (border police), 112

Magnes, Judah (first president of Hebrew University), 150, 190

Maiersdorf Faculty Club, 37

Mandel School for Advanced Studies in the Humanities, 118

Masada, 92

Megastructure (the 1981-built Scopus campus), 43

Meir, Golda, 157, 185, 188, 190

Memento Park (Budapest), 188

Memorial Day, 62, 207

Mevaseret Zion, 17

Minimal-Group Paradigm, 30

Molotov cocktail, 47, 80, 81, 120, 209, 226

Moodle (trademark), 41, 106

Moscone, George (assassinated mayor of San Francisco), 149n5

Mountain biking (along the frontier of Jerusalem), 34

Mt. Rushmore, 149

Mt. Scopus Slopes National Park, 46

Nakba, 12

Nehru, Jawaharlal, 164

Neoliberal university, 1, 4, 17, 19, 203, 216n5

Netanyahu, Benjamin, 11, 62n6, 77n26, 221, 226

November 11 armistice (1918), 70, 75–76

October 7 (2023), Hamas terror attack of, 223–28

The Opening of the Hebrew University of Jerusalem (painting), 174, 175

Orphanhood, 6

Ottoman Empire, 60

Palestine Exploration Fund (PEF), 122

Palestine Rail Company (British Mandate), 202

Paratext of IR, 160

Paz, Yair (historian), 37, 43

Peel Commission, 190

Penguin Island (novel), 15

Perruque ("making due," concept by de Certeau), 53

Pilichowski, Leopold (painter), 174

Pirates, 10

The Plot Against America (novel), 51

Poe, Edgar Allan (bust of), 156

Powell, Colin, 177

Poznań (Poland), British War Cemetery, 33

"proper" (concept used by de Certeau), 3, 53–54

Rabin, Yitzhak (honorary doctorate reception), 38–39

Ramleh (British) War Cemetery, 85

The Raven (poem), 140

Restitution narratives, 15

Rhizome of narratives, 105

"Ripping off" (concept by de Certeau), 53–54

Roberts, David (painter), 35–38

Roth, Philip (author), theory of history, 51

250   Index

Sadat, Anwar, 177
Second Temple period, 50, 115, 122
Security in campus, 46n16
Sennacherib, Assyrian king, 135, 137
Settlements, Israeli, 49, 93, 103, 174
Sheikh Jarrah (neighborhood), 38n9, 43, 72n22
Shira (novel by S. Y. Agnon), 125n28
Shuafat Refugee Camp, 111, 121
Simmel, Georg, 29
Six Day War, 38, 40, 49
Social identity theory, 30
Society Must Be Defended (book), 155
Soft fascination, concept by Kaplan and Kaplan, 29
Sovereign power, 153
Sovereignty, precarious, 166
Stalin's boots (sculpture in Budapest), 149n6
Star Trek (science fiction franchise), 7
Stone of Remembrance, 74, 75, 80, 85, 87
Sun Yat-Sen, 191, 192n13
Survey of Israel, 102, 103

Taglit—Birthright Israel, 13
Tagore, Rabindranath, 161–66
Teaching Anxiety, 3, 4–7, 27, 55, 59, 139, 140, 142, 144, 173, 204, 210, 216, 218
Temple Mount, 35, 50, 124, 125, 224
Temporal frameworks, 70
Tenure, academic, 4, 5, 17, 20, 72, 108, 175, 215, 217n6
Territorial faction in Zionism, 123n24
Tilly, Charles, 65
Titus, Roman general, 35
Tower and Stockade (colonization operation), 190
Trickster (element in the course), 109

Trujillo, Rafael (ruler, Dominican Republic), 197, 198
Truman Peace Prize, 178
Tsing, Anna Lowenhaupt, 138
Tutankhamun, 185

Utilitarian academic performance, 3

Vavilov, Nikolaï (botanist, geneticist), 134
Versailles, Treaty of, 64n10, 94
Virtual teaching, 104–9
Visva-Bharati University, 31, 163n17, 166, 171
Vulnerability, in teaching and writing, 1, 4, 9, 15, 140

Wadi el-Joz (neighborhood), 43
Wagner mercenary Russian force, 66n13
Warburg, Felix (banker), 142, 190
Warburg, Otto (botanist), 127, 128, 129, 133, 135
Weber, Max, 15, 28
Weil, Simone, concept of rooting and uprooting, 116–17
Weizmann, Chaim, 158, 159, 190
Western Front (World War I), 59, 71, 72, 75, 76, 86n30
Wishnick, Robert I. (donor to the Hebrew University), 193
Writer's block, 1, 21, 26, 27, 157, 218

Yadin, Yigael (archaeologist), 92
Yaski, Haim, MD, 72n22
Yom Kippur War, 12, 41
YouTube, 29, 222

Zionist Organization, 34
Zohary, Michael (botanist), 125
Zweig, Stefan (author), 108